Winning Ways

Winning Ways

How companies create the products
we all want to buy

James Pilditch

With a foreword by Robert Heller

MERCURY

Foreword copyright © Robert Heller 1989

Copyright © James Pilditch 1987, 1989

First published by Harper & Row Ltd 1987
Second edition first published in 1989
by the Mercury Books Division of
WH Allen & Co. Plc
Sekforde House, 175–9 St John Street, London EC1V 4LL

Set in Meridien by Phoenix Photosetting, Chatham
Printed and bound in Great Britain by
Mackays of Chatham PLC, Chatham, Kent

British Library Cataloguing in Publication Data
Pilditch, James
  Winning ways – 2nd ed.
  1. Marketing
  I. Title   II. Pilditch, James. Winning
  658.8

ISBN 1–85252–042–6

Contents

Foreword

James Pilditch has played a major and pioneering role in the rise of the British design industry to its present excellence, and in the international spread of its reputation and work. In these respects, design has often been an example to clients and potential clients. James Pilditch has been ahead of all too many of the latter, both in looking beyond the narrow British market and in knowing that managing to win is no longer an option, but a necessity.

This book most effectively combines the two themes. Its examples and lessons are drawn from close observation and understanding of the wider world of business success. The author's own special concern with design is conspicuous, as it should be. But the book sets design in the context of market needs, corporate objectives, human relations and development, competitor analysis, organisational dynamics, research and development, engineering and manufacture, etc. – and, above all, meeting and overcoming omnipresent competition. Anybody who wonders what all or any of these have to do with design hasn't got the message – and hasn't much hope of surviving the turbulent years ahead.

The Japanese have shown most forcefully how to win by making products perform better, in the production process and the marketplace, by the application of design for manufacture and use. The message is one that has reached the British Government: the book takes as its starting point one of Margaret Thatcher's typically personalised interjections. Design for use has consequently joined the school curriculum. But design-happy politicians would be well advised to read these pages to broaden and deepen their understanding.

When the Prime Minister talks of going into a shop to buy something for the kitchen and finding 'it is made in Holland or Italy or Hong Kong or somewhere else', her two apparently simple questions, 'Why isn't it made here?' and 'What can we do about it?', actually go deep into the heart of the complex British economic problem. Nor is the difficulty only British. All over the West, firms have failed to mobilise their own resources effectively to meet the needs of fast-changing and increasingly demanding markets. And of all those resources, the human ones are decisive.

The fact that foreign companies now account for a startling 40 per cent of Britain's supply of manufactured goods is both condemnation and challenge. Where British businesses – and James Pilditch names several, from Penhaligon cosmetics to J. C. Bamford's excavators – have succeeded they have followed universal human principles. His book contains many invaluable guidelines, but none more important than these three: 'These companies succeed partly by remembering that they exist to make what we want, partly by sticking with the basics of business, partly by having an inexorable will to do better every day in every way'.

These are all attitudinal precepts: they don't tell you what to do, but how to discover what is required. They are as vigorous as anything they don't teach you at Harvard Business School, but are also fundamental to everything taught there that is worth learning. Their validity recurs again and again in these pages, in matters as seemingly far apart as small companies and microelectronics, training and Japanese visiting cards – so irrepressible are the users that they may even carry waterproof ones in their swimming trunks. But that indefatigable behaviour, too, is attitudinal; and the closing chapter (Why Change the Way You Do It Now?) is therefore crucial.

It follows a resumé of the many and varied winning ways of plainly victorious companies. Of course, there are no infallible methods. But here, too, attitudes – above all, commitment – hold the key. As James Pilditch writes, 'What we have to do to win is obvious. The ideas have been bandied about for years. The snag is that we don't follow them.' People get snagged partly because, like the many maxims and methods in his book, the ideas don't come singly. In fact, the way in which Japan leads the world in terms of competitive advantage is that of integrated management. The seemingly far apart are actually close together.

Everything must cohere, as it does in these chapters – microelectronics and training, product and process, marketing and motivation, overseas and 'domestic' sales: indeed, in the modern world, there are no export markets. The world market is the only one, and the standards of global competition are increasingly those which determine success nationally and regionally. More than that: the global game is constantly changing, in ways that can land even the largest and ablest practitioners gasping on the shore.

The by now familiar setbacks to giant corporations from IBM and General Motors downwards have been accompanied by a strong philosophical movement (a philosophy James Pilditch shares) in favour of the smaller company and of outward-looking, collegiate management of a kind very different to the habits of the past and passing giants. This author, though, rightly does not hold with the inevitability of failure. Rather, he is convinced of the eternal possibility of designed success, using 'design' in every sense of the word, and in every aspect of the corporate life. His book fits excellently into that overall and all-important design.

ROBERT HELLER

Preface

Winning Ways was first published in 1987. This is the second edition. It has been both updated and expanded. How Amstrad has grown a hundred-fold in eight years, why Anita Roddick's Body Shop was made Company of the Year in 1988 – these are among a number of new cases in this revised edition. Small companies are looked at as well as some of the world's largest. The driving businesses of Korea and other newly industrialised countries have lessons for us and are included. So, of course, have Japanese companies. There is a lot here about the winning Japanese companies: Sony, Sharp, Honda, Canon and others.

Saying that, the aim of this book is unchanged: to show how the winning companies in the world win. Small companies, big companies – some are doing things right. So steadily we don't notice, they are carving out their future. We, as shoppers or buyers, prefer to buy what they make. Day after day, our buying decision is going their way.

As one by one the easy explanations explode (cheap labour, unfair competition, and so on), we are left wondering how they do it. This book gives the answer. The good news is that there are no secrets. These winning companies have nothing we lack. In the end, they just have a different point of view, another way of doing things. That is what this book shows, through dozens of examples. There is no question: every company, whatever its size, could improve its performance quickly by doing as the winners do. They can. Sooner or later, if they are to survive, they must.

Winning Ways grew from a study I chaired for the National Economic Development Office (NEDO). The brief was something like this: what can be done to encourage industry to use design more effectively as an instrument of competition?

Within days it became clear that wasn't quite the right question. More to the point was this: how do some companies manage to deliver one marvellous product after another? What makes winners win?

We set out to discover whether the companies that claw larger and larger shares of our markets behave differently from others. If they do, what is the difference?

To find out, we did a number of things. First, we invited James Fairhead, an independent consultant, to look at driving companies around the world, including the UK. We also commissioned market research into some 8,000 British manufacturing companies. The same research was replicated, though using a smaller sample, in the United States. Experts kindly came from the United States, Germany, Italy, France, Japan and elsewhere. We held innumerable meetings with specialist engineers, designers, teachers and others. We talked to a lot of people and read a great deal. Our heads spinning with information, we held a two-day 'brain-storming' session, led by Ron Baker, at Ashridge Management College, to pull our ideas together, and Edward de Bono kindly gave us a day to look for new approaches. I then went to Japan to look at how companies there develop new products.

To give you the answer at once: winning companies behave differently from others. What is more, although they operate in many countries and all sorts of industries, they are all doing the same sort of things.

Does it matter, if we're all doing quite well? Yes it does. The subject is timely. Today Britain spends over £2 billion a week on goods made abroad and imported to this country. It is a huge sum; think how many hospitals we could build, roads we could repair, schools we could improve, jobs we could provide with the money spent on imported goods.

While it is wrong to be too glum (Britain is still the world's fourth largest exporter of manufactured goods; in the decade to 1988, British exports doubled), the simple point is that others are doing better.

Yes, it does matter. A year or two ago I chaired a panel to select design awards. It was clear that great swathes of British industry are being pushed out altogether, or pushed to the periphery of the market-place. We gave an award to a beautifully engineered fishing reel and another to an ingenious plastic bulldog clip: 'sad, slight, useless things to calm the mad', as Robert Lowell, the American poet, put it.

In other fields there were products of scale and importance, it is true. A flight simulator that sells around the world, for example. But there were few high-volume consumer goods to stem the flood of imports. The high ground now belongs to someone else.

There are those who say that a decline in manufacturing doesn't matter. The future, we are told, lies in servicing global markets with brain power and software. That is not the view of economists at either Oxford or Cambridge. Aside from the fact that service and software companies use hardware, Oxford economists Roger Bacon and Walter Eltis argue that Britain's problem has been and remains too few producers. According to the Cambridge Economic Policy Group, 'If Britain gives up industry as well as agriculture, it will become a really poor country'. Strong words. The report goes on:

> If manufacturing continues to be squeezed out of both home and overseas markets at anything like the past rate, there is no plausible growth of earnings from the export of services and technology that will rescue Britain from severe recession within the next two decades.

Nor is this confined to the UK. The American deficit worries the Western world. Akio Morita, founder and chairman of Sony, told *US News and World Report*:

> Right now in this country [the United States] service industries are booming. But if America goes to services and forgets manu-production industries, you must not complain about an imbalance of trade, because you are not producing. American executives . . . are moving into the 'money game' – buy a company, sell a company, take over a company. If you continue this, American industry will completely deteriorate.

Modern Britain, at least as much as the United States, is in the grip of that same 'money game'. Morita, who has created in his lifetime a company with annual sales of $11 billion, puts his advice simply: 'Produce real things well.'

When Sarah Hogg was economics editor of *The Times* she wrote, 'We desperately need a manufacturing future.' She described the notion that the UK has a choice between manufacturing and services as 'the smelliest of red herrings'.

To prosper, in short, we need to make more products that people who are free to choose want to buy. That seems self-evident. It is also clear that a number of companies in other countries are doing so better than all but our top companies.

There is a larger perspective:

Unless we understand that we must make what people want to buy, not attempt to sell what we think we are good at making, we had better get used to continuing decline. And, in its wake, social and political decay, and perhaps even democracy itself struggling for survival.

That was not said by some panicky alarmist, nor some marketing guru from Harvard, but by Sir Edwin Nixon, chairman of IBM in the UK. It might sound high-flown. The simpler point is that all companies need to satisfy customers in highly competitive conditions. This book shows how the winners do just that. To set the scene, I talk about that competition and then look at how to respond.

APOLOGY AND THANKS

There are many more excellent companies than are described in this book. I hope they – and readers – will forgive obvious omissions.

Many people have helped provide material for this book. Their names appear in the Acknowledgements. I thank them all wholeheartedly. They will perhaps understand if I mention here Anne, my wife, and Robert Postema and Rachel Pyper of WH Allen, whose support and help with this new edition has been wonderful.

James Pilditch
1989

1

The New Competition

'Japanese growth slows to a gallop.'
New York Times, 19 January 1968

Margaret Thatcher invited sixty people in the design world to 10 Downing Street. She held up a glass. 'It makes me mad,' she said, 'when I go into a shop to buy something for the kitchen and I find it is made in Holland or Italy or Hong Kong or somewhere else. Why isn't it made here?' And she asked, 'What can we do about it?'

She pinpointed what had become a major threat, not only to tens of thousands of companies, but also to the British economy as a whole. In Britain, once 'the workshop of the world', imports of manufactured goods cost double all the expenditure on education and health put together (Figure 1). And that is in a country that provides free health care and free education for everyone.

This is not only a British problem. Economies around the world are being knocked sideways by the devastating impact of a relatively few high-powered companies, the new competitors. Forty years ago, for example, the UK and the United States each exported over a quarter of all the world's manufactured goods. By 1986 the British share had fallen to 8 per cent. By 1988 it was 6.9 per cent. The US share is down to 14 per cent.

Saying that, British exports have doubled in the last eight years. Indeed, this country still exports more of its production than most. Over the last decade the UK has exported between 25 per cent and 30 per cent of its production. This compares with the 7–10 per cent for the US and 12–15 per cent for Japan. Other European countries are much like Britain, only Germany being ahead.

It sounds all right. The trouble is that these big numbers hide a bigger truth: the inexorable rise in imports. It is those that cost jobs and wealth we can ill afford. In Britain they have risen 60 per cent in five years. In the US between 1980 and 1985 they rose 70 per cent, while American exports

1

Figure 1 Expenditure on imports of manufactured goods, health and education

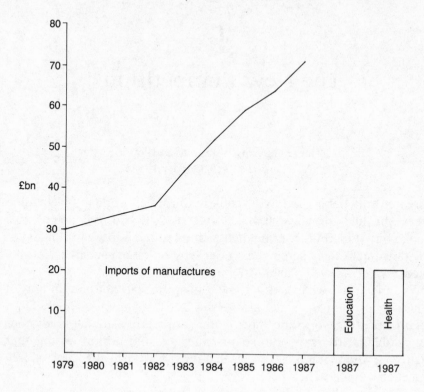

SOURCE: DTI and Amalgamated Abstract of Statistics (1989)

fell 14 per cent. Look deeper and you find that these imports are often in high-calibre, large-market growth areas. Tomorrow's wealth is being clawed away from us. Look deeper still and you find that this is not occurring because others work harder or charge less. The theme of this book is that some of our global competitors, expecially the Japanese, are simply superior. They are aiming at longer-term targets and going after them in ways that are plainly better.

For a while this superiority may not be obvious. As Western companies (US and British in the lead) grow by acquisition and rationalisation, you can't see the difference. But there is a difference. You come across people who grimly see the scale of the competition (you can hardly walk down a high street without being aware of it), but think it won't affect them. It will, in every dimension one can think of.

2

People in small, local companies can hope the gale will blow over their heads. For some that may be true, but not for many. The consultants Arthur D. Little, who have studied global competition as much as anyone, put it this way:

> Some companies believe they can create a refuge from competitors by burrowing into one market. This kind of niche in the context of global competition becomes analogous to a pot-hole. When a strong competitor targets a market section that includes that niche it will have the effect of a steamroller paving over the entire sector.

The experience of America, remembered as 'the arsenal of democracy', admired as the world's innovative and advanced industrial leader, tells the story. Today its trade deficit is the worry of the world. In 1985 nearly three quarters of all TV and video cameras sold in the USA were imported. Over one third of all cars, clothes, machine tools, telephones and semi-conductors were imported. Nearly half of all car radios and more than three quarters of the shoes were imported (Figure 2). In the third quarter of 1984 the USA imported more high-tech products than it exported.

Is this to do with low prices? Maybe yes, maybe no. A Gallup poll in the US showed that people would pay 135 per cent more for a pair of shoes, 66 per cent more for a television, and 36 per cent more for a car if it were seen as a quality product.

DANGEROUS ANALYSIS

There are as many explanations for all this as there are people to give them. Some say it is all the fault of the exchange rate. In the United States, an economic report to the President in 1983 considered an overvalued dollar to be the only problem. The report was wrong. In August 1986 Commerce Department officials said the – by now – lower dollar had little or no effect in reducing the deficit, which was heading for another record. Imports were strong. By comparison exports continued to weaken (Figure 3). The same trend can be seen in the UK.

The simple conclusion is that people in other countries are making the products we all want to buy. Put it another way, despite all the energy, all the competence, all the business schools, all the supporting infrastructure

3

Figure 2   US imports are rising (imports as % of domestic supply)

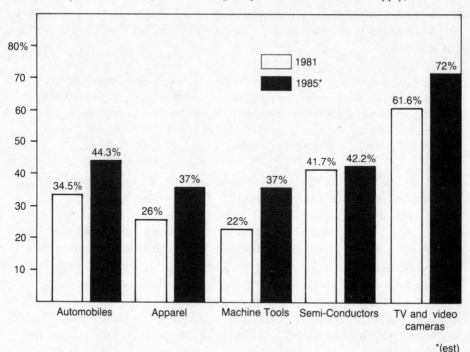

SOURCE: US Department of Commerce

of some of the most developed countries in the world, many business people are failing to do what they are there to do.

It is popular to blame unfair competition. Jerry Pearlman, chairman of Zenith Electronics Corporation, one of only two remaining US colour television manufacturers, expresses a common view. In the *New York Times* he wrote, 'A major portion of the colour TV market has been stolen by foreign competition whose unfair trade practices are emboldened by our government inaction.' No doubt he was thinking of the Japanese. Though it has dropped a little since, in 1986 the US deficit with Japan was $60 billion, a stunning amount. But as this book will show, if we put Japanese success down to either low wages or unfair practices we're missing the point completely.

Robert Christopher, a former *Time* and *Newsweek* editor, has been a 'Japan watcher' for forty years. In his book *Second to None: American Companies in Japan* he punctures a number of myths. Christopher took Lee

4

Figure 3   The alarming gap between imports and exports

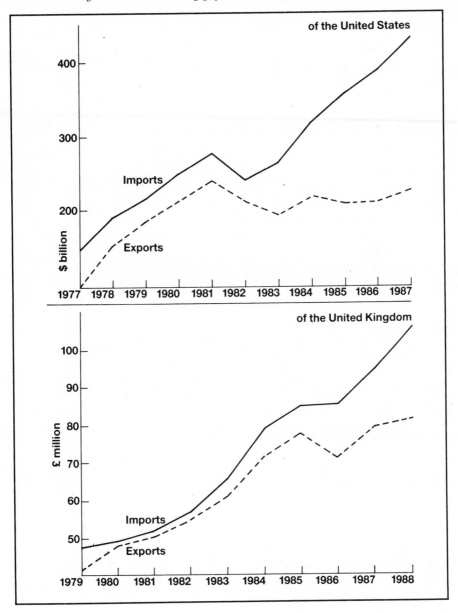

SOURCE: US Department of Commerce
SOURCE: Overseas Trade Statistics

Iacocca, chairman of Chrysler, to task for promoting 'the view that Japanese rip-offs are largely to blame for America's record trade deficit', a view that has gained currency and prompted restrictions. Christopher claims that charges that 'the Japanese capture American markets by unscrupulous means while unfairly closing off their markets to American products are at best vastly overstated and more often just plain wrong'. Despite its protectionist reputation, he claims, Japan buys more from the USA than does West Germany and a number of US companies excel in Japan. IBM in Japan has sales of $2 billion, Xerox's Japanese affiliate has sales of $1 billion. Coca-Cola produces 60 per cent of all Japanese carbonated beverages.

In 1984 the USA exported $27 billion worth of goods to Japan, from data-processing equipment to snow-making machines. Nor is this just high-tech. Seventy per cent of the razor blades sold in Japan are made in Connecticut by the Schick Division of Warner-Lambert. Half of the disposable nappies worn by Japanese babies are from Procter & Gamble.

Between 1982 and 1987 Japan's imports of manufactured goods more than doubled, only a fifth of them coming from newly industrialised countries. Indeed, Japan's Ministry of International Trade and Industry (MITI) wrote recently, 'the burning issue for domestic industries is higher added-value achieved through design as a means of coping with rising imports of manufactured goods'. Not much hint of unfair practice in that.

Not everyone in the West understands that clear view. Complacency comes into it too. One well-known commentator told me in Boston that General Electric 'could lead in consumer electronics if it chose to'. A second man talked about cars: 'As for Japanese cars, when they first came into the US they were a mess. It took a West-coast dealer to set them straight.' Well, if so, he did a convincing job.

SHAPE OF THINGS TO COME

Let's look at cars. If America isn't the home of the car nowhere is. But see what is happening. Nearly one car in every four sold in the USA is imported from Japan. Even though the rising yen has put up the cost of Japanese cars some $2,000, every one that is permitted into the country by Japan's self-imposed quota is sold. Detroit's share of the US market, 68 per cent in 1986, is expected to drop to 55 per cent by 1990. Add to that a million trucks, not limited by quota.

Of course, this thrust is not only towards the USA. Within a decade, by their own estimates, Japanese car makers will supply one third of the world's cars. The current figure is a quarter. In addition, Japan now registers the largest number of automobile patents. That speaks well for their future.

Look at Britain. In February 1986 *Car* magazine splashed across its front cover the headline: 'These new Japanese cars are poised to tear the heart out of the car industry in Europe.' The cover showed the Honda Accord and the Celica GT. In the leader, the editor said that he and his colleagues had thought hard about whether they should print such an alarmist view. They decided it was the truth and was necessary. Since then *What Car* has voted Toyota's Celica GT the best coupé two years running.

Over 2 million cars were sold in Britain in 1988. Over half of them were imported (57 per cent). That means, according to a Nissan estimate, that in

Ford's Probe V also aims to cut drag. This car, claim Ford, has less drag than an F-15 fighter. Improving aerodynamics, they say, is the most cost-effective way to fuel efficiency.

seven months of 1988 alone the motor industry was responsible for £5 billion of Britain's £8 billion trade deficit.

Imports come from many countries, of course, but it is the penetration by Japanese firms into Western and other markets that is most dramatic, even shattering. They have laid down the truest marker of the new power of global business.

Harvard Business School runs a course on country analysis and scenario planning. Speaking at the course in 1983 Professor Bruce Scott said, 'Most people do not yet believe we have a competitive problem.' He added that through the creative combination of technology, capital and skilled labour the Japanese have created a strategy of dynamic comparative advantage. They are gaining a share in high-tech, losing it in low-tech. They have 'upgraded their national portfolio'.

It is perhaps irritating to dwell on Japan. But many of us still haven't grasped the scale and force of its industrial competition. In 1985 the Department of Trade and Industry (DTI) published the report of a study tour to Hong Kong, Japan and the United States. It posed the question, which country has more than 50 per cent of world market share in the following products: shipbuilding, motorcycles, zip fasteners, pianos, colour cathode ray (TV) tubes, cameras, plain paper copiers, hi-fi, electronic typewriters and calculators, artificial leather, robotics? The answer, in every case, is Japan. It makes more than half of all of those products sold in the world (Figure 4).

The DTI report, bravely, was called '. . . *You won't do it'*. Where had that come from? As the British study team finished its work, its leader thanked their Japanese hosts for their warmth and openness. 'But something puzzles us,' he said. 'You have been wonderfully frank, answered all our

Figure 4   Share of world markets held by Japanese companies

35mm cameras	84%
Watches	82%
Motorcycles	55%
Telephones	66%
VCR	84%
Colour TV	53%
Microwave ovens	71%
Calculators	77%

SOURCE: The PA Consulting Group

questions, told us everything we wanted to know. How is that possible?' The Japanese reply, couched in courtesy, was this: 'We feel able to tell you everything because we are ten years ahead. By the time you catch up we will be another ten years in front. And anyway, we know you won't do it.'

Look at facsimile machines, sure to outstrip the boom enjoyed by personal computers a few years ago. The technology, which transmits copies of paper documents over telephone wires, was created in 1842 by a Scottish clock maker. In the 1920s German inventors improved the process, then US companies took the lead. Fax was used for sending cables and for other professional uses. Who has turned that specialised technology into products for everyone? That has been a Japanese achievement. Sharp, Canon and Toshiba have sold over 3 million machines.

Two Japanese companies, Sony and Matsushita, have between them half the US market for compact discs. The first, second and third largest microchip manufacturers in the world are all Japanese, according to Dataquest, a California market analysis firm. Toshiba is now assembling a one megabit chip in California, four times as powerful as the currently dominant chip. Hitachi, too, is producing chips in Texas. NEC is expanding its memory chip production in Roseville, California, to 5 million chips a year. In Tokyo, the same firm built a supercomputer called SX-2. Problems that would take a normal mainframe computer a week take the SX-2 a mere 23 seconds, it is said.

Nor dare we think that Japan's penetration into world markets is over. They are focusing now on new areas. Computers, aerospace, pharmaceuticals, banking and cosmetics are among those listed by Philip Kotler and colleagues. Indeed, already all ten of the world's largest banks, judged on assets, are Japanese.

There is a kind of twentieth-century colonisation going on. Just as both the United Kingdom and the United States in the past spread plants across the world, so the same is now happening to us. In 1986 *Business Week* reported that some 500 Japanese companies now manufacture or assemble automobiles, VCRs, telecommunications devices and other products in the United States. Nor will it stop. Speaking on US television in October 1986, Akio Morita, chairman of Sony, forecast that his company will 'put more capital into America'. Since then, in 1988, Sony paid £2 billion for CBS Records, which has manufacturing and sales operations in every EEC country.

The American Electronic Association estimated that in 1986 Japanese companies made about 400 investments in the US electronics industry.

One hundred and fifty Japanese companies are producing auto parts in the USA now – triple the number in 1984 – and analysts say there could be 300 by 1990. Already at least 250,000 Americans work for Japanese companies in the USA, a figure expected to triple in the next decade.

CLOSER AND CLOSER

According to the Ministry of Finance in Japan, between 1985 and 1987 Japanese companies have invested £7 billion in Europe. Year by year Japanese investment in the UK has grown: in 1980 the figure was £125 million; in 1986 it was £578 million. By 1987 they had invested £1,454 million in Britain.

The point of this is that from now on our competition won't come from across the world, but from across the street. There are said to be one hundred Japanese companies in Britain now. The British Government expects that figure to double. One company alone shows the salutary effect they can have. Nissan opened a plant in Sunderland, Tyne and Wear, in 1986, with a production goal of 24,000 rising to 100,000. Thanks to the rising yen, Nissan's profits were down 56 per cent in the year ending 31 March 1986, but that didn't stop them from continuing to invest. Indeed, by 1988, they put up their production targets in Britain to 200,000 cars a year. Nissan now employs 2,000 people in Sunderland. Toyota, too, plans to invest £650 million in a car assembly plant and engine assembly plant in Derby. They will produce 200,000 cars here, they say, and employ 3,000 people. Already linked in to Austin Rover, Honda is building a £300 million plant in Swindon.

Nor is that the end of their influence. One obstacle to Japanese investment in Britain is the difficulty of finding suppliers of the quality Japanese companies are used to. Local manufacture has the effect of raising local standards. That's true in other ways. Nissan's Sunderland plant will soon be making 40 cars per person per year. That is twice the productivity of competitors. Absenteeism is 2 per cent, which compares with 10–14 per cent in the car industry generally.

Ryuzaburo Kaku, chairman of Canon, says that from his point of view the rise in the yen has been 'a national calamity'. The irony is that as the yen increases in value, more Japanese companies will want to manufacture abroad, bringing them closer still to our markets. Sony and others intend to respond by shifting plants overseas and by buying more components abroad. As well as wanting to come close to our markets, Japanese companies are being driven to seek lower cost manufacturing. Yamaha, the $2 billion a year company, now makes guitars, tennis rackets and golf clubs in Taiwan – for sale in Japan. Matsushita, too, makes air conditioners in Malaysia for sale in Japan. Casio goods are now made in Taiwan, Hong Kong, and Korea too.

In recent years Japan's imports from the four 'dragons' of the Far East – Hong Kong, Singapore, South Korea and Taiwan – have risen 50 per cent a year in dollar terms. Now, richest of all, in 1988 Honda started to export cars *from* the United States to Japan. Their target is 70,000 cars a year. This must confound critics who say Japan keeps exports out. They're accused of being unfair, although some in the West are not above wanting to introduce their own restrictions. One response to imports, of course, is to impose restrictions. The French Government's Poitiers ploy was an inspired example. It required that all Japanese electronic goods should pass through this sleepy town for clearance. It was too bad that the customs officers were in Paris or out to lunch or otherwise engaged. More seriously, in 1988, the US Congress voted to stop all increases in imports of textiles. A bill passed by the Senate restricted increases to 1 per cent, the rate at which the US market is growing. It also tried to freeze all shoe imports to the 1987 level. But neither the Japanese, the French, Americans nor British need think restrictions will right the balance.

Quite the reverse. Krish Bhaskar, author of the University of East Anglia's *Japanese Automotive Strategies,* reports that the Japanese will be able to raise their profit per car by between £200 and £400 by making them in Europe. In North America Honda's production is already 440,000. (Their millionth car rolled off the Ohio assembly line in April 1988.) Nissan and Toyota each produce nearly 300,000, figures bound to rise. Now Isuzu has companies in Michigan and California.

MORE THREATS

Nor should one ignore what Dr R. D. Schraft of Stuttgart calls the 'threshold countries' – Brazil, Spain, South Korea and Taiwan, among others. In 1987 Taiwan's trade surplus was $19 billion. Korea's exports totalled $47 billion.

As a portent of what is to come, South Korea's Hyundai sold 130,000 Excel cars in the United States in the first nine months of 1986, its first year of entry to the market. In December 1986 *Business Week* described Hyundai's Excel as 'the hottest-selling import in US history'. Notice that in 8 months in 1988 – from January to October – 377,000 Korean cars were sold in the US. There is more to come.

The rising yen is helping Korea. With 1985 sales of $8.2 billion and as the country's leading automobile manufacturer, Hyundai expects to market the equivalent of the Toyota Crown for less than one third of the price. 'At the moment,' the head of Hyundai told a startled audience of Japanese businessmen in 1986, 'we can barely keep up with production of our autos headed for Canada and the US, but we also plan to penetrate the Japanese market in two or three years' time.'

Hyundai also sold 50,000 personal computers in the USA in 1986. By 1988 it had climbed to sixth in market share. It also signed a joint-venture agreement with Tandon Corp., of Chatsworth, California, to manufacture disc drives.

In 1987 Daewoo, Korea's biggest exporter, with exports totalling $3.28 billion, increased sales to the United States by 49 per cent over the previous year and to Japan by 38 per cent. As if that wasn't dazzling enough, it planned to increase total exports a further 40 per cent in 1988.

Japan is well aware of this new competition. Satoshi Iue, president of Sanyo Electric, on a visit to Samsung, a major Korean group, commented: 'Frankly, I could almost feel the menace. We are already reaching a stage whereby not only our conventional industries, such as shipbuilding, but also advanced technology businesses will be threatened by the Korean competitors.'

The impact of these 'threshold' countries is already being felt on a global scale. In 1970, according to Gary Shilling, an American economic forecaster, Taiwan, South Korea, Hong Kong, Singapore, Mexico and Brazil together accounted for 4 per cent of world exports. By 1986 the figure had risen to 10 per cent.

Already the need is plain to see. The US shortfall in trade with Korea, for example, 'exploded', in the words of *Business Week*, from $300 million in 1981 to $7 billion in 1986 and $12 billion in 1989. The deficit with Taiwan has increased almost fivefold over the same time, from $4.3 billion to $20.5 billion.

Facing this huge penetration of our markets, what are we to do? Clearly, something must be done; equally plainly, conventional answers are not working.

LOOKING THE WRONG WAY

A few months ago, like a new boy at school, I sat in the company of distinguished British engineers, business executives and officials. They were talking about 'Great Britain Limited'. One man said, 'We are becoming technologically obsolete.' Another, a distinguished scientist, engineer and manager, said, 'It is not technology that counts, but how you adapt it to the consumer.' Others spoke of productivity and unions and a cultural legacy that undervalues manufacturing. Finally, and symbolically, an economist was asked to sum up. He reminded me of a travel guide telling us how to drive on the motorway from London to Birmingham. 'If M1 could equal M2,' he said (or M3 or M25, I forget), 'then the economy would be in equilibrium.'

For all its gobbledegook, this struck a chord with me. I have certainly sat at board meetings where the talk is of budgets and financial plans and investments and acquisitions and P/E ratios and discounted cash flows and dividends. Somehow, what the company does, what it makes and who it makes it for, are never mentioned.

John McKay, a high-level and discreet communications consultant in London, was invited to spend a day with senior officers of a multinational company with annual sales of £6 billion. The subject was corporate strategy. At lunch the chairman asked him how he found the morning. 'May I be rude?' he asked. 'I have heard about your sales in every country, your plans for capital equipment and your P/E. But no one has said *what* he makes or what he sells.'

By contrast, winning companies keep a simpler focus, one that every company can have. Although as sophisticated as any, they have got back to basics. In a way, getting back to basics is the main message of this book. The end result, as we all know, is that these companies are pouring out the goods we all want. That, so easy to say, is the unanswerable key to competitive success.

Business schools are not noticeably better. Hot on finance, adept at numbers, fine at the elaborate analyses of marketing plans, they are so often terrible at the simple things. I knew a German lecturer who was miserable. 'What's the matter?' I asked. He replied, 'I'm doing a Ph.D. in marketing and I can't make it sound difficult enough.'

This is no argument for ignorance or even naïvety, refreshing as both may sometimes be. Business in the modern world is complex. But it remains clear that despite all the erudition and theory, many formerly fine

13

companies are going to the wall or are, at least, past their best. It is also true that other companies drive forwards inexorably.

Put at its simplest, some companies are making the goods we all want to buy. They are the winners. Still more important, the more you look at them the more you believe they are the long-distance runners. Their names will continue to dominate our stores and streets and plants tomorrow as they are doing today.

THE NEWER THREAT

There is a second and even larger threat. Winning companies are not only developing the products we want to buy, and that applies to printing plant and earth-moving equipment as much as to cars and consumer goods, but they are giving us better quality than we have ever had. In addition, they are doing it in half the time it takes the rest.

Riccardo Berla, chairman of Olivetti in the UK, said that product development in Olivetti 'used to take two years or so. Today Bellini produces mass design in two months.' That is the new way.

Opposite ideas can come together to make sense. 'Loose/tight' management is one example. Another might be the extraordinary paradox of Japanese business – 'slow/fast' you might call it. It is slow in two ways. First, anyone who has dealt with Japanese companies knows how tortuously vague and slow they seem to be. The management process seems ethereal as it feels its way towards consensus views. Second, they take time to investigate markets before attacking them. They are painstakingly, comprehensively, exhaustively thorough. These are the slow bits of 'slow/fast'.

The quick part is when they have made up their mind. Some Japanese companies have a phenomenal ability to pump out one innovative product after another. In April 1986 I asked for a photograph of the latest Sony product, seen in a magazine the day before. I expected the newest version of the Walkman. Instead, I received a picture of a girl with a compact disc player hanging from her neck. That was new. But not any more. By June the newspapers were writing about digital audio tape (DAT), which, they say, will render compact discs obsolete. Sound quality is 'spectacularly' improved. Size is 'dramatically' reduced. As compact discs, less than 5 inches across, replaced 12-inch records, so DAT is smaller

Is the world's smallest compact disc player, the Sony Discman, already obsolescent? Yes. In 1988 Sony introduced a Pocket Discman that weighs 10.6 ounces.

15

too. It looks like a slim matchbox, the size of a credit card, a quarter of an inch thick. Playing time is twice that of compact discs and likely to increase. With DAT it will be possible to record as well as play high-quality sound. And there's another quality, according to Noel Keywood of the *Sunday Times*: DAT has potential for adaptation as a computer memory – a pocket-sized digital stereo and computer, all in one.

DAT cassettes allow 'almost perfect music reproduction' says *The Economist*, but still new products are pressing forward. The hand-held video camera and recorder was one. Since 1986 Sony have sold 3.5 million. And they cost about £1,000 each. Now there is their Video Walkman.

We've been able to watch films when we want for some years. Now we can see them where we choose. This is a complete VCR (video cassette recorder). It is the size of a small book and powered by battery or mains. The cassette itself is 8mm. From Sony, it is called the Video Walkman. You can link the Video Walkman to a video camera, so that it becomes a portable recorder too.

This is a portable and complete VCR. The size of a small book and weighing 1.1 kg, it has a 3-inch liquid crystal display screen (with 92,160 pixel resolution). Power comes from batteries or from the mains with an adaptor. The Video Walkman can play a three-hour tape – and can record. The idea is this: when VCR was launched it meant you could see programmes when it suited you. Now, you can see them both when and where you like. 'Times whiled away in trains and tubes, waiting rooms and queues could now be used for video viewing,' Sony say. Observe the sheer pace and pumping persistence of such innovation. Later we will see exactly how Sony achieve it, but the point now is that Sony want this speed and can get it. Manufacturers anywhere who can't keep up with this momentum are in trouble. They have to match it.

To rub it in, Sony's swiftest introduction was their new 3-inch CD. A few months after this concept was introduced all their 1988 CD players were able to play these new discs. Two months later the D88 Discman, specifically designed for these small discs, was introduced.

The pace of change is changing. Within months of compact discs comes digital audio tape (DAT): smaller, better, and allowing digital recording anywhere.

17

This speed of product introduction is deliberate. It is designed to upset existing patterns of product life-cycles. Kenichi Ohmae, head of the consultants McKinsey & Co., in Tokyo, says Japanese firms are using speed of product introduction to 'shake out slower competitors'. Some 20,000 new products come on to the Japanese market each year. In 1985 the figure was 19,703, one third more than two years earlier.

Is all this development too fast? Some people fear it will destroy established business. When top executives from the United States and Japan met in Vancouver in December 1986 to talk about DAT, Nesuhi Ertegun, chairman of WEA International, parent of Warner Brothers Records, protested: 'It is false to assume that consumers should get whatever they want.' In reply, the head of Toshiba, Shoichi Saba, said: 'Consumers have a right to enjoy the best quality music and video, the latest developments, whenever advanced technology is available.' Behind his protestation may lie the fact that the rising yen is eating into exports of electronic goods. Japanese industry needs new products.

DON'T GET STUCK

One extraordinary consequence of shortening product life-cycles, according to the Mitsubishi Research Institute, is that companies now have to reckon not how many of the products they can produce, but how few. They don't want to be stuck with surplus stock. The other consequence is a new flexibility. If the product succeeds, they have to turn up the gas in a hurry; expand production, in other words, to meet demand.

Against this onslaught there is one encouraging point. Most of those so-called 'new products' are improvements of previous ones. Maybe only one or two in a hundred are, like DAT, radically new.

If most companies cannot match the technology of the winning companies, they can improve their existing products, and speed up the way in which they do it. People think innovation is too slow and costly. As we all know, it can be. Development programmes can potter on for years, without much fruit at the end. But we will also see, and this is one of the main themes of this book, that this need not be so. It is a matter of what you look for, where you start, how you go about it. When General Electric in the United States wanted to develop a new jet engine they appointed a team leader. He held reviews every day. A daily, typed, single-page memo covering the main events of the previous twenty-four hours was mandatory. It had to be written by the key people. It could not be delegated. The development took one year instead of the usual two.

Tales like this show what can be done if the will is there. But I must issue a note of caution. It is easy to be swept away by the excitement of this bustling change. Business, as we all know, is a complicated affair. Being simplistic is risky. But the fact is that we have to move from where we are towards this faster world, whatever the problems. It is the only way to go.

So here we see a double challenge: first, to develop products that people want to buy; second, to develop these products far faster than we used to. These fast-moving companies must be doing something right. What is it? What can we learn from them? I think the essential point is that winning companies do what we say we do. We would all say we care about our customers. We all believe we create the best products we can. We all believe in quality. But, as I will show, the hallmarks of all winning companies are the intensity and totality of their efforts in each of these areas. From an author's point of view this has its drawbacks. There is little to say that hasn't been heard a thousand times before. But that doesn't make it any the less true or timely. Quite the contrary. My defence is that if companies do the things that are in this book, unoriginal as they may sound, their perspective will alter and their performance will improve.

PRESSURE TO INCREASE

There is a third threat. Not only are Japanese companies pouring out these new, high-quality products, but they intend to step up their activity.

In mid-1985, the consultants Arthur D. Little sent questionnaires about innovation to top executives in North America, Europe and Japan. Two thirds of the Japanese respondents said innovation is becoming 'much more' important. Forty per cent of North American business executives thought the same. One quarter of Europeans agreed.

Japanese executives said innovation takes up one third of their time. And here's the nub: 87 per cent of the Japanese said they thought it would take *more* of their time in the future. So, Japanese executives both give more time to innovation now and they are going to give it still more.

When asked how much innovation needed to occur in creating their products, four out of five Japanese respondents replied 'a great deal'.

19

About half the replies from North America and Europe said the same. Innovation just doesn't figure as highly on our list of priorities as it does in Japan. Fewer than half of the UK managers and about half of the US managers who replied to the Arthur D. Little survey had any specific corporate expectation of the role that innovation would have in relation to earnings in the next five years. This compares with 87 per cent of the managers in Japan. We would do well to notice this difference. According to Arthur D. Little, 'Firms that neglect the management of innovation tend to wither and eventually die.'

In fact, Arthur D. Little listed eight possible areas for innovation: product, service, marketing, production, distribution, finance, management and social (Figure 5). In every one, except management, the Japanese replies to the survey were far stronger than the American or European ones. As if to warn of what's coming, over half the Japanese executives who replied said that 'a great deal' of innovation must also occur in their service, in their marketing and in their production, as well as in their products.

We have been warned. What are we to do about it?

SUMMARY

The amount of goods we buy from abroad is eroding both American and British prosperity. Whole industries are being decimated. While thousands of companies are involved, from all over the world, barely a handful are setting the pace. They are producing the goods we all want to buy.

For years it has been popular to ascribe all kinds of false reasons to their success. Uncritical of ourselves, these were as comforting as they were deceptive. Now, as the true scale of global competition becomes more apparent day by day, we can ask what is it these winning companies are doing to outpace everyone else? The answers are simpler than they should be. These companies succeed partly by remembering that they exist to make what we want, partly by sticking with the basics of business, partly by having an inexorable will to do better every day in every way.

To compete, other companies must do the same.

Figure 5 **Turning up the heat**
Results of this international study suggest that competition, already fierce, will grow

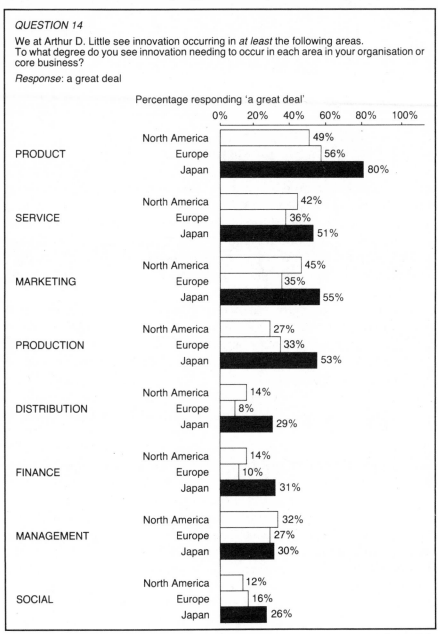

QUESTION 14

We at Arthur D. Little see innovation occurring in *at least* the following areas.
To what degree do you see innovation needing to occur in each area in your organisation or core business?

Response: a great deal

Percentage responding 'a great deal'

		%
PRODUCT	North America	49%
	Europe	56%
	Japan	80%
SERVICE	North America	42%
	Europe	36%
	Japan	51%
MARKETING	North America	45%
	Europe	35%
	Japan	55%
PRODUCTION	North America	27%
	Europe	33%
	Japan	53%
DISTRIBUTION	North America	14%
	Europe	8%
	Japan	29%
FINANCE	North America	14%
	Europe	10%
	Japan	31%
MANAGEMENT	North America	32%
	Europe	27%
	Japan	30%
SOCIAL	North America	12%
	Europe	16%
	Japan	26%

SOURCE: Arthur D. Little

2

Set the Right Goals

'Having lost sight of our objectives, we redoubled our efforts.'
Duke of Wellington

Where to start? Perhaps the first thing is to put the financial or economic view of business in its place. Company boards dwell on financial matters because that is what they think business is about, or at least some do. A comparative study of attitudes among US and Japanese directors showed that US business executives put profitability as their number one goal. Their Japanese counterparts put market share first. For them, profit comes third from last out of a long list.

Returning home at night a man lost his keys. He looked under a lamp-post. 'Did you drop them here?' asked a friend. 'No,' said the man, 'I dropped them back there, but I can see more here.' This is about tackling the easiest problems even if they are wrong, like cutting costs rather than developing good new products.

NON-PRICE FACTORS

Some people still believe that low prices are the key to competitiveness. Were that true, there is little hope. Always in the world there will be someone who can make things cheaper. Happily, low prices are not the answer. This is not to deny that pricing is a sensitive instrument of business, nor to criticise substantial efforts made to improve productivity. But the fact is that in today's world, people buy whatever they believe meets their needs. They don't always buy the cheapest.

This is not just confined to clothes and handbags and luxury goods. In 1971 a study of trade between the USA and West Germany showed that relative price advantage accounted for only 28 per cent of trade success (Figure 6).

Figure 6 People who believe price is the key to competitiveness can be wrong. Analysis of trade between the United States and West Germany showed it to be far less important than the so-called 'non-price' factors – quality, uniqueness, service.

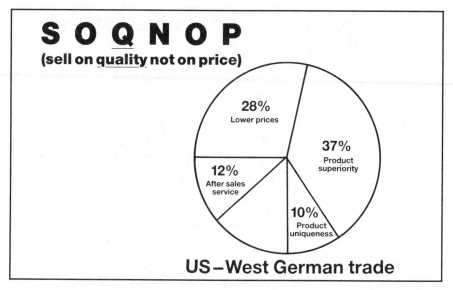

SOURCE: Kravis and Lipsey 1971

There is nothing new in this. In 1965, users of machine tools were asked by Britain's National Economic Development Office why they chose to buy imported equipment. The reason most quoted was 'superiority of foreign products' (Figure 7).

Farmers in Britain were asked in 1982 what guided their purchase of agricultural machinery. Quality factors were cited by 60 per cent of farmers. To them, quality was more important than price, according to Paul Gardiner and Roy Rothwell of the Science Policy Research Unit of the University of Sussex.

Evidence gathered in 1983 by K. Pick and K. Schott at University College, London, showed that the purchasing decisions of as many as 80 per cent of imports to the UK are based on so-called 'non-price' factors. There is more evidence along the same lines. In 1984 the Chartered Institute of Marketing asked 1,775 senior executives responsible for marketing in UK industry to think of a product successfully launched in the previous five years and to rank the factors that are most important in getting business. Fewer than one in five (17 per cent) named pricing. Six out of ten put product performance or product design in first place.

Figure 7 People may believe shoppers pay more for luxuries, but what about business executives buying machine tools? Here, too, the design of the product – its specification and superiority – is more important than low price.

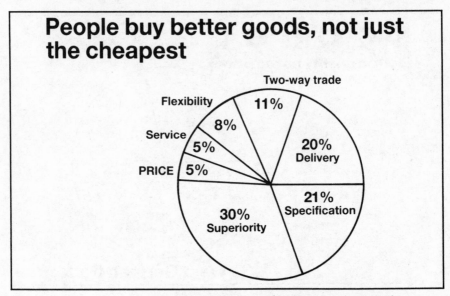

People buy better goods, not just the cheapest

Two-way trade
Flexibility
11%
8%
Service
5%
20%
Delivery
PRICE 5%
21%
Specification
30%
Superiority

SOURCE: 'Why the UK machine tool industry chose foreign goods',
National Economic Development Office

In the same study makers of industrial equipment were asked to name the factors leading to a successful new product launch in the previous five years. Eighty-six per cent named 'superior product/service' and only 28 per cent said 'low price in relation to competition'. Going further: when the same sample was asked to identify reasons for the failure of a new product launched in the previous five years, over half (56 per cent) pinpointed the product. Fewer than half (44 per cent) gave price in relation to competition as a reason for failure.

In 1983 the consultants McKinsey & Co. studied forty-five top performing companies (on a financial basis) in the United States. Of forty-three of them, they said, 'Winners compete by delivering a product that supplies superior value to customers, rather than one that costs less.' Time and again you see the simple fact that success depends on creating products people want to buy. Yet we also see, repeatedly, that companies don't think this way. They plan their money, not their products.

In the face of such evidence it is astonishing to read the findings of a study by the Open University of thirty-seven British companies and ten from other countries. Two thirds of the companies analysed in the study expressed their objectives in terms of profits, sales and (occasionally) market share. This was most marked in UK heating firms (74 per cent) and least marked in electronic business equipment firms (47 per cent). Only 17 per cent of the companies interviewed expressed their main objective in terms of meeting customer/user needs and/or product excellence.

Still more astonishing, when those companies commented on how they planned to improve their ability to sell in existing markets or expand into new markets, only 6 per cent included developing new or improved products. Eight per cent mentioned improving manufacturing technology.

In a 1979 survey of fifty-six small and medium-sized manufacturing companies conducted by the Confederation of British Industry (CBI), only seven cited low price as a reason for their success at home and abroad. Fifty-four credited 'good customer service'; forty-five named 'specialisation'; thirty-nine said 'high standard of product'. About half (twenty-nine) gave 'innovation' as their reason for success. In other words 'non-price' factors dominated the successful companies. Interestingly, almost all of those companies were very busy developing new products, either incrementally (step-by-step improvements) or more radically.

Commenting on the broader picture, Christopher Lorenz, management editor of the *Financial Times*, wrote: 'So long as British companies continue to be preoccupied with selling their products largely on price, their attitude can only spell harm for their own well-being, and that of the balance of payments.'

PERCEIVED PRODUCT QUALITY

The Strategic Planning Institute in Cambridge, Massachusetts, has the largest strategic database in the world, called Profit Impact of Marketing Strategy (PIMS). It has correlated hundreds of variables with long-term financial performance and concludes: 'The single variable far and away the most closely associated with good financial performance over the long haul is relative perceived product quality.'

But note: the perception is that of the customers. Losers, they go on to

say, 'downgrade the customer view'. They make high quality synonymous with tight tolerances. They tie quality objectives to manufacturing
flow. They 'formalise quality control objectives for manufacturing only'.

Professor Christopher Freeman of the Science Policy Research Unit at
the University of Sussex has written in *Design and British Economic Performance*, an impressive academic work:

> Many studies, both theoretical and empirical, point unambiguously to the
> fact that factors such as real or perceived quality variables related to design,
> technical service, reputation and marketing play an extremely important
> role [in international trading]. Price, in short, is only one element in
> effective competition.

He quotes Luke Soete, now professor of international economics at
Maastricht University in The Netherlands, who looked across the board at
all sorts of industries. His studies, for the Organisation for Economic Co-
operation and Development (OECD) and others, show that:

> Firms (and the countries in which they are based) tend to do well in their
> trade performance, if they are relatively more successful than their com-
> petitors in developing and designing new products and improving old ones
> and in improving the manufacturing technology by which they are made.

Theodore Levitt, the distinguished professor of business administration
at Harvard Business School, and now editor of the *Harvard Business Review*,
argues: 'Precisely when price competition gets more severe and therefore
price reduction becomes more important is when one is also likely to
benefit [the most] by incurring the additional costs of special new product
augmentation.'

AIM FOR QUALITY

Many companies compete for market share by buying their way in. They
cut prices. It is questionable whether this is still the best route. According
to PIMS, 'First achieve a relative perceived product quality edge over
your competitors. If you do you will gain share. Then take advantage of
economies of scale. Start from quality, achieve low cost as a result.'

The PIMS statement is as far from the conventional attitude of so much

26

business as it could be. It throws the focus, inevitably, away from balance sheets and towards the products a company makes. It asks the questions: 'What kind of products do you make? How can you make them better? How are you to gain the market share to build the volume to reduce the cost?'

Tom Clarke, when chairman of Silentnight, the largest bedding firm in the UK, criticised retailers whose only buying principle is 'bird seed' (cheep, cheep, cheep). Not even one retailer in ten, he complained, could answer simple questions about the specification of the products they buy.

Anthony Bamford, chairman of J. C. Bamford (JCB), one of Britain's shining companies, is emphatic: 'I don't think just being the cheapest helps at all.' His belief in so-called 'non-price' factors is manifest in every way. Take service, for example. When it comes to service, J. C. Bamford takes some beating. Anthony Bamford boasts: 'We can supply a part for any machine we have ever made the same day a customer requests it. If he orders before midday it can be shipped that afternoon. That is why we keep customers.'

In his book *The Design Dimension* Christopher Lorenz quotes Bob Lutz, head of Ford Europe. His policy is 'to get Ford cars out there that people desperately want, rather than cars they will buy because they are the lowest-priced in the market. You can't do that any more because the Japanese have taken that part of the market away from us.' That's no longer true. Honda, for example, do not discount cars as others do.

Ron Baker, a British consultant who runs brain-storming sessions to help companies arrive at their corporate strategies, says: 'When an archer aims at a target he first sees the arrow smash into the bull. Then he lets it fly.' In other words, we would do well to imagine our goal achieved. The first goal, we hear time and again, is not low price nor even profit, but reliable quality. Start there.

Talking of her car, my wife Anne said, 'It is marvellous. It never goes wrong.' Such excellence doesn't happen by accident. Michael Wolff, when president of the Chartered Society of Designers, summed it up. 'That remark,' he said, 'was planned in an office five years ago.'

If our goal is to remain in business or, better, to build market share, then it follows that we should take the steps necessary to achieve this. Too great an emphasis on profit, paradoxically, inhibits it. Companies in both the UK and the USA undoubtedly feel constrained by the insistence of analysts on immediate, short-term profit. It is a constraint felt far less strongly in Japan, where the *zaibatsu* who own companies feel able to take long-term views, or in West Germany, where banks have sizeable stakes in industry. Or in South Korea, where the top thirty conglomerates, or *chaebol*, account for one quarter of the country's gross domestic product.

One man who is credited with analysing Japan's economic ills years ago and setting it on the path of economic triumph is Dr Edwards Deming. He believes Western management 'has failed to perceive the forces of competition and become, instead, their victim'. Management style, he thinks, is the key. In the 1960s accountants and lawyers took over Western firms. Management by them, thinks Deming, only brings further decline. He hasn't any time for their short-term point of view:

> Quick returns, whether by acquisition, by divestiture, by paper profits or by creative accounting are self-defeating. In the long run they erode investment and the company ends up with just the opposite of what was intended. . . . A better way is to protect investment through plans and methods that improve product and service.

Dr Edwards Deming claims top management's use of only visible figures is the way to ruin. 'Do courses in finance,' he asked, 'teach people the importance of the unknown and unknowable loss – from a dissatisfied customer, a dissatisfied employee?'

SHORT-TERM VISION

The chairman and chief executive of Honeywell Inc., Edson Spencer, is among those who regret that shareholder value is almost entirely equated with short-term stock prices. By this yardstick the higher the share price, the better management has done its job.

> This forces management to put short-term earnings growth before such interests as market development, product quality, research and development and customer and employee satisfaction. As a result US companies find themselves operating at a disadvantage when competing against foreign companies.

Writing in *Business Week* Edson Spencer said, 'We Americans are competing like poker players, playing one hand at a time. Our foreign competitors are planning their moves far in advance.' He likened it to the oriental game called 'Go'. The aim of that game is to place your pieces so that your opponent is defeated before even knowing that he or she has been surrounded. 'Unless we change our strategy,' he warned, 'these competitors, with greater freedom to think and act long-term are going to be the final winners.'

The picture in the UK is the same. Sadly, Garth Wiseman, at NEDO, has found prima facie evidence to suggest that companies that cut back on investment in 'non-tangible' areas such as product development have seen their share price improve as a result. The practical impact of this is hard to overstate. First, many companies feel unable to take the long- or even medium-term view they need to create new products. Second, if profits have to be found it is easy to take money that has been committed to new products. Third, if and when the product does finally come to market, investors not unnaturally start wanting a return soon. One consequence can be that sound, sometimes marvellous developments can run out of money. They die on the edge of huge success. This attitude seems suicidal, except that maintaining share price is often, and necessarily, seen as a prime corporate objective.

Lord Caldecote, when chairman of 3i (Investors in Industry Plc) which is using its imagination to meet this problem, told me what can happen. 'If a company makes £10 million profit and invests half in the future, its accounts show a 50 per cent drop. The share price falls.' He knew of one company where this happened. 'It became a sitting duck for a takeover.'

Sir Alastair Pilkington, honorary life president of Pilkington Brothers, is the brilliant Cambridge engineer who drove through all kinds of adversity for twelve years to develop float glass and so change the face of the world's cities. From that development alone Pilkington earns some £40 million a year in licensing fees. Today the company is far and away the largest, most efficient glass maker in the world.

Sir Alastair believes he could never have developed float glass if Pilkington had been a public company, a remark that has an ironic and pertinent twist. Pilkington went public in 1970. In 1986, just when they announced that half-year profits were up by 76 per cent, they were challenged by a hostile takeover bid. 'It would be a disaster,' Mr Antony Pilkington, the chairman, said. 'Spending on research and development and the long-term view towards planning would suffer.' In the event, the bid was withdrawn.

J. C. Bamford, a second-generation private company with assets of

One-time chairman of a great financial institution (3i), Lord Caldecote strongly believes in investing in new products. The short-term scramble for profit, so current, is jeopardising the future of British manufacturing industry, he argues. Lord Caldecote (*left*) is seen here with Rolls-Royce managers, looking at an engine cowling.

£130 million, ploughed £35 million back into the company in 1988, on top of their high spending on R & D. Most public companies find it hard to match that scale of long-term commitment. But JCB's policy works. Sales in 1988 were £377 million, up from £296 million. Yuasa, the Japanese battery makers from Osaka, also took a long-term view when they invested heavily in their plant in Wales. Even if it achieves its target, it won't wipe off debts for several years, but Yuasa don't mind.

A study by Jetro, the Japanese Government body, revealed that 40 per cent of Japanese companies operating in Europe are losing money or just breaking even. 'You must remember,' says (Lady) Felicity Marsh, who has made a special study of Japanese investment in Europe for the Economist Intelligence Unit and others, 'that unlike most Western companies, the

The patient inventor who changed the look of the world's cities, Sir Alastair Pilkington FRS. He developed float glass.

Japanese are prepared to take a long view. Their priorities are not an immediate return on capital but to build up a sound operating base.'

If you have to deliver better profits every six months if not every quarter, come what may, you may be forgiven for cutting out investment in the future. It is, of course, a short-sighted policy.

When Victor Kiam bought Remington Products from Sperry-Rand in 1979 it had lost $30 million in three years. Sales were $50 million. In 1989 they are expected to top $300 million. Remington is listed as one of the 100 best companies to work for in America. Kiam says he can take a long-term view and remember that quality is uppermost because his is a private company. 'We don't have that Sword of Damocles – the ninety-day reporting period – hanging over us.'

Of course, growth in Britain often comes by acquisition. The numbers are blinding. Britain is now spending the equivalent of nearly 5 per cent of

31

its gross domestic product on acquisitions in the United States alone. (In 1987 British entrepreneurs spent $31.7 billion buying 262 US companies.) That is eight times the rate of West Germany, thirty times that of Japanese investors. British takeovers on the continent of Europe, too, were up 43 per cent in the first half of 1988. By the end of the year British firms had made 595 acquisitions overseas. No doubt acquirers are preparing for the new age of global marketing. 'The globalisation of markets is at hand,' said Theodore Levitt. 'Corporations geared to this new reality can decimate competitors that still live in the disabling grip of old assumptions about how the world works.'

None the less, a fear must remain that companies are relying on buying growth rather than breeding it. *Fortune* magazine found that eight out of ten major acquisitions were major blunders. While hoping that is no longer true, it remains essential to keep looking in the right direction: at

From *Company Image and Reality* by David Bernstein. *Credit*: Rex Audley

matching competitive pressure with better products better delivered.

The PA Consulting Group analysed research conducted among 176 top executives in five countries. 'It looks,' they said, 'as if the rash of mergers in Britain in the 60s and 70s (and continuing unabated) in a bid to achieve economies of scale addressed the wrong problem. British companies spent so much effort getting bigger when what they really needed was to get better.'

Sir Peter Parker, former chairman of British Rail and now chairman of a cluster of companies including Mitsubishi Electric in the UK, once lamented that 'our corporate existence has a Hobbsian tendency to be nasty, brutish and short. Never more so perhaps than now, as giant companies prowl the business world with mergerous intent. The sharp-angled view from the bottom line does not always reach the horizons of the twenty-first century.'

Writing in *The Reckoning* about the decline of Detroit, David Halberstam points directly to the rise to power of the financial specialists. He says they became a self-perpetuating cadre who stifled innovation. 'It was no longer enough,' he wrote, 'simply to make a good product and solid profit. Now, more and more, the object was to drive the stock up.'

Akio Morita, chairman of Sony, made much the same point about the debilitating power of the financial institutions when he was interviewed on US television. Asked why chunks of US business were becoming uncompetitive, he replied, 'Short-term vision, excessive focus on next quarter's results . . . Quarterly figures have nothing to do with running a business.'

Masanori Moritani, noted observer at the Nomura Research Institute in Japan, believes US corporations have become complacent. Moritani charges them with 'inadequate attention to product and process innovation and an excessive emphasis on quarterly earnings'.

Although a subject beyond the scope of this book, tax policies in many countries don't help either. In the UK, companies may 'write off' their investment in research and development, although, after the Rolls-Royce débâcle of some years ago, it is not always thought prudent to do so. But money spent beyond the laboratory, in product design and development, is not allowable. It comes straight off profits. This encourages a really outworn myth, that new products come from research and development. Sometimes it is true; mostly it isn't. As Lord Caldecote says, what we need is more 'R D & D' (research, design and development). The Australian government has shown what can be done. It has introduced a tax allowance of 150 per cent on money invested in research, design and development. In other words, encouragement doesn't stop at the laboratory door.

There is a story told of a man who had a hot-dog stand by a highway. He did so well he was able to pay for his son to go through Harvard. One day the son came home. He saw all the tables laid out, ready for customers. 'But Dad,' he said, 'don't you know there's a recession coming? You'd better get rid of some of those tables.' His father did. Sure enough, business dropped off. His son had been right. So he took away more tables. And his business fell again.

It is easy to slip into the same vortex. When profits fall companies cut costs. Design and new product development, R & D and market research and advertising are among the first to suffer. So market share goes down. This means costs rise. Profits fall. To respond, companies cut costs. Without new products, with less promotion, market share goes down. Profits fall. And so on. In time such firms rationalise themselves out of business.

The virtuous spiral goes the other way. Companies that develop high-quality products both add value and build market share. This volume enables them to invest in plant to increase productivity, which in turn leads to lower costs. With increased market share and lower costs the company makes larger profits that can be invested in developing new, quality products.

Garth Wiseman argued that 'there is a virtuous circle between a market-based pricing system and good design. Good design leads to premium prices. They lead to increased margins. They, in turn, yield higher profits to plough into investment in good design . . .' The vicious vortex, in his eyes, links cost-plus pricing with poor design. 'Cost-plus pricing limits margins. That reduces profits and leads to lower or no investment, which leads to poor design.' Companies that seek short-term profits and believe that low price is the main way to achieve them (two inimical ideas) are in constant danger of the vicious vortex.

This short-term view has other harmful effects. Companies are not only inhibited from investing in new products, they feel unable to spend enough on new technology to improve their manufacturing.

TECHNOLOGY TAKES TIME

You come back to the short-term view of the financial world. Mike Kelly, when chairman of the British Robots Association, pointed out that 'there is no doubt that it is difficult to justify robots on a two-year payback period. But financial institutions must learn that there is a payback over a four- or five-year horizon.

In 1986 the British Institute of Management surveyed the technology intentions of 250 manufacturing companies in Britain and other European countries. British companies were far less interested in investing in new technology like computer-aided design and manufacturing, flexible manufacturing systems or robotics. The key factor in this country, according to Professor Colin New of Cranfield School of Management, 'seems to be the search for short-term payoffs'. But technology is long term. As a result, 'the pressure for short-term results drastically inhibits the pursuit of long-term strategies, particularly in relation to market share dominance and new technology'.

It is suicidal. The irony is that those same companies want to increase market share and believe that the way to do it is to deliver high-performance, highly reliable products on time. Technology would help them. Its absence will hinder them.

How, you wonder, can companies with a short-term view, obsessively concerned with the next half-year's results, keep up? Many blame currency movements, of course. The pound is too high. The pound is too low. You hear both within months of each other. Although the parallel is not exact, Japanese experience is salutary. They've suffered as much as anyone from the strength of the yen. But look at Casio. In 1987/8 their world-wide sales rose less than 5 per cent. How did they respond? 'We will place even greater efforts in research and development activities,' said president Tadao Kashio. In the same year, Casio's spending on R & D rose from $69 million to $96 million.

It's a different attitude. And it pays. In 1988 Casio reported that their R & D is 'picking up speed each year, as shown by eighty-five separate announcements of the development of products using these [new] technologies in as many as 300 different models'. Or look at Toshiba, the £16 billion Japanese electronics group. Due to the rising value of the yen, although sales grew, their profits were halved in one month. But the company is not in the red. 'Until it is,' said Nobuko Hara, who writes for the *Financial Times* from Tokyo, 'the company will continue to expand its spending on product innovation, which is the key to economic survival in the long run.' Insofar as this is true, it means that companies will be squeezed out by newer products developed by their competitors. They will also be pushed aside if their existing products are not of sufficiently high quality and are not made quickly enough.

35

'Principles [of doing business] are at risk of being knocked down in the rush for short-term profits.' Sir Christopher Hogg, chairman of Courtaulds, says he has shifted a long way from that financial perspective to caring about his products. In eight years he has lifted profits from 'very little' to £2.4 billion.

Sir Christopher Hogg, chairman of the £2.4 billion chemicals and textile group Courtaulds, issued a warning that principles of doing business are at risk of being knocked down in the rush for short-term profits. 'However,' he reminded shareholders, 'companies are not just pawns to be sacrificed in some financial game of chess.'

In another way Lester C. Thurow, dean of the School of Management at Massachusetts Institute of Technology (MIT), makes the same point: 'Any elementary economics textbook will tell you that finance exists to serve industry; now we're busy making industry into a plaything for finance.'

Sell on quality, not on price (SOQNOP) is the way John Deere, the US farm machinery company, puts it. Companies that prefer to sell on price, and care less for quality, could remember the initials a friend of mine swears he saw on the label of a jacket he bought – SAOBJ. Wearing the jacket, he took them to mean 'sold against our better judgement'. Does that mean quality as an absolute or relative quality? And, if so, relative to what? There are two places to look for the answer. First, look at your customers. Second, look at your competitors.

Fortune magazine annually surveys security analysts and business leaders to check the reputation of leading companies. They find that innovation is one of the most important attributes distinguishing the leading companies within different industries. In addition, according to *Fortune*, 'a company's ability to successfully manage innovation correlates with its value as a long-term investment'.

SUMMARY

The short-term view of financial institutions, which requires companies to produce better profits every six, or even three, months, makes it hard for managers to see beyond the end of their balance sheet. This is spectacularly true and damaging in the bubbling markets of Wall Street and the City of London, and far less in evidence in Japan or West Germany, the major competitor nations.

The paradox is that too myopic a focus on profit actually inhibits it. Repeated research shows that winning companies look elsewhere: to their people, their products and their service. Get those right, the argument runs, and profits will follow. It is the safer way.

3
Care About Your Products

'I liked the product so much
I bought the company.'
Victor Kiam, Remington

Invite Akio Morita, chairman of Sony, to lunch. It won't be long, a friend told me, before he pushes his soup plate aside and shows you one of his new products. I mentioned this at a meeting of the Royal Society of Arts in London. To my horror my friend, Peter Gorb of the London Business School, stood up to correct me. 'He didn't have one product with him. He had three.' It is said he has had special poacher pockets fitted in his well-cut suits, to carry his products about with him. That may be apocryphal, but it shows where he, as chairman of one of the world's most important companies, puts his priorities.

By contrast, according to Professor Colin Clipson who runs the Competitive Edge project in the United States, 'Too many chief executives are not interested in their products.' In 1985 Rob Matthews, of Kingston Polytechnic, studied UK companies for the Confederation of British Industry. He found a sharp distinction between those companies that make fast-moving consumer goods (FMCG) and other manufacturing companies. All consumer goods companies had products in the board-room. Of thirty manufacturing companies he visited, only three had pictures of their products in the boardroom.

INTEREST IN THE PRODUCT

How refreshing and how unusual to hear Victor Kiam, who turned the US shaver company Remington's $30 million loss into a profit and multiplied sales sixfold in a few years. He said, 'I liked the product so much I bought the company.' Indeed today people in thirty-one countries (speaking

38

'Produce good things well' is the plain, yet profound, advice given by Akio Morita, co-founder and chairman of Sony. His focus has built a worldwide corporation, always in the lead.

fifteen languages) hear that on television all the time. 'We will grow,' he said, 'as long as we remember that quality is uppermost.' Stanley Marcus, former chairman of Nieman-Marcus, the Dallas-based department store group, says: 'The greatest problem American business faces is getting the boss back to work watching his customer and his product. Too many bosses are involved with long-range planning meetings.'

One cardinal difference between the winning companies and so many others seems to be that winners believe their business is about making products people want, and beating their competitor to it. 'Our job,' says Akio Morita, 'is to make our products obsolete before our competitors do.' Too many companies, there is no doubt, believe their business is about controlling finance, about acquisitions and here-and-now profit.

If you want to talk to a company about developing new products you

From loss to profit, by telling the world he loved his product: Remington's
Victor Kiam.

may have a few minutes with the boss, but soon you will be steered
towards the design department or engineering department or somewhere
else. In one company visited by a study team led by Robin Roy from the
Open University, the man responsible for product design was the tool
room foreman. Everyone will think that funny. But they should pause.
When, it might be asked, was new product development last on their
board's agenda?

When the National Economic Development Office asked 300 British
manufacturing companies how often their board reviewed a product
being developed, some companies said not at all. Some said once. Most
said twice, yet the development programme could take well over a year.

Japanese companies are different. Canon have the subject on their main board agenda every month, and board directors visit the design team at least as often. The same is true of Sony and of Sharp.

I repeat, the boards of many companies simply don't think that the products they make are their concern. This is a job they delegate. Arthur D. Little, the consultants, explain that until recently North American companies have not emphasised innovation as a key means of realising corporate growth. Managers tended to believe that:

- If new products or new ideas couldn't be developed internally, they could be bought

- Innovation was the province of scientists and specialists, not of management.

They thought that innovation is the same as any other task, where money and labour can be applied and orders given.

The consequences are all too visible. In their book *In Search of Excellence* Tom Peters and Bob Waterman said that when they looked at what makes the excellent companies excel they hoped to find that it didn't really depend on the boss. But, they concluded rather sadly, it does. If a chairman, or president, or chief executive wants the company to win customers by delivering the right products, he or she had better take an interest in those products.

Sir Christopher Hogg, chairman of Courtaulds, was brought up in the Oxford and Harvard Business School pattern. He admits that he came to this realisation fairly late. When he visits one of over 100 Courtaulds plants, he now asks first to see the products:

> You go into a factory. Instead of walking around the factory floor, which is what I did for years, you say, 'Show me the products that the factory makes.' If they can't do that you try and establish that they set up some place in the factory where the products are shown, and where people on the shop floor actually see what they are making.

In five years John Bittleston has doubled both sales and profits of Cerebos Pacific in the Pacific, South-east Asia and Australasia. At budget review meetings he asks managers by how much they are increasing spending on their product formulations. He wants them to invest more to improve products. That way, he says, they can increase margins.

41

Aware of the hazards of short-term goals, he wants to achieve a position where managers' bonuses run for five years after they retire, so they have an incentive to invest in the future.

PRODUCT STRATEGY

Once a company has created this internal interest in its products, it has next to evolve a strategy for them. Again, research shows that most companies have no clear strategy. Here are some questions to consider. They apply to makers of machine tools and marble baths, and to everyone in between:

- Do you have a strategy for your products? What is it?
- Do you intend to compete by being more advanced technically?
- Or by being cheapest?
- Or by having the best distribution?
- Or by being first in the market?
- Or by being a 'fast follower'?
- Or by having the highest quality products?
- Or by being different in some other way?

You can have two product strategies running at once. J. C. Bamford, manufacturers of earth-moving equipment, run two programmes. One aims to improve existing products all the time. It is called 'incrementalism', or 'little by little'. J. C. Bamford introduced 150 product improvements to their range in 1987/8. This may be hell for the production manager, but it gives them market leadership in fifty countries and a larger share of the US market than Toyota, producers of the biggest-selling imported car, have of their market in the USA.

The parallel strategy is to take larger steps to innovate. That is how J. C. Bamford developed the Sitemaster, a one-machine alternative to all the

A twin policy, both little-by-little improvement and big breakthroughs, has helped Britain's J. C. Bamford to market leadership in fifty countries with machines such as their innovative Sitemaster.

other equipment on a construction site. The company's focus is not on costs, but on cost benefits; not the amount they spend, but what they get for it. Chairman Anthony Bamford said, 'We had to design our company to be competitive.' He listed three factors that are absolutely essential to J. C. Bamford:

- meeting customer requirements
- high quality
- cost-effective manufacturing

43

'Design, quality, costs – the three are indivisible,' he said.

The contrast between Concorde and the Boeing 747 is another example of how the 'little by little' approach works. While Concorde was a staggering technological breakthrough, it may have been less impressive as an exemplar of new product development. The 747, evolutionary rather than revolutionary, sold hundreds more and is still developing. Nearly twenty years and several models later, the 747-400 is going into service. British Airways are spending £2.6 billion on nineteen of them.

Unless you look carefully, you won't see much difference. It lies in the extended top deck (which now carries forty-four passengers, as does a small airliner) and winglets at the end of each wing. But everything else is transformed. The 747-400 will fly from London to Tokyo or Bangkok or Singapore non-stop, up to 8,000 miles. It takes 386 passengers, giving all more stowage space.

Passengers are customers, of course, but so is the airline that foots the bill. For them, the 747-400 is a delight. In the cockpit, the two-pilot crew gets all the information it needs from six-colour cathode ray tubes. Earlier 747s had 971 lights and gauges and switches in the cockpit. The new version has 365. Once the aircraft reaches 400 feet the pilot can switch to automatic pilot that gives pre-programmed computer navigation. Another automatic system detects icing on the wings and copes with it. Quite soon communications will be by satellite, free of earth stations. And that will work both ways: the pilot is informed all the time, but people on the ground are also told of all changes, including those to engine performance.

Like J. C. Bamford, Boeing look at all the details. Brakes made of carbon rather than steel, for example, save 820 kilos in weight, worth saving.

Rolls-Royce, supplying the power, have the same evolutionary approach. Not only has engine thrust been doubled in a few years, but the new RB211 engine saves 18 per cent in fuel consumption per seat mile over the version used on the 747-200.

Of many lessons to learn from Boeing, one is to have suppliers who evolve as you do. Rolls-Royce call Boeing 'the toughest customers we have' but they're grateful for it. Boeing's ever more demanding specifications help drive Rolls-Royce to better and better performance. Another Boeing lesson is to know who your customers are and what they want.

From J. C. Bamford to Boeing, to Rolls-Royce to Sony, the benefits of little-by-little, or incremental, improvement are clear. Sony developed the original Walkman. Now there are many models for different segments of the market. While that has been going on, Sony has cut the number of mechanical parts in half and cut assembly time by 67 per cent. As part of this, they cut the number of fastenings from twenty-one to four.

When the RB211 won the contract to power the Boeing 757, the first contract for a new American aircraft ever awarded to a foreign firm, the demand was for an engine giving a thrust of 37,400 lbs. Today, many variations later, the RB211 delivers a thrust of 65,000 lbs and uses far less fuel. Orders stretch into the next century.

That kind of constant improvement is wonderful, an object lesson. But there are people who warn that it is risky for most firms to focus only on this kind of innovation. You may miss big changes in your market. As we will see in the chapter on technology, many British companies, by investing too little in R & D are in danger of doing exactly that. Today, the thrift looks clever. One day it won't.

Products, processes, materials can be improved and improved and improved, but there comes a time when limits are reached. What you have to assess (though heaven knows how) is how close to that limit you are. In *Innovation: The Attacker's Advantage*, R. N. Foster describes how Du Pont persisted in investing large sums in improving nylon for use as tyre cord when nylon was approaching its performance limits. Celanese, by contrast, focused on its superior polyester yarn, which was, as Roy Rothwell says, 'at the front end of its performance trajectory.'

There's another lesson: even when Du Pont recognised the importance of polyester cord, they persisted in nylon cord production because they'd invested so much in it. Celanese quickly became the market leader.

An alternative to having two parallel strategies, as at J. C. Bamford, is to progress from one to the other. Dr Charles Parker, former director of R & D at Ferodo, led a study of innovation for the Council of Engineering Institutions. He thought that companies should embark first on low-cost 'evolutionary' projects. Build up profits, he advocated, to invest in high-risk, high-reward endeavours.

While Baker Perkins, the British printing, bakery, chemicals and plastics equipment group (part of APV), introduce a new leading-edge product every few years, and the time gap is shortening, most of their success comes from incremental improvements. Rather than bring them in when they occur, Baker Perkins tend to collect improvements, then launch line extensions that are better in a number of ways.

Dr Tony Warren, chief executive of the management consultants PA in

North America, says any company has two choices. One is to be 'the best player in town'. That means doing what everyone else does, only better. The other is what he calls 'buying tickets for next season'. By that he means taking a quantum leap. In this case, the way to win the game is to learn the rules sooner than anyone else.

He thinks the first is not a safe option. But the other is risky too. He talks of the 'success trap'. This is, when the board is confronted with a demand for more capacity because it is doing well, it is no time to ask for money for new ventures. Yet, says Warren, it is just when a business is most success-ful that it should start doing something else. That's hard, too, for com-panies with a short-term profit view and for managers who are rewarded for short-term results.

QUALITY AND DIFFERENCE

The drive must be for constantly improving quality and for differentiation; that is to say, creating a clearly recognisable difference between your pro-duct, or company, and those of your competitors. Any difference won't do. To be effective it must be one the customer wants. Quality and differentiation build market share. They lead to higher productivity, higher margins, more profit to invest and the whole virtuous circle.

Nor, as J. C. Bamford show, is this confined to consumer goods. There is considerable evidence, according to James Fairhead, author of *Design for Corporate Culture*, who conducted my international study of best practice for NEDO, 'that even in capital goods industries products are bought much more because they are differentiated through effective design than because of price factors'.

In fact pricing comes into this. Should it be needed, a commercial rationale for differentiation is that it opens the way to premium pricing. This, in turn, leads to improved margins and profits. It is said that the norm in large parts of British manufacturing is to price on a cost-plus basis. This may sound safe, but companies who do this will not reap sufficient bene-fits to invest in their future. 'Product differentiation is almost always pos-sible,' Fairhead added. By contrast, 'only one firm can be cheapest'. And there is always someone.

LOOK FOR YOUR 'DIFFERENTIAL ADVANTAGE'

The University of Bradford compared British and Japanese companies in Britain. British companies said their advantage was that they were British and they had good brand names. The Japanese companies pointed to their quality, reliability and service.

When the Chartered Institute of Marketing asked some 200 makers of industrial products what is important to them when they make a marketing plan, only 21 per cent gave 'product differentiation' in their first three answers. But then, according to the same survey, fewer than one fifth of them survey their customers, and only one in eight surveys its distributors. They can't be expected to know.

For the benefit of those small companies that feel they haven't the basis or means to differentiate their products in this way, the case of Penhaligon's, London perfumers, is encouraging. In 1975, Sheila Pickles, a theatrical agent who spent five years as assistant to Italian film producer Franco Zeffirelli, acquired, with his encouragement, a small business. It had been started in 1870 by an ambitious Cornishman who made his way to the capital to start a gentlemen's hairdresser in St James's. In time he came to prepare perfumes and colognes for his clientele.

By the time Sheila Pickles arrived, revenue was down to £6,000 and the cupboard was bare, except for, and this is the point she seized upon, the name and the original formula books. For many of us that would hardly have been a promising start, but Pickles had vision. 'I saw the firm as very small and very precious; essentially English and left over from another era,' she recalls. Her first step was to recreate a 'Victorian' shop in Covent Garden. Then she set about reviving some of the products.

From the beginning, she explained, 'quality was all-important'. Her golden rule was 'never to change the [original] formula'. Modern substitutes and synthetics wouldn't do. One line of products followed another. One day a designer went into the shop. What she needed, he said, was a 'corporate identity'. His company, Michael Peters, advised her how she could afford it by clever economy – one range of designs, limited colours and so on. In Sheila Pickles' view this would have reduced the expression of quality and uniqueness. So she went for the best. Together, she and the designers created a range of beautiful and nostalgic Victorian and Edwardian packages. 'For a small company,' Sheila Pickles later said, 'this was a major investment, but one which I have never regretted.'

Design, always of the highest quality, pervades Penhaligon's business.

Not only have their packages won awards on both sides of the Atlantic, but in 1983 the company received a coveted Presidential Award for Design Management from the Royal Society of Arts. Year after year her accountants tell Sheila Pickles that she spends too much on design. But are they right? There is no doubt that her insistence on excellence in every part of the company has helped position it at the top of the highly competitive big-spending perfume and toiletry industry. And here is the revealing sentence: 'No matter how successful a design, Sheila Pickles once said, 'it needs loving attention to implement it.'

The exclusivity she created attracted 'tremendous interest' in the United States. 'I was fortunate enough,' she recalls, 'to be able to select which New York store to go into.' Instead of selecting one that would have given them tremendous turnover, she chose Bergdorf Goodman. 'They gave us much less business, but have the exclusive clientele and are themselves world-wide leaders in style and design.' Nieman-Marcus in Beverly Hills followed. Today the company also has equally carefully selected stockists in Canada, France, Italy and Japan. In the United Kingdom it has a concession at Harrods and five shops of its own in London.

In 1987 Sheila Pickles sold her business to Laura Ashley, while remaining in charge of it. Its turnover then was £1.2 million. In retailing or manufacturing terms that was small. But by turning the roots to advantage, by securing a niche for itself, by insisting on high quality, Pickles secured for Penhaligon a place in the market and a price freedom Laura Ashley found attractive.

GROWTH BY ACQUISITION?

Rather than rely on acquisitions, which are both harder and harder to find and often bring no joy, company boards would do better to resolve to grow through their own products. The corporate policy at 3M (a name derived from Minnesota Mining and Manufacturing) is to derive 25 per cent of their business each year from products or services that are less than five years old. Don Osman, vice-president, Commercial Markets group, said, 'That may sound like an ambitious target, but we do attain this average each year.'

The experience of IBM bears out the value of this approach. In recent years IBM has felt competition from DEC. One analyst, Michael L. Geran of E. F. Hutton & Co., noted that 'about 40 per cent of IBM's current product range is less than eighteen months old, versus 85 per cent of DEC's'. Thanks to DEC and other competitors, IBM's unit share of the worldwide IBM-PC and personal computer-compatible market slipped to 22.5 per cent in 1986, which is probably where it sits now. While IBM's resilience should not be underrated, the competitive challenge is biting. Enough for IBM's chief scientist, Ralph E. Gomery, to be moved to quote Shakespeare's 'sweet are the uses of adversity'.

John Kerridge, chairman of Fisons, the British pharmaceutical and scientific equipment group whose profits since he became chairman eight years ago have grown from £3.8 million to £132 million, believes that growth through a company's own products is much the best policy. 'Organic earnings are quality earnings,' he said. None the less, Kerridge has made a number of acquisitions. His point is that the *basis* of growth should be organic. Only when you are sure organic growth is not frustrated by lack of investment should you invest in acquisitions. It is 'dangerous', in John Kerridge's view, to grow solely by acquisition, and 'particularly dangerous' when acquisitions have a priority call on finance.

One example shows the Fisons' approach. By 1980 the company had struggled to build a pharmaceutical business in the USA for a decade. It consistently lost money and had a minuscule share of its main market. By 1988 Fisons was market leader in its therapeutic area, has a highly profitable business and is growing at 30 per cent a year compound. *Only then* did it make an acquisition. It doubled the business. It is a mark of how well Kerridge's philosophy works, that that one purchase cost £270 million. When he became chairman the whole group was worth £50 million.

When Dr John Constable was director of the British Institute of Management he analysed acquisitions throughout Europe. He wrote:

While it is difficult to prove that the UK approach to diversification and acquisition is the major cause of the UK's poor performance, it can be argued that the high level of strategic energy devoted to acquisitions and mergers results in:

1. The creation of an illusion of growth. The acquiring companies invariably proudly tell their shareholders about the rates of growth which are being achieved. From a national standpoint though, the reverse is often the truth. As a result of the acquisition the total growth achieved may well have slowed down.

49

2. Too much importance being given to the financial aspects of strategic expertise as opposed to the operational and market based aspects of strategic expertise. Greater emphasis is certainly placed in the USA, Germany and Japan and probably also in France on strategic aspects of product development, low cost delivery systems and marketing.

3. A disproportionate amount of top management time being focused on seeking and implementing acquisitions and also conversely avoiding being acquired.

4. A diversion of investment from internal developments which are more likely to focus on the long-term needs of the business and which research findings suggest are inherently more profitable.

In the long run it would seem that strategy should focus less on creating apparent growth through merger and acquisition and more on effective internal development.

It comes back to caring about the products you make – and making it clear to everyone that you do. Steps to take include:

- Appointing a director responsible for developing market-winning products

- Making sure your products feature on the main board agenda this month, next month and every month

- Visiting the design team often

- Telling your designers your strategies and your plans, so they can use their initiative to help you achieve them

- Putting your products, or models of them, in all functional areas in the boardroom and in plants.

In a company in South Wales called Power Sport, makers of sports and gymnasium equipment, everyone in the firm is supposed to stay fit. Why? Because when they sell the products they know them, believe in them and are therefore credible. At J. C. Bamford everyone learns to drive a JCB. That is part of it, too; making sure everyone in the company knows about the products the company makes and cares about them.

SUMMARY

There seems to be one great divide between executives whose prime aim is to make money and others who think that if they make the products people want to buy then healthy profits will follow. The first perspective, force-fed by the stock exchanges, justifies apparent, rather than real, growth by acquisition and share massaging. The latter impels a focus on customers and competitors and the people in the business. Some company chiefs spend their time with financiers and bankers. Others are more often with their designers, engineers and marketing people. These leaders put product development firmly on the agenda. There is no question where the winning companies find themselves. Their steadily increasing market share tells its own story.

4

What Do People Want?

'Marketing is the key factor in
business. [It] is not only the fuel,
it is the compass of the ship.'
Sir John Harvey-Jones, former chairman of ICI

Make what people want. That sounds common sense. Unless they are
lucky, companies can hardly expect to create goods that will sell in quantity if they don't bother to find out what people want. Yet most don't try
to. According to a survey conducted by the Institute of Marketing in 1984,
among makers of consumer durable products, fewer than one fifth spend
anything on consumer surveys or qualitative research or field experiments. Makers of capital goods spend even less (Figure 8).

The main reason manufacturers gave for not using market research was
that 'they knew all they needed to know about the market already'.

Figure 8   How UK companies find what customers want

Use of market research techniques

	FMCG	Consumer durables	Repeat industrial	Capital industries
Company records	76.7%	72.4%	72.6%	67.9%
Survey of consumers	42.1%	19.0%	20.8%	18.7%
Survey of distributors	17.7%	23.1%	19.9%	13.9%
Qualitative research	39.0%	19.9%	19.1%	22.0%
Field experiments	25.0%	17.1%	17.4%	12.0%
Laboratory experiments	22.8%	9.1%	12.3%	4.8%

SOURCE: Chartered Institute of Marketing 1984

NOTE: The Institute of Marketing study used these definitions: *consumer durable goods:* private cars, domestic
appliances and household equipment, domestic electronic equipment, white goods, domestic textiles, carpets,
glassware, etc.; *fast-moving consumer goods:* food, drink, tobacco, toiletries, pharmaceutical products, etc.; *repeat
industrial goods:* building materials, raw comodities, iron, steel, fuels, lubricants, etc.; *capital industrial equipment:*
industrial plant, office equipment, building and construction, shipbuilding, machinery, etc.; *services:* insurance,
banking, transportation, specialist marketing services (e.g. advertising and market research agencies), etc.

What do people want from you? Be 'obsessive' about customers, Tom Peters and
Nancy Austin say. 'Not markets, not marketing. Not strategic positioning.
Customers.'

Perhaps they are luckier than others. Eighty-seven US companies took
part in a survey of 'business opinion and experiences'. They admitted not
only that three out of ten major new products marketed in the previous
five years failed to live up to the hopes placed in them, but that the principal reason for failure was 'inadequate market analysis'. 'Failure in most
instances,' an oil company executive said, 'can be attributed to faulty

judgement of the market situation.' An executive from an aircraft company echoed this:

> In almost every instance our new product failures have been due to lack of
> sufficient knowledge of what the market would absorb . . . we feel that a
> major portion of the difficulty could have been anticipated in advance had
> we spent enough on, and properly directed, the marketing analysis.

CUSTOMER FEEDBACK

An obvious snag of not listening to customers is that you can get things wrong. Roy Rothwell looked at the textile machinery business in Europe. Its international competitiveness declined markedly from the 1950s on. Rothwell said this was because it didn't keep its technology up-to-date. But even the firms that were innovative, he says, often got it wrong. Professor Rothwell conducted a comprehensive survey among people who make textile machines and those who use them. He asked them to list product qualities that mattered to them, from 'not important' to 'of crucial importance'. Sometimes they gave the same answers, but the importance attached to them varied. For example, both sides said the rate of production was important. But it was more important to users than producers. Users were much more interested in equipment that improves quality than machinery makers were, and much more interested in the cost of labour to work the machines. The profile that emerged was that users are more interested in life costs. Manufacturers are more interested in the initial price. Such mismatches, which let imports in, could have been avoided.

Consider the case of two firms that made engines for military equipment. One designed a new engine that was half the size of the one in use – a brilliant piece of engineering. Still, the customer chose the old, larger, engine. Why? Because the larger engine was easier to service. And keeping on the road was more important than size. That's a good example of clever people solving the wrong problems (theirs) because they haven't looked for the right ones (the customer's).

In 1986 the Open University studied thirty-seven British companies and ten from other countries. The companies were in three contrasting sectors: office furniture, domestic heating equipment and electronic business equipment; that is, a traditional design-based industry, an established engineering-based industry and a new-technology-based industry. Most were small or medium-sized.

The Open University team asked these companies to say how they manage new product development. Most operated in the same sort of way. The differences lay in the details, but they were important. Significantly, all the foreign companies used what was called 'customer feedback'. To quote from the report: 'The two Japanese electronic business equipment manufacturers went furthest [to learn from their customers] having a "special monitoring system" ' – a panel of users and customers who would meet regularly and be consulted on what new products they wanted. 'This was part of an elaborate system of product planning in which marketing, design and engineering staff were involved.' Only two thirds of the UK companies used 'customer feedback' from any source. Many thought formal market research 'too costly' (27 per cent) or 'of dubious value' (16 per cent).

Saying that, the Open University noted that there is evidence that 'user orientation in product planning was linked to business success. Firms with high asset and profit growth rates were likely to be gathering market intelligence from several sources, both systematically and ad hoc' (Figure 9).

Figure 9 Companies that care about their customers grow faster

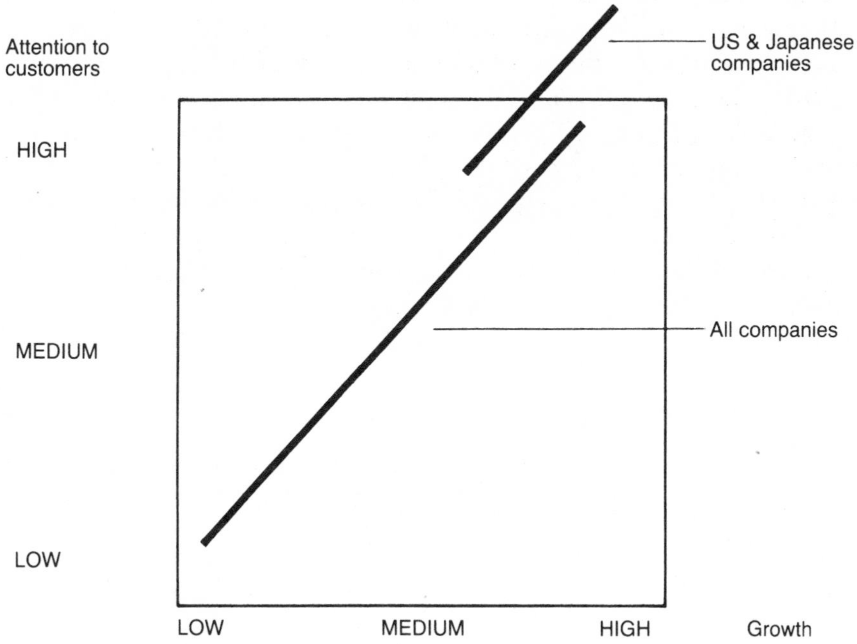

SOURCE: CBI's 'Management for Success' sample

55

LARGE OR SMALL?

James Brian Quinn, of Dartmouth College, New Hampshire, who won the McKinsey Award for the best article in the *Harvard Business Review* in 1985, has studied highly innovative companies in the USA, Japan and Europe. He said:

> More striking than the cultural differences among these companies are the similarities between innovative small and large companies and among innovative companies in different countries.
>
> Effective management of innovation seems much the same regardless of national boundaries or scale of operations.

There is an immediate and obvious gap between many manufacturing companies and makers of 'fast-moving consumer goods' (FMCG), generally taken to mean food, detergents, cosmetics and the like. The large companies making FMCG spend heavily. Indeed, almost all the money spent on market research in the UK is spent by them. 'Engineering companies,' Gordon Heald, managing director of Gallup in the UK, told me, 'don't do market research. They don't believe in it.'

When the Chartered Institute of Marketing commissioned extensive research among companies of all sorts it found that half the sample's 'capital industrial' manufacturers (of items such as industrial plant, office equipment, buildings, ships, machinery, etc.) never conduct market research. Almost half (47 per cent) of 'repeat industrial' companies don't either. Still more surprisingly, nor do four in every ten makers of 'consumer durable' products. Eighty per cent of FMCG companies do. The study also found that companies that use market research generate higher profits.

CAN PEOPLE SAY WHAT THEY WANT?

One argument you hear is that customers don't know what they want until it is in front of them, so there is no point in asking. Dr Liz Nelson, an American who runs the Taylor Nelson Group, a respected market research firm once noted that 'there is a belief among many researchers that if you ask consumers directly what they want they may not be able to tell you.' The answer, she believes, is to study lifestyles. She quotes Lancia and

Renault, who both did this exhaustively before launching successful new models.

Designers are among those who think that market research can only give yesterday's answers. Some even think that to listen to the market is to reduce everything to its lowest common denominator. They see something vulgar in that. Other designers believe they know better than the public. Sometimes they are right. Intuitively, designers can sometimes see ahead of the market. This is an asset to prize, even though the timing is hard to judge.

Even so, there are ways to see what people think of new ideas now. Years ago an American colour expert, Louis Cheskin, wanted to know which colour handbags women preferred. He gathered women for a discussion group. At the end, to thank them he said, 'There are some handbags outside. Please take one.' Their real choice, he felt, was a guide. The experiment, apparently casual, was carefully controlled.

My own firm did a great deal of new product development work. Often designers created 'concept' boards which showed ideas for new products. These were shown to typical users, for their opinions. On more than one occasion potential customers criticised the manufacturer because 'of course they wanted the product' and 'why wasn't it on the market already?'

For a household-name company that makes hand-held machine tools, designers in my firm developed products which, for the first time, were battery-powered. To test them they made wooden models, then used them in simulated TV commercials. With realistic sound, music, voice over and photography you couldn't tell they weren't real working products. Viewers were asked about the performance they'd like, the price they'd pay and more. The critical point is that these tests guided the company towards customer demand, and did it before committing a penny to manufacturing.

Years ago Beecham bought Badedas in Germany. In the corner of the plant they found, to their surprise, a small glue factory. Without knowing it, they had bought UHU. They realised the value of this brand-name. To help support their position in a new market, they asked my firm to think of new DIY products. Among many steps was a lunch we held for 'gurus' in the DIY business, editors of trade journals and others who knew the business.

Trade journals receive lots of enquiries, but we asked, 'Aren't your enquiries a bit like a doctor's? That is, you may get a rare complaint, but most of the time you are dealing with the same problems?' They agreed. When they left, we asked if they would send us the ten questions they were asked most often. Eight people sent lists. All eight had the same questions. More amazing they were, with slight variations, in the same order.

While not a substitute for larger-scale research, this quick view from experts told us in a day or two the main problems faced by people struggling with DIY.

TECHNOLOGY PUSH?

Engineers and scientists often develop new ideas from their own knowledge of what is possible. At a high level, this glories in the name of 'technology push'. It stands to reason, does it not, that you have to have something before you ask people about it? Well, no.

Another common reason for not conducting market research is that people in companies think they are the best judge. Who knows more about cars than the people who make them? 'The driver and the passenger' is the answer that Don Peterson, chairman of Ford in the USA, would give. He says they are now 'the centre of the Ford universe'. That is plain soap-company language and has been for sixty years. According to Procter & Gamble 'the market place is everyone's responsibility'. Winning companies are on the same wavelength. Repeatedly you hear how they are 'obsessive' about their customers.

CUSTOMERS NOT MARKETS

'Obsession with customers,' say Tom Peters and Nancy Austin in *A Passion for Excellence*. 'Not markets, not marketing. Not strategic positioning. Customers.' Having looked at seventy or more companies that outperform most others, that is the phrase Peters and Austin use. While those companies have since had their ups and downs, that should not encourage sceptics to doubt the basic truth.

It really is back to basics. Every stallholder in a street market knows the need to satisfy customers. We have become too complicated to remember.

Obsession with customers is a hallmark of the most successful companies, claims Tom Peters, who, with Bob Waterman, wrote *In Search of Excellence*.

But there are other blocks. The first is that people think they care about their customers when they don't. 'FMCG companies frequently use the full range of marketing skills. But many industrial companies restrict themselves to advertising and PR, which tends to suggest that this is their interpretation of marketing,' remarked Anthony McBurnie, director-general of Britain's Chartered Institute of Marketing.

The second block is that people confuse marketing with selling, and believe selling is less meritorious than making.

Marketing, I was told at INSEAD, is concerned with the problems of the market. Selling is concerned with the problems of the seller. Of the two, the former is unquestionably the better focus. If you keep your eye on the customer you will change as he does. If you keep your eyes on your own concerns, polish your own skills, you may find the market has gone away. Many firms have.

A third problem, in the words of Joseph Bower of Harvard Business

School, is that 'marketing has trivialised itself.' I'd put it another way: it has complicated itself. To too many people in the profession, marketing has become another set of theoretical techniques. The fourth block is the misunderstanding, if not arrogance, we started with: the view that people in the business know better than their customers. Even Yasuo Kuroki, the courteous head of the Product Planning Centre of Sony, was moved to say that 'UK manufacturers must research their markets better in the future – and produce better quality products'.

'Find a need, then fill it', the six-word prescription for success at any level of technology, appears to have been met by this Garden Tidy. Designed to take the strain out of gardening, 'specially for older people', it combines a kneeler, a refuse bin and tool store, with strong support handles. Ian Walsh, who designed this while still a student, has used polypropylene and bright colours to take away the hospital appliance look. Final year students' work is often both original and practical. Companies should cuddle up to colleges to benefit.

The same is seen in West Germany too. Dr R. D. Schraft of the Fraun-hofer Institute for Manufacturing Engineering and Automation, Stuttgart, says that because 'the wishes of the customer are becoming more and more important on the market', mechanical engineering com-panies must 'realise the features of a service company'; increase flexibility. He calls for meeting customer requirements by permanent readiness for delivery.

Dr Schraft's view is borne out by research in 1982 among machine tool manufacturers in Germany and Britain.

> In the West German companies in the sample, customer involvement in the product design and development process was seen as axiomatic if the com-pany wanted to be successful. In contrast, in the British companies the pre-vailing attitude was not to involve the customer in the process until the product was put on the market.

What happened was that British firms talked to their customers about price and delivery. The Germans swapped ideas about 'user needs' and technical data. Look at the machines in almost any factory to see which way has worked best.

Alan Sugar, founder of Amstrad, endorses Tom Peters' view. Everyone who knows him speaks of his 'remarkable feel'. Said one analyst, 'He, more than any other player in the consumer electronics market, has a sense of what consumers want.' Says another, 'He has an almost uncanny ability to read market trends and a forcefulness that can switch Amstrad's sales emphasis from one product area into a completely new direction, virtually at the drop of a hat.' Sugar hasn't much time for the complexities of marketing thinking. He relies to a considerable extent on his own 'gut feel', as does his company. But that's him. Gut feel definitely isn't enough for most mortals.

HOW PEOPLE LIVE

If your business is to focus on your customers, then market research is inescapable. But you have to be careful. Because we pin our faith on numbers, however spuriously arrived at, amateur research is worse than none at all. Even when market research is carried out most assiduously, there are still dangers. In *The Design Dimension* Christopher Lorenz describes how in 1978 General Electric, after extensive market research, concluded that there was no market for small TV sets in America. Within a month Sony launched an 8-inch TV set there. They sold a million in the first year.

Was it luck? Was it intuition? Maybe. But Sony, who say they do no market research but in fact do lots, look at the market in another way. They study social trends, and go where their customers are. It is said that chairman Akio Morita avoids expensive dinners when he is abroad. He prefers to visit discos or go wherever his customers congregate. His company, like others in Japan, has a 'consumer satisfaction' group that includes psychologists and sociologists. It also has a panel of 'Mr and Mrs Doer', members of the public who try every new product idea. Other companies have teams that study 'lifestyles'. Still others have 'futures' groups.

Why do they do this? Theodore Levitt of Harvard Business School has the answer: 'The surviving and thriving business is a business that constantly seeks better ways to help people solve their problems . . . functionally better, valued better and available better.'

Of course. But here is the twist: 'To create business requires knowing what customers think betterness to be. This,' says Levitt, 'precedes all else in business.'

Finding out what customers want is how Xerox turned their business around. From 1976 to 1982 their share of the copier market in the US exactly halved – from 82 per cent to 41 per cent. Competition from Japan did that. Xerox fought back in a number of ways. One, always the Western answer, was to cut costs. Another was to cut in half the time it took to develop products. They created a Strategic Business Office, reporting to the president. The design boss at the time, Arnold Wasserman, said, 'There had to be a shift in the way Xerox designed its machines, from thinking about the machine as the centre of the design, to thinking about the user as the centre of design.' The SBO was responsible for business planning, product planning, market research, forecasting and pricing. Design and 'operability', as they called it, were in there.

During the first six months of this new regime, the designers didn't draw a thing. They did something which, incredibly, had never been done before: they went to places where Xerox copiers were installed and saw how their machines are used in practice.

What they found was that the typical users were secretaries wanting two copies of a single original. They didn't need a professional operator to reproduce complex publications on a big machine. Xerox also found their complicated manuals were incomprehensible to people who actually used the machine. People had stuck signs on the machines to say what to do. The 1075 copier, introduced in 1983, was the first outcome of this new approach. It was the second most successful copier Xerox ever made. Market share moved up to 52 per cent.

Firms that don't research their customers because they 'know enough about them already', as they say, 'cannot', in the immortal words of tennis player John McEnroe, 'be serious'.

HUMANWARE

Ricoh, the Japanese manufacturer of computers, copiers, facsimile machines, typewriters, cameras, watches, daisy-wheel and laser printers, and other products besides, including gas meters, is a truly innovative company. In 1988 their dazzling new Mirai SLR camera was described by *Amateur Photographer* as 'probably the most advanced zoom camera yet'. One feature was an infra-red, auto-focus beam – to take pictures in total darkness, should you want to. Ricoh say, 'We have moved from the hardware age (1965–75), through the software age (1975–85) to the human age.' By this they mean that 'the user's requirements will take over as the major dictator of a product's capability. Companies are concentrating now on the input of "consumer lifestyle" into the product.' Their aims are 'to make technology more intelligent, more flexible for users of different cultural backgrounds' and generally to consider the social context of their products.

Kiyoshi Sakashita, corporate director and head of all design activity at Sharp, the Japanese electronics giant, talks of 'humanware'. 'Today,' he says, 'many companies have shifted their marketing strategies from a merchandising to a "needs oriented" basis. As a result, the role of the designer has changed. "Humanware" is the consideration of the product in terms of the total environment in which it will be used.'

LIFESTYLE

Sony develop new products by combining the technological flair of the development laboratories with a study of the way people behave, and are

Kiyoshi Sakashita directs Sharp's design and development. In 1987 Sharp introduced 2,000 new products.

likely to behave. They don't believe so much in conventional market research, but are masters of 'lifestyle' and social forecasting. Sharp have learned to study and revise their notions about how people live and behave. They now design products, Kiyoshi Sakashita claims, 'on both a material and psychological level'.

If that sounds fanciful, too elaborate for every day, then hear it from another source. When John Bloxcidge was at Wilkinson Sword, whose products ranged from swords and shears to razor blades, he warned, 'Lifestyle trends advance towards us at a visible rate, but are so often ignored by those cultures about to receive them.'

Japan's Ministry of International Trade and Industry (MITI) commented on this in a paper it published in 1988 about the growing need for design:

> People no longer base their decisions for purchase only on fundamental criteria such as function, economy and safety. Now there is a growing tendency to select on the basis of secondary criteria such as comfort, warmth, elegance, humour and personal statements conveyed by individual life and taste. It is expected this tendency will increase. . . . Young people buy what they like or what they feel suits their lifestyle almost regardless of expense . . . the future of design would seem to indicate greater individualism and design diversification, possibly leading to an inordinate variety of products.

MITI talk too, about the ageing population. In the past, industries that targeted the elderly operated on a small scale. That will change. MITI forecast a booming 'silver market'. Demands for design in this field, in contrast to previous focus on miniaturisation and multi-functionalism (products doing several things), will emphasise the importance of 'user-friendly' and 'error-proof' functions.

The growing and changing role of women is also touched on:

> Thanks to labour-saving devices, the amount of time needed for housework will decrease. Focus will shift from 'housewife-oriented design' to 'family-oriented design'. Men will also spend more of their time buying household necessities.

A plan, budget or forecast made without understanding changing social patterns is bound to be simplistic and probably wrong. Since 1973 Taylor Nelson Applied Futures, part of the Taylor Nelson Group, have researched social trends in nineteen advanced countries. They divide society into seven 'social value groups', each showing different patterns of behaviour. These groups, they say, can be lumped together in three main philosophies for everyday living: 'sustainers', hanging on to their existing standards of living; 'outer directeds', the majority of the population, though rapidly being eroded; and 'inner directeds'. 'Outer directeds' express material success. Conspicuous achievement and consumption typify them. In West Germany, Japan and parts of the United States, it is said that they are still the majority. But their numbers are being eroded by the third group, the 'inner directeds'. These 'inner directeds', argue Taylor Nelson, are more interested in self-development than the rat-race; they are looking for a balanced, complete existence. They are concerned with a sense of meaning and purpose, and with individualistic, caring, quality-of-life questions.

Illustrating this, futurist Francis Kinsman describes how each group would answer the question, 'Why are you eating less?' The 'sustainer' would say, 'I can't afford it.' The 'outer directed' would say, 'Because I can't get into my trousers.' The 'inner directed' would reply, 'Because it is healthier.'

Why should harassed executives take a minute to bother about such esoteric notions? First, because, according to the researchers, the 'inner directeds' could easily outstrip the other two groups by the end of the decade, and second, because these shifting patterns will unquestionably alter purchasing behaviour in a thousand ways. There is a third point, obvious as soon as it is said: demographic or socio-economic analysis is no more than a starting point for understanding what is happening. 'And,' Dr Liz Nelson adds, 'not always a very good one at that.' To decide what people are going to want on the basis of where they live, how much they earn and how well they are educated, won't get to the heart of anything.

Nelson wrote, too, about our inability to see the growing complexity of consumer behaviour, which 'seriously challenges the sacred rule of marketing'. She summed up the importance of studying changes in life-style: 'It is necessary to identify the opportunity in time to take advantage of it. This is the cornerstone of successful new product development' (Figure 10). Studying social and cultural change can reveal possible niche markets in highly competitive sectors as well as the emergence of completely new areas of opportunity.

Figure 10   Will changing lifestyles make these growth markets?

Growth markets	
Electrical, etc. VCR, etc.	Furniture
Holidays, DIY, eating out	Security
Telephone (to 95% of homes)	Home improvements
Credit	Tourism
Motoring	Hobbies of all kinds
Health	Energy
Defence	Space
Biochemistry	

SOURCE: Professor Morrell, Henley Centre for Forecasting

If researchers understand consumers' needs from an analysis of basic values and if they can communicate these needs to creative people, creative communicators or R & D people, the result is likely to be 'magical' says Dr Liz Nelson.

The first point is to look outside the company and, still better, outside your own industry. In 1960, in his famous *Harvard Business Review* paper 'Marketing Myopia', Theodore Levitt pointed out that major innovations come from outside an industry. Yet even today in the UK the furniture industry still thinks that plastics are not quite part of its industry, and the Engineering Industry Training Board, I was told, sees as its universe 'things that are made in metal'. They have few electronic engineer members.

LEARN BY GETTING OUT

Designers can help you to find out about your customers and competitors, but not by sitting at a drawing board. If you tell them your plans, they can use their initiative and imagination to address them. Get them out, to visit customers, retail outlets, trade shows (of other industries as well as your own) and conferences.

Honda director Nobuhiko Kawamoto told a US/Japanese design management conference that designers must be 'those always in action'. At Honda they are 'not allowed to stay as mere design specialists in a room. From time to time they are given the opportunity to drive at 200 km per hour in Europe, to experience the driver's psychology, sense of security in the car and investigate driving conditions in other cars. It is necessary for designers to investigate car markets, to have opportunities to talk to customers and to listen to claims or complaints about the cars.'

Designers at Honda have to be present when new models are exhibited and criticised by journalists. They must survey how the design is implemented and how the products are delivered to the customers. Designers must be responsible for their designs and the products as manufactured in the factory. 'The ultimate target of designers with high sensibilities,' Kawamoto summed up, 'is to catch the customer's mind.'

J. David Power, of Californian consultants J. D. Power & Associates, talked about how Honda find out about their customers: 'While I don't think they do a ton of market research the way some companies do, they get all their decision makers down at the consumer level, where they do a lot more hands-on research.' He cited one design team that spent a week at a shopping mall talking to shoppers as they loaded bags of groceries into their cars. One result, he claimed, was the redesigned Honda Civic hatchback.

Is it a coincidence that the US magazine *Car and Driver* named the Honda Accord among the year's best cars in 1985 and in the same year Honda's Civic won the prized Car of the Year award in Japan itself?

Japanese firms like Honda often have elaborate systems to evaluate prototypes. Many other companies, according to an in-depth study of forty-seven companies by Britain's Open University, 'rely on the intuition of senior management and marketing staff to assess product acceptability'. This, the study noted solemnly, 'seems ill-advised given the evidence that firms with high turnover and profit growth were significantly more likely to subject prototypes to customer and user feedback than those who relied on intuition or indirect methods like asking sales staff for comments'.

LISTEN TO CUSTOMERS

A study published in 1983 by Robin Roy and Vivien Walsh at the Design Innovation Group at the Open University described a Danish toy manufacturer. The company tests every new product idea among children. If they don't like the toy, the company doesn't make it. In other words, let people who are closest to your customers in age, experience and inclination think which product ideas to develop.

David Carter runs one of Britain's largest and most thorough industrial design practices. He was retained to develop products for people setting up their first home. He couldn't understand why his clients wanted old-fashioned design. Then he saw they were the generation of the parents of their potential customers.

Contrast this with Honda. To develop a car to appeal to young people, Tadashi Kume, the president, appointed a design team with an average age of twenty-seven. When he saw their proposals, he found them 'quite a diversion from our idea of a car. But the young people seemed confident, so we decided to let them go ahead with it.' Honda's president is well aware that however hard people of his generation try, they can never fully keep up with the younger set. The important thing to do, he emphasised, is to assess the amount of work they do before arriving at their idea. 'After that, all you can do is trust them.' He did well. The car was an unqualified success.

Merrick Taylor is chairman of the highly successful UK company Motor Panels (Coventry), Europe's largest independent designer and producer of truck cabs. Leyland, Ford, Seddon and Scammell are some of their customers. They also turn their hand to manufacturing special bodies – Bluebird, which held the world land speed record, was one; General Motors' XVR show car was another. Taylor makes the same point as Tadashi Kume. He likes to have young people such as apprentices and young graduates involved in design and manufacturing, partly because their ideas will be 'unfettered by middle-aged pressures and constraints'. You can measure the benefits. Merrick Taylor points to the Leyland Roadtrain cab system. His new design was built with 30 per cent fewer parts than the nearest competitor, and the drag coefficient was reduced by 25 per cent.

I asked the managing director of one of Britain's largest furniture companies how he found out what his customers want. He said he couldn't afford market research. Nonsensical as that is, there are still things that he – and anyone else – can do. IBM talk of 'the joy of complaints'. That is one way they learn what their customers want. 'For every customer who complains,' they say, 'fifty walk.' In other words, people who complain are just the tip of an iceberg of dissatisfaction. Unknowingly, they speak for others who may be less vocal or determined.

Listening to customers was one way that Jaguar Cars came back. In 1980 the company was losing $1.5 million a week. Sir John Egan, brought in as chairman and chief executive, decided that the company's future depended on the US market. He brought over parties of dealers, and stunned them by saying he had established 250 areas for improvement. In the USA itself, the company, by now down to sales of only 3,000 cars a year, hired Californian consultants J. D. Power & Associates to carry out telephone conversations with several hundred buyers each month. They talked to drivers who had owned Jaguars for thirty-five days, for eight months and for eighteen months. Some interviews were taped. 'The service stinks,' said one customer. 'I don't like being treated this way,' shouted another. Michael Dale, senior vice-president for Jaguar Cars Inc., was horrified and sent the tapes to his managers. They fed them to district service managers who, in turn, went to their customers to see if their complaints had been dealt with. All too often they hadn't. The message

Merrick Taylor, with Leyland's Roadtrain, says his company spends 'lots of time trying to find the real needs and aspirations of end-users'. Voted European Truck of the Year when it was launched, by 1986 the Roadtrain had become UK market leader.

started getting across to the dealers, by now in danger of being dropped. By mid-1983 Jaguar was climbing up the service charts – thirteenth out of twenty-seven marques measured by J. D. Power & Associates. The next year it climbed to sixth place, and the following year to fifth, ahead of all luxury cars except Mercedes. By 1987, sales of Jaguar cars in the USA had risen to 23,000. The company had edged out Scotch whisky as Britain's biggest dollar earner. Although teething problems with their new model pushed Jaguar down the Powers scale in 1988, by the end of the decade Jaguar intends to make 60,000 cars a year of which 35,000 will go to the United States.

Well up to plan, Jaguar made almost 52,000 cars in 1988. Heavily exposed to the US dollar, they reported profits sliced in half early in 1989. It didn't take long, of course, for financial journalists to warn of predators. Sir John Egan, who also reports sales up 11 per cent in the United States in the early part of the year, is responding by slicing £50 million from his costs.

The City's rejection of its former favourites, as the *Sunday Times* reported, is a fact of life in a bear market. The Stock Exchange is as much a victim of fashion as any other community, it added. And as short-sighted, might one say.

IDEAS TO TRY

When General Electric in the United States set out to build up their share of the railroad business they held workshops on their customers' premises. Together with their customers, they wrote lists of desired features of new products. Then they divided them up: those the customer could do best, those General Electric could do best.

Other companies get their sales force to add a new heading to their sales reports: 'best three potential product (or line extension) ideas heard about on a customer's premises'. What is important, they say, is that the chairman should read them all monthly. His or her next step is to make sure that the design, marketing, engineering and manufacturing people in the company pay attention to those ideas.

At 3M everyone in the R & D department makes regular sales calls. Other companies get their managers to spend time in their customers' shops, offices or factories. When Anthony McBurnie, now director-

General Electric held workshops on customers' premises to develop new products for the railroad industry.

general of the Institute of Marketing, joined a bakery making cakes, his first two weeks were spent in Marks & Spencer, one of their large customers.

The essential point is that business itself needs to be turned inside out; it must work from the customer in, not from the factory out. Companies can only survive by making what their customers want. They are unlikely to prosper by offering people what the factory chooses to make. No one would deny this logic. It is just that it is rarely followed. One hard nut to swallow is the fact that your customers' perceptions are more important than your superior technical knowledge.

John F. Akers, chairman of IBM and former Yale hockey player and Navy pilot, stated, 'We do, we make, we buy, we sell,' trying to breathe urgency into the $54 billion revenue giant that is now sniffing competition in the air. During 1986 he set up a series of task forces to look at the company. One question he asked was: 'Has IBM become too bureaucratic and slow?' Another was: 'Is it too concerned with selling what it makes rather than making what customers want?'

Nixdorf ranks among the top five data processing companies in Europe. It produces systems solutions, services and software for everything except mainframe computers. It sells more computers and terminals to European banks than IBM and has a sizeable niche in retailing. The company doubled sales revenue in the four years to 1983 and plans to do the same again. (By the end of 1987 it was £1.7 billion.) Nixdorf attributes much of its success to 'close co-operation with the customer, leading to rapid assimilation of market needs – and their swift translation into innovative products'.

Merrick Taylor, chairman of Motor Panels (Coventry), believes 'it is no good being right and irrelevant'. His company spends a lot of time trying to find out the real needs and aspirations of the end user, particularly their routine, day-to-day needs. It assumes that the most knowledgeable or influential person is not necssarily the buyer or any director, but more often the driver or the mechanic. Further, when Motor Panels (Coventry) meet customers, or exhibit at motor shows, they don't just have marketing or design people there, but people from the finance, purchasing, manufacturing and quality control departments.

Speaking to the Royal Society of Arts, Merrick Taylor said:

> All importantly the complete team is introduced to the exciting first stage of the process – identifying the customer's needs and selling the idea. This process of early, enthusiastic involvement with the end user by a well-informed, multi-disciplinary team enhances confidence in the development of the design, giving the best possible motive for achieving cost effectiveness.

Kenichi Ohmae of McKinsey & Co. in Tokyo advises:

> Unless the company objectively views its customers' intrinsic needs as they change over time, its competitors will some day challenge the status quo. There is no doubt, therefore, that a corporation's foremost concern ought to be the interest of its customers rather than that of its stockholders and other parties . . . It often pays to pick a small group of key customers and re-examine what it is they are really looking for.

ANTICIPATE

Bosch, West Germany's largest private company, is a prime example of a company that has triumphed by anticipating and focusing. They foresaw the growing importance of fuel economy and of air pollution. They pioneered fuel injection and now have three quarters of that fast-growing market.

Others have the notion of 'lead users'. In other words, some people are first to buy new products. They can be years ahead of the rest. Carefully spotted and followed, they can be a fertile source of leading-edge ideas. But, warns, Jim Utterback at the Massachusetts Institute of Technology, 'the initial use and vision for a new product or service is virtually never the one that is of the greatest importance commercially'. When television was first transmitted publicly in Britain from Alexandra Palace, north of London, in 1936, one of its benefits was claimed to be 'apprehending wanted criminals'. The mayor of one US city, more perspicaciously, spotted the merits of the telephone when it was new. Every city, he said, should have one.

Tracking the behaviour of lead users can be another answer to the people who say that market research will only tell you about yesterday's needs. Professor Peter Doyle, of Warwick University, says the big successes in recent years, such as the Sony Walkman, Swatch (the Swiss watch), BMW cars, and retail concepts like Next and Conran:

> have very little to do with capital investment or manufacturing efficiency or low unit costs. These successes have much more to do with innovative marketing positioning. Success seems to be due to the imagination and professionalism that management have had in identifying emerging market opportunities and then aggressively and incisively capitalising on them.

SUMMARY

Mark Twain once said, 'Everyone talks about the weather, but no one does anything about it.' In the same way, few companies would deny the need to find out what people want if they aim to sell to them. Yet many manufacturing companies continue to believe they know better than

Understanding 'lifestyles' and with brilliant design and marketing flair, Swatch Watch has helped the Swiss watch industry to fight off fierce competition.

their customers. Perhaps as bad, others, knowing market research would be helpful, feel they cannot afford it.

Without true knowledge of customers, product development is bound to be risky – a lottery, a lucky dip. Intuition and experience might lead a company to making the right products, but the odds are poor and getting worse. Markets are now so competitive, so precise, yet so extended, that it is impossible to know what people everywhere will prefer.

First, the conventional way of analysing the population, by socio-economic groups, is a very blunt and probably out-of-date instrument. 'Psychological segmentation', as I have called it elsewhere, is likely to be far more telling. Second, we can pin too much faith on numbers. Third, older and newer ways of finding out about customers are proving highly effective. On the one hand, leading companies are finding 'lifestyle' a more revealing guide to forecasting human behaviour than the normal head-counting survey. On the other, business executives are remembering that there is no substitute for getting close to the customer and staying there. The idea is to 'stand in your customers' shoes'. If more people, at all levels, in more companies spent more time out of their offices and among their customers, the results could only be good and would show quickly. With or without money, that is something all of us can do.

5

Find the Right Niche

'If you're not thinking segments,
you're not thinking.'
Theodore Levitt, Harvard Business School

Peter Doyle, when he was at Bradford University, studied a matched sample of British companies and Japanese competitors operating in the UK. Among his 1985 findings was that customer targeting is the basis of marketing. Doyle said it was 'somewhat alarming' to find that many UK companies did not know how they segmented the market. Many of them did not think it important. He asked the marketing director of a British consumer durables company to say how he approached the market. He replied, 'I don't know if we segment the market, or how we position ourselves against the competition. But I expect our advertising agency knows. Why not ask them? I think we are probably up-market because we advertise in some very posh magazines.' If that is a horror story, it is not unique.

The Japanese companies that Doyle looked at were very clear on their strategy. They had identified their markets with precision. The British entered the market because they saw problems with existing products; the Japanese because they saw opportunities. Eighty-seven per cent of the Japanese companies interviewed by Doyle said their goal was aggressive growth. They were after market share. The British, Doyle claimed, 'didn't really seem to believe in market share as an objective. But what they did believe in was short-term profitability.'

The conventional concept of 'mass markets' is collapsing. Global marketing, a current cry so espoused by the world-wide advertising agency Saatchi & Saatchi, does not mean that everyone in the world will buy the same products. Instead, under global brands perhaps, companies may now, thanks to computerised manufacturing systems, be able to provide the precise products that people everywhere want. Ricoh, in Japan, is an example. It can make copiers in batches of 50. It then alters the details

Mass production, like mass marketing, is out of date. Amazing flexible manufacturing at Ricoh lets it adapt its copiers to suit the precise needs of customers in different markets and segments.

and switches to manufacturing another batch for another market. With this technology, the same company has become the leading supplier or facsimile machines in the United States, with 15 per cent marketed under its own name and another 15 per cent under the AT&T label.

THE TRUE VALUE OF MICROELECTRONICS

In 1987 Sharp, the Japanese electronics giant, launched 2,000 'new' products. Not all, by any means, were true innovations. Most were variations of basic models, tailored and designed to suit particular groups of customers, or, to use the jargon, 'segments' of the market.

Looking ahead, Dr Bruce Merrifield at the US Department of Commerce, talks about the 'make-anything' factory. Thanks to the total

78

flexibility of computer-integrated manufacturing, 'a given plant will make hundreds of products for different companies. It will run for thirty-five minutes on one thing, twenty minutes on another. Manufacturing itself will become a service function.' Being able to go to a factory that can readily switch to making what you want will lead to still more new products for still more niche markets.

According to Dr Liz Nelson, of the Taylor Nelson Group, companies find it hard to perceive the development of micromarkets because they run contrary to our strong beliefs in standardisation (economy of scale, long production runs and mass marketing). The important point about microelectronics has been overlooked. It is not that everything can be the same, but the opposite. Today everything can be different. That is what computerisation has given us.

This new insistence on trying to satisfy customers faster and better than anyone else affects the way people have always looked at business. The attitude of mass production, of thousands or millions of products all being identical, because that is the cheapest way to make them, is going out of the window. 'You can have any colour you like as long as it is black' had a good life, but it is dead now. All the economists and managers who still strive for economies of scale had better be careful.

We need high productivity, yes. But we also must tailor products more and more precisely to suit ever more selective customers. Flexible manufacturing systems (FMS) are the key. The car industry is using FMS for batch series production. But installations are very expensive. In 1984 Japan had 100 installations of FMS, the United States forty. According to Dr R. D. Schraft, West Germany had twenty-five in place. But numbers are growing. An unofficial estimate put the number of FMS systems in place in the UK in 1986 at fifty.

The complexities of global marketing are crystallised in the problems of designing truck cabs. The market is declining, if anything, in the northern hemisphere, but expectations for styling, comfort and quality are very high. 'Reliable simplicity' (a phrase of Merrick Taylor's), by contrast, is the priority in the southern hemisphere. Further, developing countries, where the growth potential lies, often want to make their own trucks. Taylor's imaginative company has designed a way to meet all these requirements in one, modular way. Their cabs can be built by robots or by a pair of hands, using simple jigs.

LAST-MOMENT DECISION

In 'Managing the New Product Development Process: How Japanese Companies Learn and Unlearn' Ken-ichi Imai, Ikujivo Nonaka and Hirotaka Takeuchi studied five companies: Fuji-Xerox, Honda, Canon, NEC and Epson. One of the outstanding characteristics, they found, was the way these companies deliberately delayed making decisions on reducing the options on a product line. 'Variety reduction', as it is called, is only undertaken at the last moment. The aim is to take advantage of the latest state of the market into which the product is being sold.

The Italian knitwear and clothing firm Benetton have made this their competitive advantage. What happens in the clothing industry is this: before each season buyers see new designs and colourways. They buy. Manufacturers make garments to fill these orders. Then end customers choose. Some garments will be more popular than others. So retailers run out of stock. They have to wait for new goods to be made. Benetton have sliced this delay by using a process first developed over 100 years ago; they dye the garments *after* they are made. That means they can wait to see which colours shoppers prefer, then provide them in a day or two. The undyed goods are already made. Benetton can colour them and ship them in no time. By so doing, they avoid carrying stock people don't want and serve retailers and shoppers faster. Benetton's manufacturing, distribution and marketing are stitched together, one might say, to keep options open as long as possible – and to provide better service.

On the same theme, the National Institute of Economic and Social Research looked at the kitchen furniture industry. In the UK, German manufacturers dominate the high price, high quality, high added-value end of the market. The research found German firms maintain regular contact with customers, which British firms generally do not. The British companies work in cramped conditions with large stocks. They are geared to mass production. The German kitchen furniture manufacturers, by contrast, organise production around small batches. The reason they give is to minimise stock levels and be more responsive to customers. Productivity in the German firms is 66 per cent higher than in the UK companies. And they have the market leadership.

SEGMENT THE MARKET

Market share comes from segmentation, and segmentation comes from market knowledge. Peter Doyle of Warwick University warns, 'If a company fails to segment the market, the market will segment the company.' 'If you're not thinking segments, you're not thinking,' says Theodore Levitt.

The majority of British companies in Doyle's study had 'very unclear objectives and very low expectations of success. Most of them had no clear market positioning strategy, nor could they describe their target market segment and the majority could not define a rational differential advantage.' 'The boards of British companies,' Doyle argued to a national marketing conference, 'do not understand marketing. They feel uncomfortable with it. They do not press their managers to produce marketing strategies. Consequently, marketing strategies do not get articulated.'

We come back again to the boards of many companies being mainly concerned with finance. 'With the Japanese companies, by contrast,' Peter Doyle said, 'short-term financial and cash-flow objectives are very secondary indeed. They judge their managers on their ability to understand the market. They know that if they get the marketing right the bottom line will come right in the long run.

Four characteristics of the winning companies were identified by Doyle in this study of Japanese companies in Britain. He said they focus on:

- Professional marketing orientation

- Decisive entry strategies

- Commitment to market share

- Organisation to motivate people.

Graham Hooley, James Lynch and Christopher West of Bradford University conducted a major research programme in 1983. It was called *Marketing in the United Kingdom* and compared high performers with low performers. They wrote:

> The core of good marketing is to isolate a market segment, where the organisation's distinctive competences find a profitable match with unsatisfied customer need. The best performing companies demonstrate an unwavering focus upon the marketplace and relate all their major operating decisions to the dictates of customer needs. . . This kind of market orientation is not possible without the genuine understanding of the marketplace, which is derived from sound market research. Many companies which claim to be market oriented neglect this fundamental truth.

81

It is no coincidence that the weaker performers often show a low level or reduced commitment to market research, allowing short-run financial pressures to obscure the centrality of the need for updated market information.

BACK TO MARKET RESEARCH

Philip Kotler and his colleagues claim that Japanese devotion to product improvement is reflected in their commitment to listening to and learning about their customers:

> They will spend long hours in discussion with customers about what limitations and weaknesses exist in their present product offerings, how products might be improved and how the customers might react to possible product modifications. Product development never occurs in complete isolation. Products are developed and modified with particular markets in mind.

In the copying machine industry, US companies concentrated on sophisticated products at high prices. Then the Japanese companies, Ricoh, Canon and Sharp, came in with smaller, simpler equipment. The policy of market segmentation and focus is clear. The Japanese focused, for example, on computer peripheral equipment. In five years they captured 75 per cent of the US market for computer printers costing under $11,000. In the motorcycle industry, while Harley Davidson, Norton, BSA and others worked on producing more powerful motorcycles, Honda and Yamaha developed smaller, lighter, less expensive machines. In each case the Japanese chose entry points where the competition was, in the words of Philip Kotler and his colleagues, 'weak, complacent or non-existent'.

Soichiro Honda, founder and builder of the $26 billion Honda empire, told *INC.* magazine how it happened. 'Our marketing people were told that Americans would never buy motorcycles. Then we started thinking: how can we build motorcycles in such a way that the Americans would like to buy them? Well, let's build a motorcycle that can go in a car.' He was thinking, he said, of the natural desire of humans to get to remote places, where fish are biting or wildlife is plentiful. 'If you want to go fishing, you don't expect to find many fish in areas that are accessible by car.

So you want to get out of the car and ride on a motorcycle to where you can catch many fish.'

Honda created a new market, one that widened. It was this kind of original thinking that shattered the conventional industry, fixed as it was on producing large, powerful machines.

Baker Perkins, the food, printing and chemicals equipment group (part of APV), might be going the same way. Ten years ago their printing business introduced heavy plant that prints 32-page spreads at a remarkable 1,800 feet per minute. It was aimed at the biggest magazine publishers in the world and won over 60 per cent of the US market and over 80 per cent of the British market.

There's more than a sporting chance that the American magazine you pick up was printed on equipment supplied by Baker Perkins, the Peterborough-based firm. To break in to the US market, the company went to great lengths to find out what their potential customers wanted, then studied, really studied, their competitors. Design is at the centre of their insistent product development; teamwork their key to speed.

Six years later they brought in a sixteen-page web offset machine that cost some 30 per cent less. The savings come from design, not lower standards. That has already captured over 30 per cent of its markets. In June 1986 they introduced new equipment that, harnessing microprocessor controls and the world's first fibre-optics applications, is aimed at printing houses wanting shorter print runs, more flexibility, less down time. The payoff of this determined product policy is not only to spread risk but to achieve a sales growth of 50 per cent a year compound and profits up by 62 per cent compound over five years.

I remember working for a biscuit firm. It wasn't very large, yet it sold biscuits in sixty-seven countries. It collected export markets like stamps, each with about the same, slight value. That is not the Japanese way. They choose their markets and point of entry carefully. They think about where to strike. They look for attractive opportunities. Then they develop appropriate products. They choose their market entry points to gain a foothold. Then they aim to broaden their base and build market share. When they achieve market leadership, they develop strategies to hold it.

According to Kotler and his colleagues, 'the Japanese have used product proliferation as a major market penetration strategy in many industries'. This allows them to appeal to a large number of niches in the total market, to people with different tastes, preferences, income levels. Further, 'every industry in which the Japanese have been successful is marked by their capacity to furnish a sequence of product improvements in performance style, features and quality'.

Britain's National Economic Development Office commissioned market research to find out how manufacturing companies develop new products. One question asked what they put into a brief. Did they describe the potential customer and the need being served? One third of the companies said no. A parallel study was conducted in the United States by students at Boston University, under the guidance of Peter Lawrence of the Corporate Design Foundation. The reply was much the same. However, almost all the US firms (91 per cent) said they describe the product objective and key product characteristics. In both cases, UK figures were lower. Showing their concern for price, four out of five US companies said they state the target selling price in the brief. So do six out of ten British firms, according to the NEDO study.

It is axiomatic that before you develop a new product you should state your expectation of its customer benefits, as well as its market and price. Segment the market according to user objectives (people buy your product for different reasons). Then develop differentiated strategies and products. Find the right niche.

The notion of mass markets is long gone. All markets can be segmented. Choose the slice where you are likely to be strongest. Within that, go for market share. Secure it with quality, reliability, service, not by underpricing. When Peter Doyle asked the Japanese companies in his sample their definition of 'differential advantage' (why should the customer prefer your product?), they all gave one of two reasons. Most said 'superior quality and reliability'. The second reason was 'customer service'.

The fascinating element about Doyle's study, so black and white in its conclusions, is that the comparison was not between companies on different sides of the world, imbued with all the cultural differences we hear about, but between British companies in Britain and Japanese companies in Britain. Their employees come from the same cultural background. They work in the same environment. The difference is a managerial one.

Akahi Minamimura, chairman of Sumitomo, the Japanese trading group, recently reported that Japanese executives in the UK found that productivity and absenteeism match levels in Japan 'pretty well across the board'. When all the talking is done, we come back to the elementary point: if we want to make products people will buy we had better find out what they want. We know that, but case after case shows we don't always do it.

LADDER OF BUSINESS

You can't help feeling that people who pay little attention to their customers, whatever they say, are still far down the ladder of business that has been evolving over centuries.

The first level of business may be called 'agrarian'. You grow food, or make things, where it is convenient to do so. As competition enters, you move further from base, further, in farming terms, up the hillside. Returns diminish the further you go. Maybe eighteenth-century farming was like that. It was replaced, was it not, by the age of *production*. People learned to produce in quantity. They needed to find and fill 'empty spaces', reaching out, for example, to the old 'empire' countries. For many years, the ability to produce was the key to prosperity. Evey today it is unquestionably one reason for Japan's current success. Although not by itself. Companies, and government departments, come to that, that pin too much faith on productivity are missing today's point.

None the less, large-scale production leads to lower costs. But in time those 'empty spaces' become saturated markets too. Then people compete with *sales and service*. One way or another, companies and governments try to manipulate markets. As we see now, protectionism crops up.

Up to now, all those have been problems of the company; the company looking out from itself. What happens when all of that fails to preserve a company's competitiveness? You then shift from your own problems to those of the market. Companies start to find and solve *customers' problems*. That is the current phase. If a company does this well, it can then create its own markets. Polaroid, IBM and Xerox are examples of three companies that did just that. Move, as they did, from products to systems. View your product as part of a total package: design, corporate image, service, financing, distribution, convenience. All these are parts of the customer-satisfying complex.

But you need information to identify the right problems to solve. The company has to become what is termed knowledge-oriented. Problem solving, or finding new problems to solve, leads to creating a demand. You see what a priority that puts on the people in your business rather than on the equipment.

A German lecturer at INSEAD, Dr H. Gross, once remarked that in a climate of change, future-mindedness is created by 'our fantasy, our planning'. Marketing, as he saw it, is more than an extension of selling. It is 'the strategy of decision making'. First, decide the tactics of doing the right things. Then do them right.

There are at least three ways of going about that. One is to say, 'I make this product. I have always made it, and I will make it in the future.' Another is to look for problems you can solve within your existing competence. 'I develop competition within myself. That means I spread my overheads over the same customers.' Better still is to see that the closer you come to the market, the less you can specialise. Production, ever important, shifts from being dominant and standardised towards making whatever the 'de-specialised' market-focused company wants.

It is possible to lift the subject to high levels of theory. Market analyses can become mathematicians' delights of arcane obscurity. Simpler ways are better. Indeed, marketing departments can become too removed from reality. It is vital that their feet should stay on the ground. Everyone in the business should know they are there to serve customers and should be encouraged to think of ideas to do so better. 'We love our customers', the sign in a New York shop reads. 'They pay our wages.'

The chairman of another company makes it a rule to phone three customers every week, and to phone another three people who didn't buy. That doesn't cost much. Nor may it be statistically reliable, but it is a start.

British Airways has turned around in the last few years. One reason: a sustained effort to improve service. 'Service,' says chief executive Sir Colin Marshall, 'is another means of providing value for money.' Further, 'People will pay for better service.'

Sir Colin has a monitor on his desk which tells him of all departures. He can see which are late. A phone call tells him why. And that is the boss of the world's largest international airline. If he can bother, why can't the heads of smaller businesses?

'If the company consistently succeeds in serving customers more effectively than its competitors, profit will follow,' claims Kenichi Ohmae, head of the consultants McKinsey & Co. in Tokyo. 'Too many corporations lose sight of this,' he adds, 'even to the point of forgetting what business they are in.'

SUMMARY

The notion of mass marketing is dwindling. It is being challenged by targeted, 'segmented' marketing made possible by flexible manufacturing. The key is the way rising education, wealth and independence are all giving people more time and opportunity to be themselves. More and more, winning companies are those that identify and cater for this spectrum of individual tastes and preferences. The age of 'any colour you like as long as it's black' is over. It comes back to finding out what the customer wants more rapidly and precisely than your competitors do – and then providing it.

6

Know Your Competitors

'Be a Jack-of-all-trades
and master of one.'
The late Sir Misha Black, senior partner
of the Design Research Unit

Focus on your customers, yes, but keep more than half an eye on your competition. It is your competitors who set the standards. If there were no competitors there would be little need to strive for higher performance. Competitors introduce new designs, satisfy customers' needs that much better, lift the quality of service, introduce new technology, and sometimes find ways to sell a product for less than you can make it.

Competitors introduce the need for strategy. 'The sole purpose of strategic planning,' says Kenichi Ohmae, 'is to enable a company to gain, as efficiently as possible, a sustainable edge over its competitors.' Japanese companies are masters of competitive product and strategy analysis. James Goodson, former vice-president of ITT in Europe, said, 'We used to smile at all those Japanese wandering around with their cameras. But we don't any more.'

WHAT ARE YOUR COMPETITORS DOING?

No self-respecting manager would admit that he or she doesn't know the competition. Of course not. They meet each other at industry functions, if nothing else. The question is: how well do they understand their competitor's business? In February 1986 American consultants Korn/Ferry International studied the relative importance to directors of a number of issues. Over half (56 per cent) put financial results in first place. Just over 1.5 per cent thought 'industry competition' that important. Fewer than one in five (17.5 per cent) put competition in the first three places of importance. That is an answer.

'The difference between effective companies and others is not so much what they do,' said Robin Leaf when he was at McKinsey & Co. in London, 'but the depth and dedication they apply to doing it.' At a meeting of chairmen of UK companies, he described how some companies look at their competitors' performance and, as much to the point, what they do about it.

Leaf described a British margarine company. Not only did they use consumer panels to evaluate their own and competing products, as many companies do, but they developed a reliable quantitative guide to what were, after all, subjective consumer reactions. One of the things they did was to build an artificial tongue that measured the melting rates of different margarines. Their homework paid off when a US competitor decided to enter the UK market. The UK company knew enough about the incoming product to develop the right strategy quickly and see the competitor off.

That's the best way. To have your defences in place by knowing what competitors are up to before they strike. Xerox in the US didn't do this. They came from behind. They had to react after their market had been gouged away from them. In 1976 Xerox had 82 per cent of the US copier market. By 1982 that share had halved. Surprise, surprise, Xerox responded by cutting costs. But the limitations of that became obvious. They resolved to fight back by raising quality. How did they do it? They started to look at their own Japanese subsidiary. Learning from it, they developed a system of what they called 'competitive bench-marking'. They identified the highest standards among any of their competitors and, wisely, among industries related to theirs. Then they made those targets their own. Every key operation had to match or improve upon the performance achieved by any other organisation.

Similarly, although not waiting for trouble, British Airways has a whole department whose sole job is to study competitors. The idea is to know the standards they have to beat.

REVERSE ENGINEERING

Ford buy competitors' products and strip them down. Every removable component is unscrewed or unbolted, even rivets are undone. Individual spot welds are broken. They make detailed lists of all the parts and analyse the production process that must have been used. Then they build up the costs. Parts are costed in terms of make or buy, the variety of parts used and the extent of common assemblies.

The number and variety of components and the number of assembly operations are two of the critical pieces of information, therefore. Then Ford cross-check this information with the number of cars produced, the number of people in the plant and so forth. From this they can assess the economies of scale. Thanks to this painstaking effort, Ford decided not to compete with the Mini. They realised that the British Motor Corporation (BMC), as it then was, couldn't be making money from the Mini. Further, that they shouldn't enter the market while prices stayed where they were.

This kind of reverse engineering can provide many benefits. When Sir John Egan took over as chairman of Jaguar Cars in 1980, he had several Mercedes brought into the plant. He told his engineers to 'acquaint themselves with every detail'. They took each car to pieces and rebuilt it several times. Today, Jaguar feel confident enough of their quality to advertise that their cars are 'worth any number of Deutsch marques'. Further, by stripping down competitive products, a company can identify how costs are made up. You sometimes find components that could be made for less. This, in turn, can lead to a price advantage. If you can assess how much the product must have cost to make, you also know whether the competitor can afford to reduce its prices if it wants to. Japanese companies have used this information to undercut competitive products, knowing their lower prices cannot be matched.

That's part of the secret of Alan Sugar's success. He says, 'We look at the competition, take it to bits and see if we can engineer something similar or better – usually better and cheaper. We identify the facilities that aren't useful and we ditch them to reduce costs.'

All this may sound too theoretical by half, but it is true. In 1986 I went on a study tour to Japan. It had been organised by the Design Council, working with the management consultants PA. The aim was to see how Japanese companies develop new products. We visited Sony, Seiko Epson, Minolta, Sharp, Matsushita, Brother, Yawasaki and others. Everywhere our hosts were generous with their time and information. At one company I asked, 'Tell us, do you buy all your competitors' products and reverse engineer them? Do you find out how each component is made and how much it must cost?' Warming to my theme I pressed on, 'And do you look at their marketing, how they distribute and what discounts they offer and what media they use to advertise?' Our host looked blank, puzzled. After a long pause he replied. 'Of course.' It was one of a number of silly questions we asked.

Indeed, when IBM in Britain started to focus on quality it wasn't because they thought it had deteriorated. They saw that some of their competitors were achieving higher standards. That is where they started: looking at their competitors. 'We concentrated on looking outside our own operation,' explained Peter Doran, former assistant plant manager at Havant. 'Some examples were under our noses in local industry.' They 'bombarded' themselves with the 'hard facts' of the quality performance of their competition.

Another area to look at is competitive marketing and sales and service. This, too, can provide valuable guidance to shaping a fighting strategy.

HOW ONE FIRM ALMOST GOT IT WRONG

Just as this kind of thorough and continuing examination of the competition can yield marked results, so can the absence of such knowledge. Many companies have experience of making what turned out to be wrong decisions because they didn't know how their competitors would react.

Frederick Gluck, managing director of McKinsey & Co. in New York, was called in by a US electronic manufacturer. Sales and profits were falling. The company decided to respond to a vigorous competitor by reducing prices to maintain market share, and then developing a new product to fight back. After extensive study, Gluck deduced that the company's strategy was based on false assumptions. First, reverse engineering showed that the competitor enjoyed a 13 per cent cost advantage. This meant that any hope of maintaining market share by cutting prices was forlorn. The competitor could follow them down.

Next Gluck found that although the competitor had a lower purchase price, its 'life cost' (the cost of owning the product through its life) was higher. But his client had never used this as a sales feature. So they retrained the sales force. Seminars were held with customers to tell them the value of 'life-cost' advantages. The other part of the company's strategy was risky too. It was based on developing a higher-performance product. But analysis revealed that customer needs were changing. In place of high-speed, high-reliability products, which the company intended to produce, the market was shifting to low-speed, medium-reliability products. New strategies were evolved, based on these findings.

This example shows how such study is vital. In brief, without this thorough knowledge of both the competitor and market trends, the company would have made disastrous decisions.

FORGE NEW LINKS TO FIND OUT

The fascinating difficulty of finding out about competitors is that responsibility falls between existing stools. Talking about studying competitors at a conference in London, Robin Leaf picked on areas of prime interest: how their products perform, what they cost and how they are delivered, and the competitors' sales systems and service. Product performance, he explained, lies between marketing and technology; cost and delivery, measured by product teardown, lie between technology and production; analysing competitors' sales and service falls between production and marketing. Any one of your existing departments will find it hard to form the right picture. It is necessary, therefore, to forge new links, to create special task forces, to address each question.

WHICH ROUTE IS BEST?

To bring alive his analysis, Leaf described the experience of two companies. Both received the same intelligence from their marketing departments, that a dishwasher (it wasn't; that's a disguise) represented a major new market opportunity. One company took what Robin Leaf described as a 'traditional' approach. The chief executive asked the R & D department to develop a product. The R & D director set up a series of pilot projects: to look at the merits of different solvents, to examine the cleaning action of different jets, the best way to arrange crockery, and so on. At the end of a year the R & D director knew a lot about it and even had a pilot machine running.

This is a fairly typical approach. Marketing identified a new market, the technologists developed a prototype. But there were no links forged between other functions. So when the prototype and design concepts were produced by the technologists, the marketing and manufacturing people started to suggest changes that delayed the development of a marketable product.

The competitor company was Japanese. It started with the same market information. Here is what it did. First, it bought three models of every available dishwasher. Second, it formed four groups:

- a product test group of marketing and technical staff

- a design team of technologists and production people

- a distribution team of marketing and production staff

- a field team of production staff

The product test group was given one of each model. Its task was to evaluate the performance of each. How well did it wash dishes? How easy was it to use? What was the period between breakdowns? What were the reasons for failure?

The design team was given the other two models of each product on the market. It tore them down, as Ford do. It stripped all the machines in one set to calculate the number and variety of parts, to assess the cost of each part and the ease of assembly. The other set was stripped down to 'life test' each part, to identify design improvements, and to develop a comprehensive picture of the competitors' technology.

The third team looked at each competitor's marketing and distribution system. It looked at the number of outlets each was sold in, the service offered and the availability of each product.

The field team of production staff, interestingly, was charged with looking at competitors' factories. It had to evaluate competitive production facilities in terms of cost of labour, cost of supplies and productivity.

At the end of the same year, the Japanese still didn't fully understand how fluids cleaned dishes. But they knew enough to put together a product design superior to that of any competitor. Based on a pre-production prototype and design for the production process, it cost 30 per cent less to build. Within the year they also had a marketing plan that positioned the product in relation to the competition. They also defined the amount of stock and service needed to meet the needs of the distribution system. Finally, they had a plan for building a new factory, establishing contracts with suppliers and training the workforce. As a result, the Japanese company came to the market two years ahead of the traditional company. It achieved its market share. The traditional company, according to Robin Leaf, 'lost some money and dropped out of the market'.

ASSESS COMPETITIVE STRENGTHS

The dishwasher story underlines another reason for looking at competitors. The history of business is replete with examples of companies that introduce wrong products or services. Some are just wrong. Others are wrong for that company. Still other products, perhaps good in themselves,

Kenichi Ohmae, head of McKinsey & Co. in Tokyo, advises us to study competitors intensely. They set the standards we have to beat, he points out.

could be seen off by competitors. It follows that when you think about a new product you need to assess not only your own strengths and weaknesses in relation to it, but also those of your competitors. Are they dominant in that area? Are they sleeping? Are they too strong for you to fight? Do you have a more appropriate scale than they do? That is to say, do you need to be large, with substantial research and development facilities, to seize a lead, or is it better to be quick to change, a quality sometimes easier for smaller companies to achieve?

This kind of study is one reason for the success of Baker Perkins in the United States. Before they brought in their massive G-16 printing presses, they sent engineers from Peterborough in the UK to Chicago to analyse competitive equipment. They defined where the competitors were weakest. Speaking of it now, director Michael Smith says they do a lot of competitive product analysis but, he thinks, they now need to spend more time looking at their competitors' business strategies.

The same applies to new technologies and trends that may provide opportunity. Can you develop faster, better access to that technology? Can you ensure continuity of supply of components?

The lessons are plain. Winning companies enjoy an absolute advantage because:

- They take the trouble to find out about their competitors

- They use cross-functional teams

- They develop products at great speed

The need for such speed and such teamwork is central to this book. We will look at it later in more detail.

COMPETITIVE TRIANGLE

Kenichi Ohmae urges us to think of a triangle (Figure 11): the customer, the company, the competitor. The struggle is for us to increase the value of our products in the eyes of the customer and to increase the difference between our products and those of our competitors. Most companies have a number of ways open to them to do this. Should you make your product smaller? Or lighter? Or faster? Or more powerful? Or cheaper? Or should

Figure 11 The competitive triangle

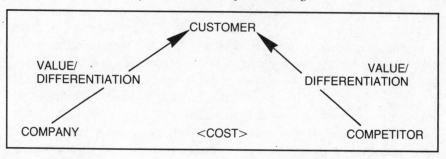

SOURCE: Kenichi Ohmae, *The Mind of the Strategist*

you extend existing features? And how do you choose? Often technical people decide. But can that be as good as finding out what your customers' true needs are, and how well your competitors are able to meet them? It is worth listing every aspect of your product, then asking which aspect, if improved, would make the most competitive difference. But that difference mustn't be for its own sake. It must match a perceived customer need.

You have to choose where to focus effort. Chief executives who invest in improving all functions may achieve a desired operational improvement. Yet they may still end up losing if the performance of their product in a single key function is still inferior to that of the competition. People will buy the other person's product.

KEY FACTOR FOR SUCCESS

The late Sir Misha Black of the Design Research Unit used to say that a designer should be a 'Jack-of-all-trades and master of one'. This idea seems to fit companies too. The notion of identifying the key factor for success (KFS) comes in here. What is it in your company?

In any business high standards are needed in all departments. But often one stands out as vital to success. It may be distribution, having the product on every street corner. (One US firm that sells perishable goods guarantees its outlets 95 per cent daily delivery, anywhere from Alaska to New Mexico.) It may be cleanliness. It may be speed of service. Tom Peters

Don't aim where the bird is, but ahead of where it is going.

tells how he had occasion to telephone Federal Express twenty-seven times in the course of a few weeks. Twenty-six times they answered the telephone the first time it rang. The twenty-seventh time he had the wrong number. It may be innovation or reliability or price ('We are never knowingly undersold' claims the John Lewis Partnership). The right one is the one feature that customers want; go for it. That phrase 'that customers want' is the key. You can often see companies promoting products in ways that are of little interest to their potential customers.

Is this the result of knowing better than their customers what they ought to want? Surely it shows a lack of appreciation of market segmentation. It comes back to finding and exploiting that competitive edge. But it is not enough to aim to beat your competitors' existing products. They will be developing new ones too. Yet that is what commonly happens. People take a brand leader or market leader and tell their designers to copy it but do a little better. This is shooting backwards. You mustn't aim where the bird is, but ahead of where it is going.

A study led by Dr Robin Roy of the Open University among British and mostly other European firms found that nine out of ten used competitors' products as a starting point for their own designs; half as a source of ideas. Rather fewer, 46 per cent, said they would adapt or try to improve on the competition. Six per cent admitted they would copy them.

Interestingly, companies that modified competitors' products were significantly associated with overall financial success. The Open University concluded from this that even companies that cannot aspire to be technology leaders can do well this way.

A MYTH EXPOSED

Michael Frye was chairman of Rotaflex, a UK-based lighting and electronics company known across Europe for its excellent products. Rotaflex achieved an average annual compound increase in profits and earnings per share of 60 and 75 per cent respectively over five years. In 1986 Frye sold the company to GTE. Shares that he bought for just under 13p in November 1980 he sold for £4.90. Frye says it is a myth that the way to reduce risk is to make the product less advanced than the designer would like it to be. Managers tend to bring it back from outside the 'paradigm' of today's thinking into what is acceptable today. This, he believes, substantially reduces the reward without significantly reducing the risk. Why? The answer is the time lapse between a concept and a product on the market. It means that 'by the time whoever is going to buy it comes along, it's now not just a "me-too" product, but runs the risk of being a "me-too" product two or three years old'.

Michael Frye went to school in Britain, spent six months as an apprentice engineer in Germany, then four years at the Massachusetts Institute of Technology. He believes that reducing risk also reduces the reward by a higher proportion. In short, it is better to be in advance, to take a lead. This gives a better mix of reward/risk/investment. 'Start on your ideas, your concepts, as far ahead as you can.'

The difference between running a tidy company and aggressively studying and fighting competitors was summed up by Kenichi Ohmae of McKinsey & Co. He said the mind functions differently. When one is striving to achieve or maintain a position of relative superiority over a dangerous competitor, the mind functions very differently from the way it does when the object is to make internal improvements with reference to some absolute model. It is the difference between going into battle and going on a diet.

This book dwells on the fundamental of competition: creating products that people want to buy. It is the basis, but only a start.

LOTS OF SPRINTS

Two business-school academics, C. K. Prahalad and Gary Hamel, spoke in 1985 in Barcelona of the way Japanese companies go about, as they put it, 'killing your opponent with a thousand cuts'. There is a growing tendency for the Japanese not only to do the things we say we do, but to invent new ways of competing. They try to take their Western competitors by surprise and to build not one, but several layers of competitive advantage.

Prahalad and Hamel took as an example Canon eating into the Xerox copier business – with different technology, different design, different production costs, different distribution and sales arrangements, and different pricing. This sort of competitive innovation, argue Prahalad and Hamel, is now a fundamental way of doing business in industries as diverse as cars and construction equipment, computers and consumer electronics. 'The Japanese win marathons,' they said, 'with a series of 200-yard sprints.' Against a 20-year view of where they're going, these companies develop layer upon layer of strategy. Now it is better product development. Next it is global marketing. Then it is cost reduction, and so on. The point of this is that by the time we have rumbled one strategy and built a response, they have moved on to another.

One-time rally driver Uwe Bahnsen, former head of Ford Europe's successful design team, gives practical advice. See his checklist.

PRACTICAL CHECKLIST

Here are some practical suggestions from Uwe Bahnsen, former head of design of Ford in Europe. This list will help you to assess both your own and your competitors' performance.

First, form a small product group from your best people, not necessarily the highest ranked, in engineering, design, planning if available, manufacturing and marketing. Then ask the group to evaluate, jointly, each of the products your company produces, by asking:

- How is the product seen by your customers who actually bought it? Why did they buy it and for what attributes?

- How is the product perceived by customers you would like to have but

100

who bought a competitor's product? Why didn't they buy your product, and for what lack of attributes?

- Does the product, and through the product your company, enjoy the image and reputation you planned? If so, or if not, why?

- Does the product use your company's capabilities most efficiently? Is it designed for most effective engineering? Is it engineered for most efficient and quality manufacture?

- Is the product correctly communicated to your potential customers?

Next, Bahnsen advises, ask the group to compare all the findings with the best competition. They should establish the strengths and weaknesses of your products versus those of the competition. Then ask this product group to recommend how to improve the product's competitiveness in the market-place. Finally, let them discuss their findings with you and your key staff in a participative atmosphere. Together identify the actions the company needs to take to develop a firm product proposal or action plan.

It is important, Uwe Bahnsen emphasises, that all members have the same status in the group regardless of their actual status in the organisation, and that decisions are reached by consensus. As we have seen, it is our competitors we have to beat. They set the standards. They win the customers – or don't.

SUMMARY

We talk of the prime need to focus on customers, who they are, what they want. Scarcely less important, however, is the need to know our competitors. This is not the same as meeting them at trade shows and industry conferences. It means taking the time and trouble to study, meticulously, their strategies for products, their marketing, distribution, manufacturing, pricing and more. Why is this necessary? Because it is our competitors who set the standards we have to beat.

7

Go for Swift Results

'The aim is not to avoid failure,
but to give triumph a chance.'
The late Sir Huw Wheldon, when
head of documentary programmes, BBC

Going about your business in the usual way won't do. It is like running a mile. Taking ten minutes wins nothing. Perhaps if we had our own, closed market it might, but today everywhere is an Olympic stadium. Some of the best products in the world are in your local shops; theirs are the standards to match. One company after another is winning world-wide markets by developing excellent products at high speed.

The case of the 'dishwasher' in the previous chapter shows how a company sliced years off the normal time it takes to develop and market a new product – and won as a result. That is very much the game today, as that example made clear.

SPEED AND QUALITY

According to Yasuo Kuroki, head of the Product Planning Centre of Sony, their lead time for developing a new product from concept to market is six months for a low-tech product, one year for a high-tech one. Production development is geared to that objective. Success equals keeping ahead, he said.

In Japanese companies the model life for facsimile machines is now down to less than four months, according to Kenichi Ohmae. For all audio components, he says, it is less than six months. When Brother in Japan launched their first electronic typewriter they had a lead of two and a half years. Now, a study team from the UK was told in September 1986, when they launch a new product Brother expect to have a lead for only four weeks.

102

Philips, European leader in electronics with sales of $25 billion, have cut the time it takes to develop some products from thirty months to twelve months. Olivetti, now second or third in the production of personal computers, used to take over two years to develop a typewriter. Now much more sophisticated equipment comes out in months.

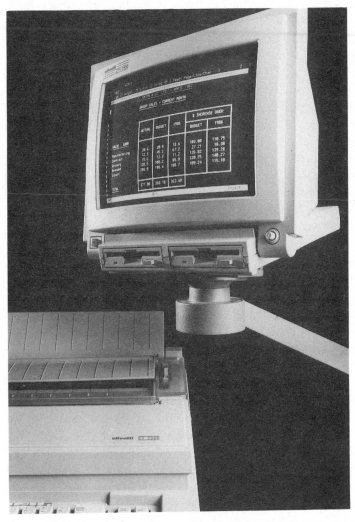

At Olivetti, well designed new products now proceed from concept to market in half the time they used to take. Here is the Olivetti ETV2900, a video typewriter screen module which transforms electronic typewriters in Olivetti's ET2000 range into video typewriters.

Carlo de Benedetti, chairman of Olivetti, twice named Manager of the Year by 8,000 Italian executives, wants his company to become the IBM of Europe. And speed is one way he'll do it.

Speed coupled with quality. That is the point. The time it takes to create and market new products is becoming one of the key factors in business. Somehow we think such speed is incompatible with quality. Whether it is relevant or not, Mozart wrote *The Marriage of Figaro* in six weeks. Who would think an unheard opera that took six months or six years must be better? Quality and speed can be handmaidens. We have to make them so.

'To develop rapidly is not an option. It is necessary to success,' claims Jocelyn Stevens, ebullient rector of the Royal College of Art, whose former students include David Hockney, Len Deighton, Bridget Riley and Zandra Rhodes − and senior designers in most European automotive companies.

In winning companies there is a constant, insistent drive to develop one new product after another. These, as we know from our own experience, are not thrown together. Highly reliable, competitively priced products can be created far more quickly than one might think possible.

The legendary 'Kelly' (Clarence L.) Johnson, at Lockheed in the USA, is said to have developed the first US jet fighter, from spec to airborne, in 143 days. Johnson, who, in the words of design historian Stephen Bayley, 'brought science fiction to reality', developed the twin boomed P-38 (Lightning), the C-130 (Hercules), the U-2 spy plane and the SR-71 (Blackbird), among the most technically advanced aircraft in the world. In 1985 the Royal Society of Arts acknowledged his achievements when it welcomed him as an honorary Royal Designer for Industry.

After Kelly had left Lockheed, the 'skunkworks' he set up (see p. 126) developed the 'plane that didn't exist'. All reports that it did were denied until the end of 1988, even though three were known to have crashed. The F-117A Stealth fighter looks unlike any aircraft you ever saw. It is a nasty, black, angular thing, sharp as a paper dart. The angles make radar detection harder, as do the secret RAM (radar absorbent materials) used. Subsonic, not spotted by radar, the Stealth fighter is designed to sneak in and knock out communication systems. It, in turn, will be superseded by the B-2 Stealth bomber. This can fly at 50,000 feet for 10,000 miles and, although huge, not be seen. Its radar signature is less than a man's.

Xerox, according to Tom Peters and Nancy Austin in *A Passion for Excellence*, created a new product in twenty-eight days that has since earned them $3 billion. Hewlett Packard are said to produce substantially

Lockheed's Kelly Johnson with the spy plane he developed. He brought 'skunkworks' to high technology.

new products at the rate of eight a week. Not all succeed, nor make a major impact, but many set in train developments that lead to breakthroughs. One major instrument took seventeen weeks from conception to debugged prototype.

The Sharp Design Centre in Osaka deals with 2,000 designs a year, from innovative, lifestyle products, through to road traffic systems, satellite and solar programmes, automated office products, optical products, and devices for energy, medicine and security, from home computers to high-tech components. When Ken Sadler, the British industrial designer, visited them he was astonished to learn that for many of these products they allow six months from concept to marketing.

More than 50 million Swatch watches have been sold since 1985. A production advantage is one reason – the Swatch is made from only fifty-one parts, compared with ninety or 100 parts in any other quartz watch. Constant innovation is another. 'We know the importance of always coming up with surprises to retain our position as market leaders,' chairman Ernst Marquardt explained.

There are many more examples to quote. Even if they are all exceptions, the general drive is clear. There is something else too: that speed cannot be achieved within the conventional company organisation. If a company wants to compete, it must alter its structure. It must be prepared to innovate here too.

THE OLD WAY WON'T WORK

Figure 12 shows, in a simple way, how most companies are structured. That pyramidal, hierarchical shape is usual. The business may be divided into product areas or market areas, which is healthy, but invariably it is then divided by function. You will find a finance department, the R & D function, an engineering department, under one name or another. Marketing and sales are somewhere. So are manufacturing, corporate affairs and the other activities. These departments grow up over time. Each becomes a fortress to defend. All are presided over by the board which, indeed, spends much of its time balancing competing claims from these departments. They are like hedgehogs. Sir Peter Parker thought it might have been Schopenhauer who remarked about hedgehogs that in winter they want to get together, but their spikes keep them apart.

So far so bad. When it comes to developing new products a company finds it needs people from almost all these departments. It needs R & D. It needs marketing. It needs engineering. It needs design and finance and manufacturing.

The most usual way manufacturing companies develop new products runs like this: R & D invent something, engineers make it, marketing or

Figure 12 The people you need to develop the new products sit in all, or most, parts of the company. The usual departmental organisation keeps them apart until their turn comes.

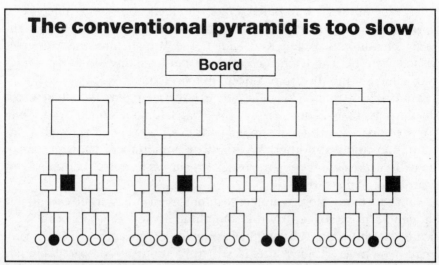

The conventional pyramid is too slow

SOURCE: National Economic Development Office

106

sales people sell it. The process is linear, which means it is slow, and it is back to front, which means it is risky. That makes it both slow and costly. Traditional company organisation inhibits rapid product development; there's no doubt about that.

As we saw in the 'dishwasher' case, some firms look to R & D to develop new products, which is mostly a mistake. Others, and research suggests this has become a pattern in Britain, give the marketing department the lead. That sounds far better. Marketing is meant to be close to the customer. But Robin Roy's study for the Open University described what happens when the marketing department leads. The result is often 'a neglect of inputs from the production side and potentially (or actually) a product that is more expensive or difficult to make than is necessary'. In any case, the point is the same. One department does its job, then passes it on to the next. If you look at the pyramid you can see how ideas come down the ladder of each department, then up again before passing on to the next. It all takes time. Worse, communication between departments is often poor. The conventional company in the 'dishwasher' example is typical. R & D thinks of something, engineering designs it. The drawings pass to manufacturing, who want to alter them. So back it goes.

WHY ONE PROJECT FOUNDERED

Nick Butler, who runs one of the largest product design offices in the world, and who works in the USA and Japan as well as in the UK, told me how puzzled he was when a product development programme he was working on started to founder. Nothing was happening. Why? He discovered that the head of marketing and the head of engineering had not spoken and would not speak to each other about the project. He used a ruse to get them in the same room. That product line carried an investment decision of £65 million. As an independent consultant designer, he was the catalyst. He untangled the mess and got the project going. Indeed, Robin Roy found that all the companies that are highly regarded for the design of their products use highly qualified designers either within the organisation or from consultancy offices.

James Brian Quinn makes another point about the normal hierarchy: 'If there are five layers between the designers and the decision makers, you need five "yeses" to go forward, but one "no" will stop you.'

'The most important problem,' said Nobuhiko Kawamoto, managing director of Honda Motor Co., 'is how the design created by an individual designer can survive in the process of planning new products,' because many people check the design in the planning stage. 'Individual design work can easily be revised, changed or crushed by the power of systems or the ideas of top management.'

THE MAN WHO SPOKE UP

The opposite can happen too. Donald Massaro, when president of the Office Products Division of Xerox, told how his company decided it wanted to 'get into the personal computer market-place'. He came up with a product specification through 'the ordinary process'. It was, he said, 'reasonably unreasonable'. Then he gave it to the engineering group.

> The engineering group was convinced that the management was watching programs that are not in *TV Guide*. So we kind of put it on the shelf and every couple of weeks we'd get it out again and go back to engineering and say are you sure you can't do this? And they'd come back convinced we were smoking stuff.

But there was a way out.

> As it turns out we had this one individual in the engineering department who stood up and said 'I can do it'. Actually he was a designer, not really a fully-fledged engineer. Of course all the engineering managers laughed. But we said, 'OK, here's $25,000 . . . go do it.' He came back four months later with the project all done.

He had ten people working on the project, in the evenings and Saturdays because they had their normal jobs to do. Perhaps by accident, Xerox broke out of the conventional mould and tapped into a different, more innovative culture.

THE WINNING WAY

The winning way to develop new products, and you come across it time and again, is to be fast and flexible. Select goals, select people, establish a few critical limits and decision points. Do not attempt any elaborate planning or control. 'Few if any major innovations result from highly structured planning processes,' says James Brian Quinn. 'Innovations,' he says, 'are best managed as incremental, goal-oriented, interactive learning processes.' The key objective, easier to say than to do, is to permit chaos. Avoid what Quinn calls the 'tyranny of paper plans'. Unless you are lucky, like Xerox, it takes time and determination to alter the historic shape of companies. It means dismantling privileges and stripping away departmental walls that can be defended skilfully.

Innovative companies go to great lengths to cut through this hierarchy. At Texas Instruments they ran an IDEA programme (identify, define, expose, act). Any young engineer could get $20,000 to test a new idea simply by convincing any one member of a large group of authorised

Peter Lawrence has studied many winning companies. Excellent communications, he says, are common to them all.

technical staff that it was worth following. 'Speak 'n' Spell', the voice synthesising device, was developed in this way.

Peter Lawrence of the Corporate Design Foundation, Boston, Massachusetts, has studied many successful corporations. He is clear that you cannot lay down simple organisational patterns. He says, 'There are so many kinds of firm that doing well is a matter of context, not structure.' One common element he has found, however, is 'excellent communications'.

There's another point. Angela Dumas, as a researcher in the Design Management Unit of the London Business School, analysed the management of design in industry. Picking her way through the varieties of method, she deduced that there are, in any company, what she calls 'silent designers' – people engaged in the design process, and influencing it, without being aware of it. The tidy organisation chart, and pigeon-holing of responsibility, never say quite what happens. 'Managers,' consultant Alan Topalian has pointed out, 'are the most influential designers in industry.'

The first task is to tackle those boxes on the organisation chart. Peters and Austin talk about 'smashing engineering, manufacturing and marketing functions together'. That, they say, 'overcomes the most important source of delays in innovation'.

Kenichi Ohmae, from his perspective in Tokyo, wrote in *The Mind of the Strategist*:

In many companies today, functional activities such as design, manufacturing and sales, which are usually divided from one another organisationally, devote more energy to guarding their own territories than to looking for ways to co-operate. As a result, the full potential for major profit improvement that typically lies in the inter-functional border areas tends to be overlooked.

Don Osman of 3M calls this self-protection 'turfyness'. Colin Clipson, leading the Competitive Edge project in the United States, has found the same thing about border areas. 'All the important decisions,' he says, 'are made at the point of overlap' (between one function and another). McKinsey and Co.'s Robin Leaf once said, 'Companies that compete successfully forge links between functions.' When a business is small, he explains, a single person at the centre typically sees the business in relation to its competitors, and is able to

110

mobilize the separate functions to meet the competitive challenge and provide the link that co-ordinates and directs the different parts of the business
. . . however, small, successful companies grow and growth brings complexity and specialisation to each function. The result of this is to push the functions further and further apart.

As it grows it tends to fragment increasingly into separate functional
islands, each trying to solve its own problems, each using its own special
language and having its own priorities.

There are, as Leaf points out, some notable examples of company chiefs
who manage to keep hold of the reins, but on the whole it is impossible.
What the chief executive can do, Leaf says, is insist on competitive
measures and focus on competitive results while, at the same time,
building communications and teamwork between functions. Speaking in
1977, which is a while ago considering the way these ideas are moving, he
advocated three sets of links: between marketing and technology, perhaps
an ad hoc project team to look at competitors' products; between technology and production, in the form of joint design teams; and between
marketing and production. The need for permanent links here is great, he
thinks, but they are apt to get bogged down in procedure.

WINNERS DO IT HORIZONTALLY

However it is done, the new organisation is much less hierarchical, much
flatter (Figure 13). Communications whizz across functions. Ideas flow
from side to side at least as much as up and down. People work in teams.
Time and again you see in winning companies that all the departments
that are necessary to product development (R & D, engineering, design,
marketing, manufacturing, finance) work together all the time. Many
Japanese companies employ social scientists to work with their product
designers in the product planning centres. Sony have a 'cultural
anthropologist' helping to brief their software engineers for their range of
personal computers. They also have sociologists who study lifestyles on
their product development team. Olivetti have someone concerned with
customer service on the development team.

The level of information flow across divisions or departments is very
high in winning companies. When Honda was developing its City box car,

Figure 13 Winning companies create teams, with all the right people together from start to finish of a project. Ideas whizz across functions.

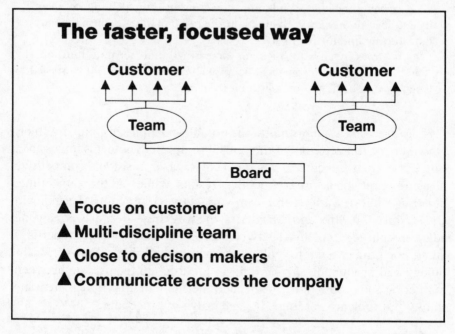

The faster, focused way

▲ Focus on customer
▲ Multi-discipline team
▲ Close to decison makers
▲ Communicate across the company

SOURCE: National Economic Development Office

2,000 visits were made between production engineering and product development, even though the two departments were 300 miles apart.

This teamwork is the faster way. It is also more profitable. A study by the Chartered Institute of Marketing, published in 1984, demonstrated that 'when co-operation is high [between functions], companies are much more likely to make higher profit margins'. Where co-operation is low they are much more likely to be making a loss or low profit margin.

'Teams are what win in our business,' said Michael Leggatt, managing director of the printing machinery division of Baker Perkins. Engineering design leads their product development team, which includes in-house industrial design and production engineering. They work daily with people from marketing, sales, machine design, manufacturing, machining and process design, production, costing, purchasing, subcontracting and field engineering. Former chairman John Peake explained: 'There is a constant iteration within the core team and with others in the organisation which goes on in parallel and not in series, as before.'

As a result of such teamwork, Baker Perkins have cut development time between 30 and 50 per cent, sliced the production cycle from fourteen to seven months and reduced inventories. Both productivity and profitability have improved as a result. As proof that the new products, developed so much more swiftly, are meeting customer need, Baker Perkins' revenue from the manufacture of printing presses grew between 1981 and 1987 from £8 million to £57 million.

'Communications are an integral part of the product plan,' says Uwe Bahnsen who, until the end of 1986, headed the multi-disciplined design team of Ford Europe. At Ford Europe the engineers used to develop the basic product. When they had done this, then the designers had to put on the 'wrap around' as they called it. Then manufacturing had to make it. Ford have altered that. Now, as well as industrial designers, there are 100 engineers in the design department and people with other specialisms.

Perhaps as a result Ford, too, have cut a year or more off the time it takes to develop a new model. The first of the new reign, the Sierra, was voted 'No. 1 in Europe' – and they're getting better. In 1985 *Fortune* magazine wrote, 'The mainspring of Ford's revival is its new boldness in design.'

Six thousand executives, surveyed by *Fortune* magazine in 1983, voted Hewlett Packard the second most admired company in the USA – after IBM. Their management style encourages individual autonomy and entrepreneurship. Responsibility for R & D, design, marketing and manufacturing is pushed out to their fifty-one small divisions, which are organised into six groups.

The engineer, marketer and manufacturer are together at Hewlett Packard, from the inception of the project onwards. By contrast, a study done by NEDO among British manufacturing firms in 1986 showed that one third of companies do not have their designers present at the start of a project, nor are they there at the end.

At Olivetti designers are in at the very start of a project. Ettore Sottsass and Mario Bellini, the most famous, have worked with the company for many years but they are consultants and are encouraged to have other clients. In their offices they have four or five rooms for Olivetti employees. When Olivetti want a new product, a 'card' is written. This is put together by people from R & D, marketing and design (they call it 'CI'). This drafts a specification, including costing. The chief executive approves it. Then a plastic model is made and presented, together with details of timing, cost and so on.

How do other companies manage this? In Casio's case, the strategy is to

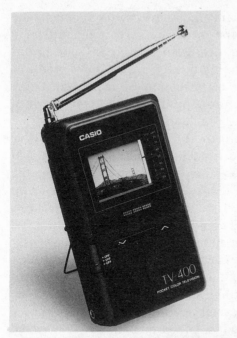

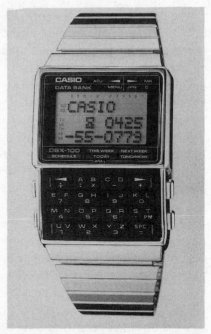

Casio develops new products at incredible speed, pushing its technology forward. *Above left*: Casio's pocket colour television. *Above right*: DBX 100 watch/calculator. *Below*: the SF 4000 digital diary. .

integrate design and development into marketing so that, as they say, 'consumers' desires are analysed by those closest to the market and quickly converted into engineering blueprints'. Because Casio have this function so well developed, they can afford to make products obsolete quickly. Any competitors, organised vertically, on the assumption of a one- or two-year life-cycle for this kind of product, are at a severe disadvantage.

DIFFERENT METHODS OF ORGANISATION

The way you develop new products depends, of course, on the kind of business you're in. Big groups may have one policy in one activity, a second in another. Fisons make the point. They are in three main areas: pharmaceuticals, scientific equipment and horticulture.

In the gardening business they have a conventional product management marketing system. It initiates new products with the R & D team, using conventional consumer market research. But even that is more complicated. In parallel they look for 'breakthroughs', developments gardeners do not know about and therefore can't say are needs when you ask them. Their soil-less composts (Gro-bags) are an example. This innovation came from technical knowledge. But the company made sure it fitted a consumer need before going ahead with it.

Fisons scientific equipment division is another case. Here, it aims for niches. Much of their new product development is done by working closely with customers. They work hand in glove with people in the steel industy, in food and drink, pharmaceuticals, biotechnology and others. Together they develop very accurate instruments to measure, or even control, precise chemical reactions which are peculiar to that industry. In other words, they identify the clients' needs, then apply their knowledge of measuring to them. Often, they say, this leads to applications in other fields.

In such a highly technical field conventional market research, according to John Kerridge, 'just does not work. Nevertheless, designing a highly technical product costing £300,000 or £400,000 in a vacuum is a recipe for disaster. Orienting towards the customer is as appropriate in its own way here as it is in the lay consumer field.'

Then, within the same Fisons group, turn to pharmaceuticals. To bring a new product to market can cost anything from £50 million to £100 million . . . and can take five to seven years. On top of the difficulty of finding new compounds, there are other problems. For one thing, often health authorities around the world won't register a new product for their country unless it demonstrates scientifically a positive advance on existing therapy. Marginal improvements or minor product variations won't do.

Many breakthroughs start from existing knowledge within the company. Scientists decide whether that knowledge could lead them to a new discovery. Then general management judges whether they are being optimistic and whether there would be sufficient profit at the end of the day to justify the costs. Kerridge insists that this is a decision for general management to make, not the marketing department. Even in this highly scientific field there are ways to go about things. Echoes of the word 'skunkworks' and small teams apart from the main bureaucracy of the business are not out of place.

One of the great discoverers is Sir James Black. Millions of people owe their well-being to him. At ICI he developed Beta-blockers, which have transformed the treatment of heart disease. For Smith Kline and French he developed the anti-ulcer medicine Tagamet, called 'the first billion-dollar drug'. Notwithstanding their patronage and support, Sir James claims that 'big institutions are destructive of people'. They drive out what he calls the 'Friday afternoon experiments', the unscheduled, random ideas. 'All mould-breaking research begins controversially,' he says. In 1988 he won a Nobel prize. He has now set up a small team at King's College Hospital in London. He marches in, colleagues say, and booms, 'Now let us do something different today.' The papers say he is on the edge of another breakthrough. His work is being funded, without strings, by Johnson & Johnson, who believe that 'wherever that fertile mind goes it will be beneficial'.

The rules for geniuses are different. They may be: big money, small team, freedom and faith. Perhaps that is straying too far from the central, down-to-earth mission of this book, but big companies need to accommodate the occasional genius.

There are many ways to organise design and development. Until a few years ago, Sony had designers out in divisions. Now they have pulled them back into what they call a 'marketing centre'. This has 470 people grouped in a horizontal structure – market research, engineering design, merchandisers and industrial designers (Figures 14 and 15). According to Sony, 'Designers in the plant can understand the engineers' problems too

Figure 14   Product development cuts across divisions at Sony

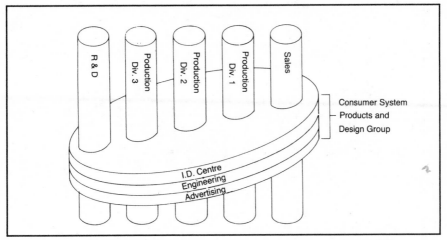

SOURCE: Sony ID Centre

well. They can be immersed in problems. Designers need to see from a distance and from outside the company. That's interesting. Tom Karen, head of Ogle Design, a long-established British product design consultancy, agrees with that. 'If design is under engineering it doesn't work,' he told me.

Sony call their design centre 'PP' (product planning). In 1984 activities in its headquarters included, in addition to product planning and advanced product design, corporate identity, packaging, display, computer-aided design (CAD) and 'customer satisfaction'.

What does the 'customer satisfaction' team do? According to British designer Ken Sadler, the team conducts research to establish which specifications are most needed and which features are acceptable or not. It interviews consumers, and runs panels and clinics to test product acceptance. It analyses market needs, trends and surveys and correlates data for designers.

At Sony the designers propose future products without relating them to existing technology. They take a three-year view, and pass their ideas and information to their R & D divisions. According to Peter Lawrence, there is a very strong feeling in Sony that technology innovation is short lived. Real success comes from a combination of technology and design. 'What is important,' says Lawrence, 'is this link to the customer.'

Figure 15 How Sony organise their product development

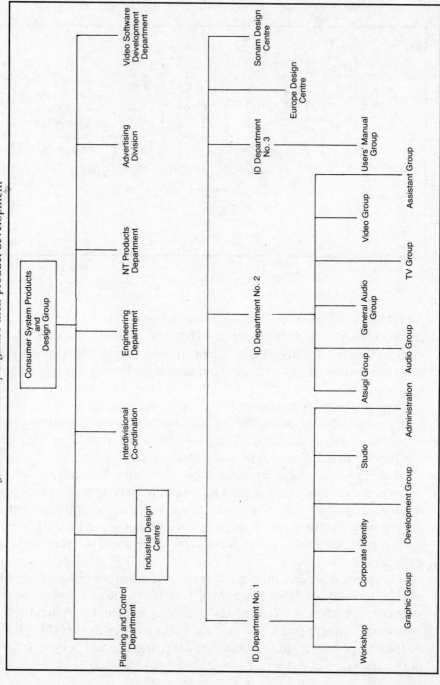

SOURCE: Sony ID Centre

At Sony ideas for both the Walkman and the Watchman pocket television came from the designers. In 1986 the vice-president for Sony design in the USA heard a group of marketing people regretting that they had no products for children. What happened next? He got his designers to think of ideas, presented as sketches and paper mock-ups. They asked marketing for estimates of sales and profit, then they designed four products, right down to the packaging. These were shown to the management team in Tokyo and again to the head of Sony's audio division. The ideas were approved. The audio division assigned an electrical and mechanical engineer to each product. Manufacturing began some ten months after the lack of children's products was stated. Both the sequence and speed are revealing.

Christopher Lorenz looked carefully at Philips. A few years ago they were being 'battered in the market-place' as he put it, 'by more appealing Japanese products'. How have they turned this situation around? Wisse Dekker and a new chief executive, Cor van de Klugt, upgraded design to a central function in product development. They brought in Bob Blaich, design director for many years of one of the most design conscious firms in the United States, Herman Miller.

Until then, Lorenz explains, Philips had been dominated by technology. Engineers were considered the 'kings of the company'. Conscientious as they were, their products were often 'over-engineered, over-priced and late to the market', no match for the speedier Japanese. Blaich gave the 200-person design centre a more devolved role. He appointed six design managers, each responsible for working with particular divisions. In turn, they had 'contact' designers reporting to them; in advertising agencies they might be called 'account executives'. Their job is to liaise between their 'clients' in the division and the design centre.

That has evolved too. They now have designers close to product divisions working with development, production and marketing people throughout the design to marketing process, but they are also strengthening their centre. Indeed, Philips has created three 'centres of competence', in Europe, the USA and Japan. People in these centres provide lead computer-aided design, ergonomic studies and the continuing development of their people. These specialists may go out to product divisions or centres of competence with their special skills. In 1987 the whole Philips design effort, called CID (corporate industrial design), led by Bob Blaich, completed 1,348 projects.

So, not unlike Sony, Philips have a centre team with people working for divisions but apart from them. As time passed, these designers have had a catalytic effect not only within divisions, but also between them, where their technologies or products or markets converge. Here, too, design, manufacturing, engineering and marketing all work together. The other point is that the main board is in constant touch.

Testing products with users . . . see how Philips is fighting back.

REPORT TO THE PRESIDENT

Toshiba are much the same. They, too, have pulled designers in from the divisions. They now have a design division reporting to the president (Figure 16). In it are administration staff, visual corporate identity staff, design patent staff, planning (concerned with education and standards and R & D information) and a design staff for each of its operating divisions. Sharp also have a design centre, with all the disciplines in one division.

120

Figure 16   Design at the centre and close to the board: how it has evolved at Toshiba

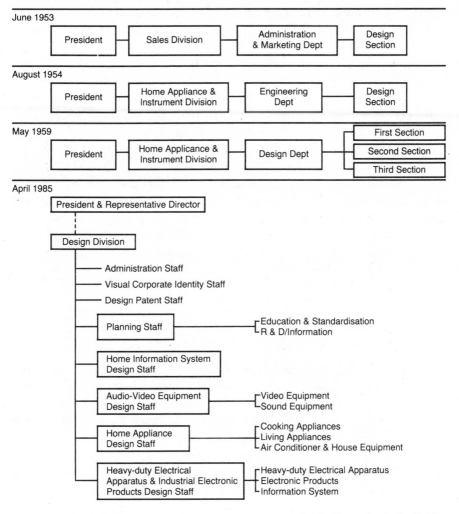

SOURCE: Toshiba Corporation Design Division

TEAMWORK IS THE ANSWER

In 'Managing the New Product Development Process' Ken-ichi Imai and his colleagues described how five companies use product development teams. They looked at Fuji-Xerox's development of the FX-3500 copier, the City box car by Honda, Canon's Sure Shot camera, NEC's PC 8000

121

personal computer and Epson's MP-80 dot-matrix printer. They found the teams were almost completely outside the normal structure of the corporation. Such teams used more production, sales and marketing people than R & D staff.

Members of a project team are hand picked by senior management. Membership of the team and their performance in it can make or break a career, they say. The Honda team, average age twenty-seven, was given virtually no brief when it was assembled to design the City box car. They just had to produce a 'small, energy-efficient car that would sell in large numbers'. They did; 160,000 were sold in sixteen months (see p. 228).

At Canon (the name is from *Kwanon*, after the Buddhist goddess of mercy there are 140 designers, most assigned to product divisions. The design department includes a planning 'human interface and trends research' group. In the 1960s part of their job was to adapt product decisions to specific lifestyles and occupational needs. Today, the design division's general manager, Hiroshi Shinohara, says that focus has sharpened:

> Since an environment is not only composed of machines and equipment, but also of people and activities, it became necessary to study the environment as a whole . . . The flow of new ideas and technology requires that designers look ahead, because the products they design in the future will precede environmental changes and decisively influence them.

Looking ahead, Shinohara expects Canon's design division to split into three parts. One will be concerned with current developments and products. A second will work on projects to be ready in three to five years. The third will consider possibilities five to ten years away. That, of course, will be impossible without an informed awareness of social change, so that knowledge becomes part of the design process. Already they put 'much more' emphasis on trends research. And this is from the company that already sells more typewriters in Europe than IBM and is the world's largest producer of 35-mm SLR cameras and office copying machines.

Listen to this teamwork story from another source. Roy Rothwell and Paul Gardiner of the Science Policy Research Unit at the University of Sussex have studied innovation in the UK more systematically than almost anyone. In 1985 they wrote:

> A notable feature of successful companies is that they integrate design and innovation widely throughout their corporate structure. The design teams are not isolated and are in close touch with the production, marketing and sales sides of the company.

No longer do you need costly cameras to take perfect pictures every time. The Canon Sure Shot came from a highly motivated team. By mid-1988 over 13 million had been sold. Canon is keeping up the pressure with newer versions.

British companies will say they have multi-disciplinary teams like this. Some are excellent; Baker Perkins, for example, who have two thirds of the US market for certain printing plant to prove it. But what about others? Why aren't their results the same? Bill Evans, who writes in *Design Studies*, believes one of the major differences is the amount of real resources that are put into product development by Japanese companies. Another is their methodology, which has 'spliced together' marketing, design, engineering and production. The emphasis is on co-operation rather than the competition we so often find in Western companies. Whatever many companies claim, this is not the case in most of them. Their departmental walls are as high as cliffs.

SMASH THE WALLS

If they want to compete, such companies must find a way to break down those walls, and the hierarchy with them. One way to do this was sug-

In many firms, each department 'flies solo'. That makes development slow. The powerful new way and faster way is to bring all the diverse skills together, to work in teams from the word 'go'.

gested by David Bernstein at a seminar at the London Business School. He runs The Creative Business, which does what its name says, in the fields of design, advertising, writing and other kinds of communication, from an old warehouse near Covent Garden. 'Think of the company like a repertory company,' he advised. 'The man playing Charley's Aunt one week can be carrying a spear in *King Lear* the next. Every problem is new and needs new groupings to solve it.'

The catchpenny phrase is that 'he who knows best should be master'. For this particular problem it is one person. For that one, another. This is at odds with the notion of the trained 'design manager', a new kind of profession espoused by some. Gordon Edge, when chief executive of PA Technology, managed innovation with impressive results. He is insistent that the team leader need not be the most senior person. RitaSue Siegel, whose company in New York finds designers for many of America's top companies and who has a day-to-day knowledge of what is going on, sees this in practice. Of these teams she says, 'They assemble, grow, shrink or disband, depending on the job to be done.'

At Canon it is the same. For each project a task force is set up. It varies in size and expertise, according to the nature of the assignment. Some teams see the project through until the product is on the market. The argument is that their work must be real, for the real world, and the design team carries the responsibility. Other companies pull together a team from the various departments. The team stays together while the product is being developed. When approvals are given, the team disbands. People go back to their departments to see that the product moves safely through them. That's a nice idea too; it spreads 'ownership' throughout the business.

IDEAS FROM EVERYWHERE

Product development is a constant, driving and accelerating process. The rate of change itself is changing. To succeed, not only must the board drive innovation, but it must encourage everyone in the business to think of new ideas. In the leading Japanese companies, according to Bill Evans, who looked carefully at a number of them,

> Ideas come from all departments, with technological breakthroughs sparking ideas from research through to designers perceiving the cultural importance of a new fashion. Marketing, by whatever name, is still pulling design which, in turn, is still pulling technology.

125

SKUNKWORKS

Others go further. 3M, who make some 45,000 products across a broad spectrum ranging from magnetic tape to cream for cows' udders, believe in 'skunkworks' (a word coined by Kelly Johnson at Lockheed). These are small, self-running hotshops, where a small team is put together to come up with new products, in any way they want. They are not little design studios low down the corporate ladder. They are closely in touch with the board. Indeed, they are the pathfinders of the business. They can be chaotic, disorderly, all the things well-ordered managers can't stand. Their way of living, if there is just one, is summed up by Tom Peters and Nancy Austin in *A Passion for Excellence* as 'lots of tries, lots of failures, lots of scrounging. But always action.'

Hewlett Packard, like 3M, develop product lines around a few products. They form units that look, for all the world, like entrepreneurial start-ups. They let many ideas come up, then test them quickly in the market. 'You must move as rapidly as possible,' say Peters and Austin, 'to real tests of real products (albeit incomplete) with real customers. That is, you must experiment and learn your way towards perfection or completion.'

Sony's Watchman pocket television was criticised for coming on to the market too soon, but that is how Sony learn. Get the product on the market, test the reaction, gain a market share and some experience, then design the next product in the range. Sony's redesigned and lighter Watchman, fifteen months later, was still ahead of Sinclair's pocket television. I asked Sony about this. 'You'll learn more in the market in two months,' replied the head of all their design, 'than you will in a lab in a year.' Although qualification is perhaps necessary, the spirit is clear: do it fast. Get it out, see what happens. By contrast, we have all seen projects that are so thoroughly and exhaustively considered, so perfected, that they are never completed. Or, if they are, interest has long since departed.

Norman Macrae, as deputy editor of *The Economist*, defined the rules of one successful venture capitalist in California:

- Test with a distributor whether this (new) product really looks better and cheaper than anything on the market already

- Get it demonstrated at trade fairs

- Try to get an article written about it in a specialist magazine, and do not mind if some of the criticism is adverse

- If and when the product looks successful, do not be chary of sub-contracting the actual manufacture

'Winners,' Peters and Austin found, 'are above all pragmatic, non-blue-sky dreamers who live by one dictum: try it now.' You can see the design team or development team as your specialist commando: a small team of resourceful, trained and determined people. They don't behave as others in your great rolling army behave. They have different tasks, different ways – and the differences no doubt help them to excel.

'Skunkworks' are a way to get small-company vitality into an established corporation. They work wonders. Products come out in weeks or days rather than months or years. One rule is that 'skunkworks' must be close to the board. They must know the company's goals and needs. Here it is again: good communication is vital. They must be removed from the head office, but not far. Their conditions should not be lavish or even very comfortable. They must be free to spend money, buying components wherever they like, including from competitors. They must be rewarded for success, but not criticised for failure. Failure is part of it. This is an important point.

LARGE BECOMING SMALLER

Some giant corporations are reproducing the characteristics of small ones. Mighty General Motors has encouraged product teams. At Buick – Oldsmobile – Cadillac (itself a newish formation) there are four product leaders. Each, in practice, runs his own business, with product design, manufacturing, finance, public relations and the rest. The chairman of General Motors, Roger Smith, has granted his managers what a consultant called 'permission to fail'. And more authority with it.

One of the merits to copy, as James Brian Quinn pointed out, is that small firms have got to succeed. They are driven by need. Large corporations often lack that sense of urgency, at least until it is mostly too late. The greatest enemy of innovation, according to Donald Massaro of Xerox, is success: 'It is easier to sit on the success they have, to manage their assets, manage their profit margins, so that all the managers involved get their bonus.'

Figure 17 Which company is yours?

Organic
   Freedom from rigid rules
   Participative and informal
   Many views aired and considered
   Face to face communication; little 'red tape'
   Interdisciplinary teams; breaking down departmental barriers
   Emphasis on creative interaction and aims
   Outward looking; willing to take on external ideas
   Flexibility with respect to changing needs, threads and opportunities
   Non-hierarchical
   Information flows downwards as well as upwards

Mechanistic
   Rigid departmental separation and functional specialisation
   Hierarchical
   Bureaucratic
   Many rules and set procedures
   Formal reporting
   Long decision chains and slow decision making
   Little individual freedom of action
   Communication via the written word
   Much information flows upwards; 'directives' flow downwards.

The organic style of organisation seems best suited to the early, creative aspects of innovation; the mechanistic form is probably best suited to effective production and distribution, says Professor Roy Rothwell, SPRU.

Xerox broke its business down into small units called 'strategic business units'. In those smaller businesses, Massaro says, you can get the focus on innovation, on risk-taking, because you can make it a matter of survival for them. Another reason we don't have a lot of innovation is that we worry too much about managing it. 'Don't worry about managing it,' Massaro says, 'worry about stimulating it.'

Paradoxically, the more you spend on innovation the less you might come up with. That is because the more you invest the more you will feel the need to monitor and control the process. Sir Simon Hornby, chairman of W. H. Smith, the British retailers, and of the Design Council, also writes articles about gardening. He warns against pulling up a plant to see if it is still growing. That will stifle creativity and originality. Unless you are careful, you will banish risk altogether, so that the whole effort fails. It is worth looking at Quinn's list of merits of small companies (pp. 238–9) to see whether we can learn from them.

SENSITIVE TO THE MARKET

J. C. Bamford has already been mentioned. In six years to 1988 its profits grew from £5 million to £37 million. Sales revenue today is £377 million (up in a year from £296 million). Ten years ago it was £40 million. The company is split into product groups. According to chairman Anthony Bamford, 'each is like a little company. Each is close to the customer.' They are organised by product group or 'strategic business unit' or by market being served – not by function.

In these individual product groups design, engineering, marketing and financial staff all work together. Anthony Bamford reports that 'employees identify more with the product. Before they identified with the department. Now the rivalry is healthier.' Another benefit is that engineers, in particular, have developed better sensitivity to both the market-place and to production and purchasing.

J. C. Bamford's plant in Wales has been described as Britain's 'first large-scale computer-controlled manufacturing plant .for engineering products'. It is producing gearboxes and axles on automatic guided vehicles (AGVs) of the sort General Motors planned to use on its Saturn project, small-car-to-beat-the-Japanese investment.

While J. C. Bamford's 'backhoe loader', a twin-ended earthmoving machine with a loading shovel in the front and excavator at the back (and power steering and a top speed of 22 mph), accounts for nearly 70 per cent of its sales and is the best-selling product of its kind in fifty markets, the company develops continuously. A second world leader went to the United States in 1986: a telescopic handler. Essentially it is a fork-lift truck with a telescopic boom. It can push goods forward or lift them three storeys high. In 1987 its world market share was 30 per cent. Never pausing, the company recently launched a range of fork-lift trucks for rough terrain and an articulated dump-truck.

The great thing is to get on. Drive for new products or for product improvement now. But don't expect it to be a tidy, well-mannered process. Tom Peters and Nancy Austin warn:

> The course of innovation is highly uncertain. It is always messy, unpredictable and very much affected by the determined (irrational) champions, and that is the important point. We must learn to design organisations that take into account explicitly the irreducible sloppiness of the process and take advantage of it, rather than systems and organisations that tend to fight it.

Peters and Austin comment on the United States. Is it better in Japan? Not according to Kenichi Ohmae: 'The Japanese winners look more like survivors of a demolition derby than meticulous strategic planners.'

That is what it is like in winning companies. Are any business schools listening? When Rob Matthews surveyed a sizeable number of large corporations for the CBI in 1985 he concluded, 'Many firms have procedures that cut out new ideas.' Of course they have. As Allen Michels of Convergent Technology in California puts it, 'what companies that want to survive, let alone grow, must do is to nurture rapid, decisive activity in a disorderly environment'.

TAKING RISKS

To put a figure on risk is not easy. Based on Arthur D. Little's 1985 study, the likelihood that a specific good idea will be successfully implemented is 38 per cent in the USA, 39 per cent in Europe, only 16 per cent in Japan. Is that because the Japanese companies have more ideas, or because they are less successful at seeing them through?

3i, believed to be the world's largest source of private capital, with investments in 9,700 companies, have invested some £2.7 billion over the past decade. They have been involved in 3,000 start-ups and 800 management buy-outs. One figure they watch is their failure rate. In the year to March 1988, 114 ventures backed by 3i went to the wall. That was 2.4 per cent of the total. But does that make them edge towards less risk? No. 'If none of them was a failure,' said Jon Foulds, the chief executive, 'that would be a clear sign we were not investing enough. We cannot be in the risk business without failures, and it is a golden rule that we never witch-hunt over an investment that went wrong.' But 3i are not in business for a fast return. The average life of an equity before they realise it is six or seven years. Sometimes longer.

Results can be spectacular for the investor, but mostly are not. 3i invested £1 million in Rodime, a disc drive manufacturer. It appreciated tenfold in five years. They put £150,000 into Oxford Instruments in 1967. Started by Sir Martin Wood in his garage in 1959, Oxford Instruments today employ 1,400 people and has a turnover of £89 million. They make high-tech equipment, from magnets for body scanners to patient monitoring systems and instruments used in advanced manufacturing and microchip production. However, the general experience of 3i is a one in three failure rate. A recent survey among investments they have held for nine years showed that almost half (46 per cent) had lower net assets. That seems more or less usual. Midland Bank Equity Group reckon their portfolio is 55 per cent above book value. Any fund, they say, with lots of young companies can expect 60 per cent to fail, 20 per cent to be 'living dead' and 20 per cent to produce returns.

3i have now introduced a scheme that encourages 'skunkworks'. Called 'Sponsored Spin-out', it invites companies with a worthwhile idea to form a new company, jointly owned by the company, by the inventors and by the bank. This gives the company funds for the new project without risking its main business. It gives the inventors a stake, and it gives the bank a chance to enjoy a substantial return on investment if the project works. The bank will sell its shares to the other shareholders at agreed times, if that is what they want. Although early days, 3i say 'considerable interest' is being shown. They are making deals of this sort in both the USA and the UK.

In Europe failure meets with opprobrium. We like to think people in the United States are less disapproving. 'A man who never made a mistake never made anything' is as true as it is trite. 'The trouble with the first-time entrepreneur is that he doesn't know what he doesn't know,' said Don Valentine, the venture capitalist who backed Apple. 'After a failure he does know what he doesn't know and can beat hell out of people who still have to learn.'

Any good product, claimed Prince Philip when he presented design awards in 1986, 'is a triumph of imagination over prudence and safety'. He quoted Merrick Taylor, chairman of Motor Panels (Coventry). Taylor had expressed concern about the 'indirectors', as he called them, managers who 'use their control expertise to exclude the possibility of creativity'. According to Michael Frye, one-time chairman of Rotaflex, there can be three reactions when you introduce a lead product concept to managers making decisions. The first is that they resist change. The second is that they try to reduce the risk. Third, they say no; it is more comfortable and so much safer.

Getting the set-up right for innovation is no small point. One man who has worked with many companies to help develop new products is Kevin McGurk (now with Michael Peters Group). He says, 'The structure of the firm must be right. If not, you throw a new idea or product into the wheel that spins in its habitual way. It gets minced up or thrown out.'

Every manager would agree that innovation, by definition, is risky. But risk is not encouraged in large corporations, as Donald Massaro, of Xerox, points out:

> We give a lot of lip service to encouraging managers to be risky. But when it really comes down to it, it really is not encouraged. The problem's even worse. We not only don't reward the risk-takers, we actually punish them. Upper management in most large corporations wants commitments signed in blood. Don't miss it. Don't give me any excuses.

SUMMARY

Companies need a steady flow of new products to be competitive. If ever there was a truism that is it, but it is one that needs saying. For forty years and more, design protagonists have been urging industry to take more trouble to develop good-quality, well-designed products. Now there is a new dimension: speed. Speed of product introduction has become a competitive weapon of its own.

This chapter has compared how many companies organise themselves to develop new products with the way some of the outstanding winners do: Hewlett Packard, IBM, J. C. Bamford, Casio, Sony, Toshiba, Philips, Texas Instruments and others. The essential point is to create teams that cut across all the usual departmental walls, then to free them from the normal procedures of the company's main business. Look on the development teams as commandos, not quite having to conform to the codes of the main army.

What about risk? Shouldn't all companies strive to eliminate it? Or is risk of failure an ever-lurking companion of triumph? Prince Philip, as well as bankers and business chiefs, warns against excessive prudence.

8
Welcome Chaos and Creativity

'Design is a funnel that opens
a company to a world full of ideas.'
Peter Gorb, London Business School

There is something unfair about asking professional managers not just to
condone chaos, but to set it up. How can they do that and, having found a
way, how do they prevent themselves from monitoring their accom-
plishment – and thereby inhibiting its success?

The unhelpful answer is that people manage somehow, as we have
seen. One of the hard parts is to change the relationships between people
in the business, not least between specialists. Today we all fly solo, each of
us with our own goals, cherishing our own measures and prejudices.
Designers, still staking their claim to a place in the sun, can be among the
worst. Design, if you are not careful, can be the answer to everything.
More alarming still, they may believe they know what the customer
should have. Designers often see themselves not as the servants of the
public, but as its arbiters: an arrogant idea made the more irritating
because it is occasionally true.

Some designers can be leaders, intuitively sensing what is coming next.
Aware of this, more than one Japanese company looks to its designers to
'imagine its future'. To dismiss the insights of creative people, as business
executives usually do, because they can't be measured or proved, is extra-
vagant. We need all the imagination available if we are to compete
successfully. Designers are not the only imaginative people in industry, as
some like to think, but the best are very good. Business executives should
give themselves the chance to benefit from their skills, but not alone.

People who lead you to believe that if you hire a designer your profits
will rise are misleading you. Profits might rise, or they might not. It
depends on lots of factors: the goals you set, how you treat them and,
more especially, how they relate to other people in the organisation.

Although some will say, with justification, that design is an attitude of mind, it is also a process. In this context, more particularly, it is the process of developing products. Peter Gorb, who set up a design management programme at the London Business School – the first of its kind – won't have it that design is just that. 'It is a passion as well as a procedure,' he says. 'Design is a funnel that opens a company to a world full of ideas' and – a theme that will recur – it is 'many short steps'.

Talking about business success, Wally Olins, of Wolff Olins, the British corporate identity and design group, says this:

> It is often the small things that matter. The difference between using and not using, liking and not liking, buying and rejecting, usually depends on how effective (and consistent) a company is in applying design to make its products function effectively in every detail.

There are said to be twenty-six definitions of design in the *Oxford English Dictionary* and it is easy to find others. Many people see design as an aesthetic or artistic activity, and so it is in part. Others believe design to be about technical performance. That is true too. Both the curtains at your windows and Concorde were designed. And, incidentally, it is astonishing how little time designers from either school have for each other.

Christopher Lorenz, the well-known writer and commentator on design, sees the word as 'virtually synonymous' with innovation. Innovation, he believes, is now taken to mean the whole process of translating an idea into a manufactured, working, marketable product. And that is how he sees design. The US Department of Commerce went further. To describe innovation, they used the term 'moving products successfully into the economy'. A development doesn't have to be a prime invention to be innovative, by the way. Incremental improvement, as we have seen, may do very well.

It should be added that a great deal of design is not to do with products. And that there are many highly effective innovations, in management, for instance, in distribution, in handling credit, that have little to do with products. Concentrating on developing fighting products, ones that will claim markets from competitors, as this book does, takes away nothing from the importance of other kinds of design and innovation.

DESIGN AT THE CENTRE

Mostly, design is seen as not central to the business. In most companies you'll find there is a design department somewhere in the hierarchy, to be sure, but apart from in avionics and a handful of other industries, it won't often be where the action is. And certainly nowhere near the decision making. Many design departments are way down the corporate hierarchy; to take a phrase from a song by Franz Lehar, 'deeper than diving for pearls'. All too often you'll find the designers in the bowels of the business, like canaries down a coal mine.

Not so at Sony, where, it is said, six members of the main board visit the design department formally every month. What Sony do affects us. Their sales abroad constituted two thirds of their $11.4 billion total in the year to March 1988. At Canon, much the same happens. They exported 70 per cent of their $8 billion sales in the year to December 1987. At IBM, whose nickname 'Big Blue' comes from its exemplary design policy, design is very much part of the corporate attitude. Design is important in all those companies that are sweeping other companies' products off the shelves.

At Corning Medical the president, Bill Toomey, drops by the design department regularly, just to stay in touch with what is going on. At Apple in its Steve Jobs days, a design council met for three hours each month. The idea was to look at everything being produced by the company. The president was always there.

Compare this with the experience of RitaSue Siegel, head of a New York recruitment agency. She interviewed fifteen General Motors automobile designers. 'To a person,' she said, 'they complained about their lack of contact with "the people on the fourteenth floor", as well as the organisational structure which frustrates, inhibits and prevents them from using their abilities to design great cars.'

Ivor Owen, an engineer, is now director of the Design Council. He used to be a main board director of Thorn–EMI, responsible for all the group's domestic appliances and lighting, an £800 million a year business. Each month he tried to bring a product to the board. Soon he realised this was seen as an irrelevance, a diversion, as though he were avoiding discussion of more serious matters: 'To talk about products, I realised, was counterproductive.'

This is in stark contrast to Japan, where, as writer Bill Evans noted,

The product planning department is really at the centre of the major com-

135

panies' structure. Generally the design department will be represented on the board, but not necessarily by the designer. Sharp may be the only large Japanese company with a designer on the board. Sony's head of product planning reports directly to the chairman.

And at Cassina, the Italian furniture firm, the vice-chairman is responsible for design, including products, and architecture.

This book is not about design in any narrow sense. It is about how winning companies win by creating a flow of products we all want to buy.

Design, of course, is part of that. So, too, is knowing what the competition is up to. Japanese industry is worth watching, and it is evolving new attitudes to design. Japan's Ministry of International Trade and Industry (MITI) recently produced a report entitled *Design Policy for the 1990s*. MITI is often credited with an almost mystical power to identify areas of future growth and to push Japanese companies into them, with the staggering success we know, so we do well to note that it has taken the trouble to look at design.

The report stresses that design 'means much more than simply shape, colour and dimensions of products. Design is the decision-making process that deals with the manifestation of objects with consideration to economy and technical function, and in answer to various consumer demands . . .' Because design works both ways, telling companies of consumer demand for a high standard of living, and delivering proposals from companies to customers, it is seen as a process of communication.

'It is no exaggeration to say that everything which surrounds us is in some way related to design'. MITI lists the significance of design under four headings.

- Fulfilling the national life. The quantity of goods has increased enormously; what is needed now is more concern with the quality of life created, at home, at work, in public places.

- Creating demand and stimulating the industrial economy. 'Superior design inspires appreciation,' says MITI. Enough appreciation on a large scale stimulates demand. Today's industries are urged, as part of their management strategy, to develop new products or services responding directly to this type of demand for creativity.

- Creating 'life culture'. In the past Japan has gobbled up Western ideas. Now, says MITI, there is a need to create a new, distinctively Japanese culture. 'Design converts material and technical values into human life values. Designed objects are the crystallisation of communication between consumers and suppliers.'

- The foundation for Japan's growth through the 1990s into the twenty-first century will be 'creativity'.

The fountainhead for development of our economic society, from technical innovation to the inventiveness with which we shape our own personal environment, is nothing less than our ability to create . . . Whereas in the past design was expected to conform to the existing environment, in this new age it is expected to be part of a proposal for a new living environment. In order for designers to live up to these expectations, it will become necessary for them to carry out careful observations of people's daily life.

That's what designers in Japan are being told.

A number of top British designers work for Japanese firms, a practice that is well-established. 'It is expected,' MITI says, 'that evaluation of their expert know-how and creative talent will continue.' British firms may not be interested in the design skills on their doorstep, but Japanese companies are.

Having said that, in Britain today there are some 2,700 design consultancies. Most are quite small, but some are the largest in the world, public companies. Their revenue is put at £1.6 billion, a figure forecast by Saatchi & Saatchi to grow at 20 per cent a year. So design is alive and well. The essential task now is to broaden the understanding of the word, to see design as a multi-disciplinary process using designers and others, all together, all the time.

DESIGN AS A TOTAL ACTIVITY

Because the importance of 'non-price factors' in products is now being recognised, and because design runs through them, winning companies are giving design the attention once offered only by a handful of high-minded companies with a sense of mission. Even then, their true understanding was largely an aesthetic one. 'Our ships aren't ugly,' the chairman of Cunard once said defensively, 'they only look ugly.'

The new lesson, and the thrust of this book, is that design is a total activity. Industrial designers are involved in the process. But so are mechanical and electrical engineers, marketing people and others who study the future, R & D, finance and manufacturing, and, of course, the board. The art is to develop new products that identified customers want to buy, in preference to all the other products available to them. At its best, the design process involves everyone.

Sir Ralph Halpern, chairman of the Burton Group, whose pre-tax profit under him has grown from £16.4 million to £183.4 million within seven years, said, 'Design is not a smart word for appearance. It is integral to the generation of profit,' because 'design is what differentiates a company from its competitors'.

All products are designed by someone, however unconsciously, however badly or well. All need to be different from their competitors'. Being cheaper is one way. But, as we have seen, non-price factors (uniqueness, quality, reliability, ease of use, appearance, and so forth) are becoming more important. The more the trend continues, as it will, the more crucial design, as an integrated activity, will become. It is by the design process that companies create superior and appropriate products. It is design that turns technology into goods we can live with and want.

Peter Lawrence of the Corporate Design Foundation in the USA points out that

> We hear a great deal about knowing and serving the customer. What we do not hear about is the process that converts that understanding of the customer into a product. That process is design. The designer provides the bridge between the customer and the company by participating in the research process and converting that information into a product . . . Design is values made visible.

The totality of this idea troubles a lot of people. Engineers think they are the designers. Develop a product that works, they say. Industrial designers think they are the ones to develop products, not engineers who have no idea what customers want. Yet many remain firmly isolationist and rooted in aesthetics. What of marketing? Marketing, as one eminent designer put it to me, is 'the art of tricking and exploiting people'. Quality? Well, that is a matter of good materials, good joins and fine finish, isn't it? Quality control is an add-on, and 'total quality control' another American idea picked up by the Japanese. Each discipline – engineering design, industrial design, marketing, sales, finance, R & D – keeps its prejudices in good repair as it remains firmly within its own walls.

David Carter, practical designer, and his team in Warwick helped design this urban transit system for Sydney, Australia; an example of 'values made visible'.

These ideas are old-fashioned and alien to the driving companies. Their notion is to put all these skills together and to keep them all together, throughout a development process. Design, warns James Fairhead, who led NEDO's international study of best practice,

> is frequently communicated in narrow terms and in a way that is either mis-leading or unconvincing for company management. The most sophisticated companies think of design as a planning process. It involves very much more than just industrial design.

Fairhead describes it as 'the process by which companies integrate a wide variety of functional skills, over a period of time, and it is only in this sense that design can be said to be central to commercial success'.

There are at least three extensions to this. First, design skills are often set to work in the absence of any disciplined strategic planning. That, Fairhead claims, is a fundamental weakness. Second, industrial design skills should be integrated with product and production engineering skills, to be sure that products are 'designed for makeability'. Third, a 'well-designed' product will fail if it is not designed to communicate well at the point of sale. As James Fairhead noted, 'A product is handicapped if insufficient time and resources have been devoted to reinforcing the product's intrinsic appeal by means of appropriate advertising and promotion.' Note that Sony have advertising in the product planning group, so that 'questions of trade and consumer communication are considered at a relatively early stage and in a cross-disciplinary manner, rather than being merely tacked-on at the end of the design process'.

ENGINEERS AS DESIGNERS

Engineers, too, can live in their confined, if not very comfortable, world, comfort being a source of annoyance when they look at the potted plants and comfortable sofas in the advertising department. Engineers feel they are the true creators, the practical people. Sometimes brilliant, too often they are encouraged to be unimaginative and repetitive, trotting out tried solutions. Much of the mediocrity you see around you can be laid at the door of engineers who don't give a button for the customer's emotions or 'impractical' needs. The thought of ordinary engineering departments bothering about 'lifestyles' and the sort of things we've been reading about, is absurd. They are not always even very good at manufacturing. There is a pecking order in engineering. Engineering designers are, in the words of Sir Monty Finniston, former chairman of British Steel, 'the aristocrats of engineering'. Well beyond the castle walls are production engineers.

It astonished Masanori Moritani, senior researcher at the Nomura Research Institute, to compare engineering graduates in Japan and the United States. In Japan, he said, when a young engineer joins a firm he goes into the plant. He can be there for eight years. When an American engineer graduates and joins a company he drives to a different car park and works in the office. Sir Robert Telford, life president of Marconi, the advanced electronics company, agrees that the same split exists in Britain. 'Manufacturing is still told what to make,' he told me.

R & D is another enclave, sometimes more akin to a university research department than part of a business trying to make money. The scientific tradition dies hard, long after most companies have ceased to be able to afford the investment needed to compete, long after the prime importance of satisfying the customer has been understood.

MARKETING

'You can't talk about design without talking about marketing,' says Jim O'Brien, former joint managing director of British Rail. But marketing, even when it is more than a grand word for selling, can be another independent box. How often do marketing people visit the factory? How aware are they of engineering difficulties? Come to that, how much time do they spend with customers, rather than with statisticians or advertising agencies?

ALL TOGETHER

While these departments or divisions or groups, whatever they are called, work in their separate fiefdoms, each will work below its potential. They cost more than they deliver, in other words. Worse, rapid, customer-loving product development is impossible. That is the essential lesson. If

141

you want to match hot competition you've got to get all these people together, to 'smash' the walls that divide them, as Tom Peters and Nancy Austin say.

Next, the focus of each group has to be switched from achieving its own honourable goals towards the customer, with what I have called elsewhere a 'laser beam' of common purpose. They have all to realise that they are part of the design team.

Some companies, such as Ford Europe, bring suppliers into the design process. Others, as we have seen, bring in sociologists and futurists. One difficulty for all of us is to forget our present comprehension of design. The designer may be, as Michael Smith of Baker Perkins says, 'the translator, bridge, catalyst in the development process', but the process involves everyone. We should try to agree that design is, of its essence, a multi-disciplinary process.

Bob Blaich, design director of Philips, believes that 'design, running from the product through environment to communications, is a holistic approach to positioning the company, in its own eyes as well as everyone else's'. Advice given by Robert Worcester, in a MORI study, was: 'See design as what the Japanese call a "parity-breaker", a way of differentiating your company and its products.' If we see design in these ways, then we can start to think of it as a vital creative resource, able to commit its imagination to a far wider range of challenges than simply applying the styling or 'wrapper' to a product.

There is another demanding role for designers. The more advanced products become, the more their technology must be translated or treated in ways people feel comfortable with. In his book *Megatrends*, John Naisbitt writes 'Whenever new technology is introduced into society, there must be a counterbalancing human response – that is, high touch. The more high tech, the more high touch.' That's why we'll see softer, rounder and simpler forms: not as a passing fashion, but to make technology acceptable.

'Innovation,' said John Bloxcidge, formerly at Wilkinson Sword, 'links us businessmen to the world of design and to those vital creative juices we do not possess.' He told an audience at the Royal Society of Arts, 'Innovation can galvanise management, inspire workforces, enthuse retailers and, from time to time, excite consumers.' None of this will happen if we see designers either as technical people in a backroom or as 'paintbrush boys', as I heard one engineer describe them.

In 1985 the Central Office of Information commissioned a market

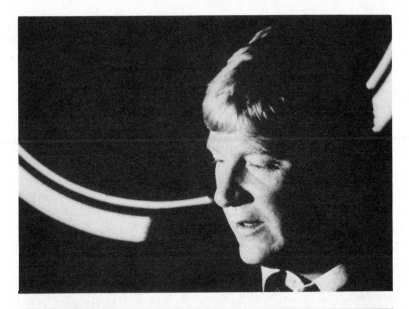

Consultant designer, Nick Butler, based in London, worked with Minolta in Japan to create their 'Camera of the Year', the Minolta 7000.

research company to study the use of design in industry. It found both that 'design lacks recognition and respectability' and that the companies interviewed had 'cut back significantly' their design departments and design effort. It will be hard to compete that way. Better by far is to create a multidisciplinary design team and in the words of Christopher Lorenz, to 'use designers to anticipate trends and to supplement the imagination of engineering and marketing'.

CONSULTANTS

With such a team, should you bring in outsiders? A growing number of companies do. There are several arguments for doing so. People from outside a company bring with them a new perspective. They have experience of materials, methods, markets wider than that of any particular company. They want to see progress, to complete the project and move on to the next one. So they hasten the measured tread of many companies. They have access to the board and so can propose changes that people in the company may find difficult. They are outside company politics. At best, they may be highly imaginative, able to look at opportunities in a new way. To use a word heard before, the talented ones can act as catalysts within a company.

More important, designers are interpreters, standing somewhere between the company and its customers. They can interpret to the company what people want, and can translate the miracles of manufacturing into products we understand and like. Bill Evans, a thorough researcher of these matters, once said that in Japan design is sometimes used as an *agent provocateur* to push a reluctant product planning or marketing department into an unfathomed area.

Riccardo Berla, chairman of Olivetti in the UK, argued that

Internal designers will never have the authority of external designers. People who make their career in a firm may say 'Yes' to manufacturing when they shouldn't. The inside of a company is conformist. You need outsiders to break this . . . But it is important to keep the same designers. Sottsass has worked for Olivetti for over thirty years. Bellini for more than twenty-five. Both are consultants. They are not on the payroll.

144

Years ago my firm worked for a company that made rivet-setting machines. They were great castings hung with exposed working parts and more protuberances than you would find on Chartres cathedral or Bondi beach. The designers simplified the product. A single column supported all the working parts on a small steel plate which was covered by a plastic box. The new design was safer to use. It cost half as much to make. It was modular, so the whole range cost still less to produce, and had other benefits. When he saw the mock-ups the company's managing director was delighted. Then he said, 'We couldn't have done that. You see, we *know* how to make rivet-setting machines.' He saw the advantage of a fresh view.

Compare him with the production people in a company making ear defenders – headsets people wear at airports when they guide aircraft to their bays. The sales director was worried about the cost of his product. It had twenty-four parts and, with screws and joins of different materials, heavy assembly costs. Our designers developed a new product. They simplified it to three bits of plastic that clipped together. Then the works manager in the factory persuaded the sales director that the product couldn't be made, that changes in the factory would cost too much and, anyway, the thing didn't work.

Within a year or, at best eighteen months, their old product was swept out of the market by an import. It was made of plastic, in three parts that clipped together.

Research shows that most companies don't bring in outsiders. According to a study by the Institute of Marketing in 1984 (Figure 18), about 30 per cent of manufacturers of consumer durables use design consultants.

Figure 18　How UK companies use consultants: the more costly the product, the fewer outsiders are brought in

Use of consultants	FMCG	Consumer durables	Repeat industrial	Capital industries
Design	53.7%	30.1%	18.8%	7.2%
Market research	60.3%	37.0%	26.8%	25.4%
Marketing	22.5%	10.6%	12.3%	7.7%
Training	24.4%	15.7%	22.5%	25.4%
Sales promotion	42.0%	16.7%	9.4%	4.8%

NOTE: For definitions see p. 52.
SOURCE: Institute of Marketing, 1984

Fewer than 19 per cent of 'repeat industrial' manufacturers do, and only 7 per cent of capital goods companies do. Even then, any consultant will tell you that it is far easier to get companies to employ you to develop packaging or graphics or corporate identity and the like, than to work on their products. A reason may be that even if many companies are bad at design, they think it is something a company should do for itself. Even odder, it is not unusual for a company to spend more on having its packaging designed than on designing its products.

DESIGN CLOSE TO THE BOARD

If we start to look at design as an integral part of product development, then see it as a strategic force, that nonsense will end. Having taken that step, the next is to keep design close to the board. We saw how at Sony six top executives visit the design department every month. The boards of Canon and Honda review every product development every month too. 'If UK boards did this,' sighed Christopher Lorenz of the *Financial Times*, 'I think there would be a difference.' Who can doubt it?

One of many lessons Peter Lawrence derived from Xerox is the need to make sure that you have an effective – and continuing – link between the objectives and strategies of the corporation and the design resource. 'It is not enough to have designers,' says Lawrence, 'they must be connected to the purpose and goals of the organisation so they can serve those as effectively as possible.' Once said it is obvious. But as the NEDO study and others have found, it doesn't happen in most firms.

It is essential that the board tells everyone on the design team its plans, takes them into its confidence, and gives them clear goals. While a research fellow at Ashridge Management College, Dr Charles Parker found that this was a distinguishing feature of successful companies: senior board members publish their plans and clearly spell out their policy on new products. Then they give the team sensible budgets. Industrial designers in the Chartered Society of Designers, Britain's professional design body, told me that not only do they have too little information to work on, but often the manufacturing companies they work for as consultants have no budget at all for designing products. The money has to be found from some other budget. This illustrates the lack of importance many British companies give to design.

Design needs to be budgeted differently. Don't look for output per hour. Look for results. Encourage 'blue-sky' thinking. Designers are not nine-to-fivers. If you motivate the team, it will work all hours – and should. Time and momentum matter. The pace, the short cuts, the insistence on forward movement are both essential and uncomfortable within normal corporate structures. Free-wheeling, too, getting out to shops, plants, to meet customers, to trade shows, just dreaming – how is the clean-desk manager to tolerate that?

Alan Topalian of Alto Design, the London-based design management consultancy, says, 'Design management is a fact of business life. It's not whether companies have design management or not. It is whether they abdicate responsibility or approach the management of design professionally.'

CHAMPIONS

Arthur D. Little, whose revenue in 1987 was some $272 million, employ 2,600 people, of whom half are scientists, engineers, economists and management specialists. They study innovation systematically. They have conducted interviews with companies thought to be in the lead in the United States and Japan and, now, in Europe. Their main findings concern corporate culture, a subject discussed in Chapter 12. About searching for new ideas, they say, 'Innovative companies do not wait for opportunities to come up. They actively stimulate the search for new ideas.' They quote Perstorp, the Swedish plastics firm, which has an 'ombudsman', whose role is to spot new ideas and help their promoters get the support needed to develop them. Also in Sweden, ASEA, the large electrical and electronics group, has appointed five senior managers from various parts of the organisation to sponsor new ideas. An important point: they have no need to go through the normal, hierarchical channels.

Dr Roy Rothwell of the Science Policy Research Unit says there must be a 'product champion', a person with both the vision and the determination to drive ideas through to completion. Christopher Lorenz looked at two quite different but highly innovative companies, Philips and 3M. Both, he said, share 'top-down' encouragement of product innovation. That includes not thinking less of people if the project they work on fails. In both companies, too, a senior person is given the job of 'championing' the product through development into successful manufacture and into marketing.

Arthur D. Little call for three 'drivers'. One is a *technical champion*, able to carry an idea through from initial concept to viable product or process. A second is a *business champion*, who provides a business framework for a technical idea. The third is an *executive champion*, who uses his or her power 'to protect and sponsor the idea at the highest level'. Most attempts at innovation would fail, they say, without the combined efforts, skills and experience of all three kinds of champion.

At the same time many of the winning companies they have studied have 'a healthy disregard' for their own organisation charts. These companies recognise that 'order and structure are important for the management of existing businesses but they accept that individuals can profitably utilise the experience and judgement of experts within and outside the company to develop new ideas'. In addition to their network of task forces and small project teams, innovative companies provide forums, conferences and internal trade shows to stimulate 'networking'.

FAILURE AND SUCCESS

Arthur D. Little say innovative companies tolerate failures:

> Coming up with new products, processes or approaches that work well over the long term is a messy process. Only in hindsight do many innovations appear to have proceeded as planned. In reality most are developed in a series of trials and errors. Managements at all levels should therefore tolerate experiments that fail, as innovation is quickly stifled.

Tom Peters and Nancy Austin reinforce this view of innovative companies: 'Lots of tries, lots of failures, lots of scrounging, but always action.'

Of course, you have to know when to cut off. That is the hardest part of all, I've found. Perhaps most of us have both cut too soon and hung on too long. One shining exception, not withstanding his present problems, is Alan Sugar, at Amstrad. Sir Clive Sinclair has said Sugar is 'absolutely brilliant' at this: 'a genius in his own field. The clever thing is he gets into markets at the right time – he also gets out of them at the right time.'

'Twenty-thousand dollar errors should not be allowed to turn into million dollar catastrophes,' Arthur D. Little say. You don't have to tell a manager that. If 'bottom-liners' have a flaw, it is that they expect profit too soon. Maybe it is best to try another tack. Keep any gems you can. Look at the issue another way.

3M foster internal competition between product groups. People in them are free to initiate new ventures in any line of business. 3M don't even insist that a new product should yield a minimum level of sales. They say they don't know which will succeed until they are tried. They also allow long payback periods. 3M can be prepared to wait five years for break even and a dozen years for full payback.

If you resolve to treat new products, and constant improvement of existing ones, as the main business of the business, then you'll want it to be close to the board. You'll want to encourage everyone, inside and outside the company, suppliers no less than people in the plant, to show initiative.

REWARD SUCCESS

Companies find it hard to bend their rules, but not much less is necessary. The conventional ways of rewarding people may not have the desired effect on creative people. According to James Brian Quinn, the driving forces for creative people, including entrepreneurs, are, in this order: independence, recognition, wealth.

The sad truth is that many companies not only get this order wrong, they don't try to satisfy any of these three forces. It is common sense to strive to create an environment in which ideas are sought and welcomed and prized and rewarded. The normal reward system is short-term bottom line. 'How can you expect executives rewarded in this way to be concerned with long-term product development?' asks Peter Lawrence.

It is characteristic of winning companies that they dwell on the importance of rewarding innovators. For example, IBM award fellowships to their creative people. Arthur D. Little remind us that base pay and annual increases are no great incentive to innovation. One tip is to provide 'advance compensation', or encouragement, at important milestones, to reward the efforts of champions, even before the project is completed. 'Rewarding only on the basis of successful results may be demotivating', particularly when projects are long term or discontinued for any reason. Effective compensation programmes, as James Brian Quinn has also found, include more than money.

Attention from the top is important, of course, but also reward successful innovators by giving them additional responsibilities and new projects. Arthur D. Little call it 'pinball'. Winners on a pinball machine get to play the game again. Many companies, they have found, use this as their main tool to motivate innovators. A sense of elitism goes with this. At Canon, one of the men associated with the successful Sure Shot camera said, 'You weren't even considered human at that time if you weren't somehow associated with the AE-1' (a previous model).

'European companies,' say Arthur D. Little, 'tend to be fairly unimaginative regarding compensation systems, typically underestimating the power of a multi-faceted and customised compensation system as a motivating tool.'

We might as well admit, too, that some of the most creative people are difficult. They can be arrogant or shy, noisy or unable to string three sentences together, introspective and moody, impatient, intolerant, vain, insecure. Lots of encouragement, lots of praise, lots of patience and — above all — support go further than a bit more pay. You need faith, too. Sometimes creative people can be right by instinct.

Years ago, a Canadian in my office designed a new shopping bag for a department store. To my horror he·put together blue and green, both strong and bright. I reminded him of the art school homily of the time: 'blue and green should never be seen'. He ignored my advice, and how right he was. Within two years every secretary in London was wearing just those colours. Indeed, his design worked for ten years at least. No one told him they were about to become fashionable colours. His innate sensitivity led him that way. It is difficult for the numerate manager to feel comfortable with such intuition. Maybe a difference between managing design and other things is to accept the inexplicable. You certainly have to try not to say 'no'.

It is usual, yes, more the rule than the exception, that the creative edge that distinguishes one product from another is compromised out of a designer's work by an overcautious board. There is not much to be said for that.

CREATIVITY

'Creativity should be positively cultivated,' noted Sir Terence Beckett, former boss of Ford and former director general of the CBI. In Canada Marshall McLuhan explained why: 'The gap between producer and consumer is closing. Ideas have become the main ingredient of the new economy.'

Speaking at the London Business School in November 1988, Lord Gowrie foresaw that economic growth in the future will come from 'the exploitation of ideas and dreams', as he put it, not from the exploitation of materials, as in the past. Sir Terence Beckett agreed: 'There is no doubt ideas are more important than functions. According to Edward de Bono, who coined the phrase 'lateral thinking', 'the quality of our future depends on the quality of our thinking.'

Who can doubt it? Strangely, though, we don't seem to expect them to come from designers. When the Open University asked companies what

Figure 19   Design – the word is growing

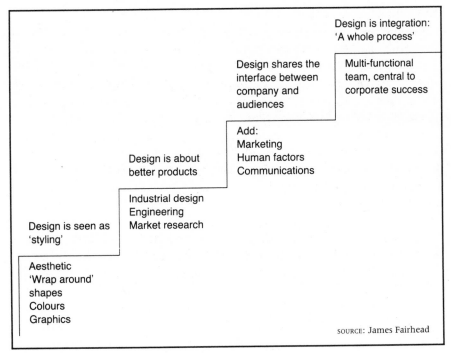

Design is integration: 'A whole process'

Design shares the interface between company and audiences

Multi-functional team, central to corporate success

Add:
Marketing
Human factors
Communications

Design is about better products

Industrial design
Engineering
Market research

Design is seen as 'styling'

Aesthetic
'Wrap around'
shapes
Colours
Graphics

SOURCE: James Fairhead

151

they meant by design, only 7 per cent defined it as creating new concepts or ideas. How can that be? We need ideas to create products which, if they are to secure market share and earn profits, must be different from their competitors. We won't get them unless we create the framework, and the climate, in which they can flourish. 'Skunkworks' are one way. Central, multi-disciplined teams with their own freewheeling rules are another. Rewarding success in fresh ways is a third.

The problem that businesses face is this: all our education prompts us to suppress imagination. The logical, numerate, literate, educated mind can kill ideas before they start. We have to recognise this and find a way through it. It matters because, as Theodore Levitt said, 'nothing drives progress like the imagination. The idea precedes the deed.' Arthur D. Little warn that new growth requires new ideas, not just efficient management of the status quo.

The most important step is to believe we are all born with creative power. The popular assumption that designers are creative but business executives are not is nonsense. Or, at least, it may be nonsense if executives give themselves a chance to dream. You see the universality of imagination at brain-storming sessions, where conditions are created to allow imagination free rein.

Pablo Picasso said it took him sixty years to see like a child. David Bernstein, the distinguished graphic designer, once told of a football match he went to with his daughter, Lucy. 'How many teams are on the field,' Bernstein asked. 'Four.' 'Four?' 'Yes,' said his daughter, 'the reds, blues, blacks and greens.' Red were Arsenal. Blue were Chelsea. Green were the goalkeepers and black were the referees.

Within the normal, numerate, controlled world of industry, scatty ideas seem out of place, their authors frowned on. Original thinkers quickly learn to be quiet or leave. The practical step is to realise that creative thinking is a different mental process; not inferior (some say the opposite) but different, to be treated in a different way. Betty Edwards at the California Institute of Technology (Caltech) crystallises the difference in a simple way. Ideas tend to come from what is called the 'right-hand mode' of the brain; but the 'left-hand mode', developed by our normal academic education, dominates when it can. If you compare the two sets of characteristics, you will see why this is likely to be so. The left-hand mode is analytic, rational, numerate, logical, linear. It uses words to define and symbols to stand for something. It keeps track of time, doing first things first. The right-hand mode, in contrast, is non-verbal, puts things together to create wholes, sees likenesses between things, has no sense of time, is not rational but intuitive and holistic. New ideas, fresh ways of seeing things, new connections, leaps of imagination, come, it is now believed, from this right-hand side of the brain.

George Bull, editor of the *Anglo-Japanese Economic Journal* and a noted Italian scholar, told me that in the Renaissance great artists and designers used both halves of their brain. 'They could paint pictures and build bridges. Look at Leonardo, Raphael, Michelangelo at the summit and scores, thousands of others between 1450 and 1550 or so.' Can we learn today from this? Bull continued, 'They got their versatility and balance from the impact of Renaissance curiosity and ambition, diversity of patronage, something in the air, something in the blood and also often being trained as craftsmen.'

If designers do have an edge, it is because imagination, latent in most of us, is encouraged during their kind of education. There is no correlation between academic beginnings and creative excellence except, possibly, an inverse one. One consequence is that you will encourage imagination to flower in your design and development team if you do not apply the measures necessary and normal to a conventional organisation.

While people are born with different abilities, hardly anyone fathoms the creative power latent within them. You can teach people to be more creative and few lessons would do more for corporate success. But what is the creative process? Are creative people different? Can you tie them to budgets and timetables? Do creative people have to wait for inspiration?

The first problem comes with definition. A child's first sketch at school is creativity at work. So is Einstein's theory of relativity. Are they the same?

Dr Irving Taylor, when he taught psychology at the Pratt Institute, claimed there were five levels of creative activity. First, what he calls *expressive* creativity. This involves independent expression. Originality, skill and quality are unimportant. Spontaneous drawings by children are examples. Second is *productive* creativity. Here, a level of proficiency is reached, though the individual's work may not differ from the work of others. When people move from the expressive to the productive level, claims Dr Taylor, they tend to restrict and control free play. They develop techniques for producing finished work. So that is creative but not imaginative.

Inventive creativity is thought to be the next level. This is when you are inventive with materials, techniques and methods. You have to be flexible in seeing new and unusual relationships between previously separate

153

parts. Important characteristics are invention and discovery.

Dr Taylor calls the next level *innovative*. This comes when someone really understands a basic principle and is able to develop it. Few can do this. Jung following Freud might be an example. You have to dig deep into principles to understand them that well.

The highest form of creativity, according to this psychologist, is *emergentive* creativity: 'In rare instances an entirely new principle or assumption, around which new schools flourish, emerges at a most fundamental and abstract level.' Picasso and Einstein were such men.

In practice, the levels that concern us most are the third and sometimes the fourth. It might be good to dwell on the creative process a moment. If we know how it works we are in a better position to encourage it in ourselves and others. First, psychologists say, raw material is gathered for the idea. It comes from the world around us, perceptions received consciously and unconsciously. Creative people glean experience from anywhere. This 'raw material' also comes, of course, from specific information fed in to solve a specific problem. Often creative people not only devour experience, they see it with a *naïveté* that surprises people. Every day is new. You have seen this innocence. It is to be prized. Non-creative people pigeonhole experience into stereotypes. We must do this to live, evidently, but too much pigeon-holing is the enemy of fresh thought. Pigeon-holes, I said recently, are for pigeons, not people. If you pigeon-hole, only a small part of what you see and hear enters the subconscious mind. Most is blocked because it is preconceived.

The creative act is to link these experiences in a new way. The essence of creativity is to organise things differently. One lesson is that if output depends on input, you should be out and about and make sure your designated 'creative' people are out and about too. Sitting at a drawing board has its limitations.

The next stage in the creative process, according to psychologists, is 'incubation'. All these experiences flow freely in the creative mind without being stereotyped. They 'bump into each other and react on one another'. From these interactions, parts start to fit together in new relationships. This phase goes on all the time. At night (many well-known creative people know this and use it by feeding in a problem before they go to sleep), in the bath, in the office.

Creative people will say how they wrestle with a problem for days, getting nowhere. Then a clear solution emerges. That stage is called 'illumination'. It may flash in the mind at any time. Archimedes and 'Eureka'.

Charles Darwin could point to the exact bend of the road where, out in his pony trap, his theory of evolution fell into place. But this flash of inspiration seldom happens except after days of apparently fruitless effort.

The final stage is 'execution'. Translating an idea into reality is often painfully hard. One thing is clear: somewhere in the creative process comes the need for great and undisturbed concentration. This can lead to odd behaviour. Schiller liked the smell of rotten apples in his desk. Stephen Spender smoked heavily and drank endless cups of coffee. Others play music to focus all distractions into one they don't hear. When creative people are in the grips of a problem, time vanishes. Hours go by as in a moment.

Too much conforming to rules doesn't help. That's one reason why 'skunkworks' are a good idea. Another thing I've learnt is the need to generate lots of ideas. If you don't, people will polish and polish their first idea, without seeing if there's a better one to be had. Finally, and this is borne out by the theory about the left and right sides of the brain, it is very important not to judge too soon. Analytical thought and creative thought are different activities. One destroys the other.

TRY THIS CHECKLIST

Look at this list. It was put together by people at the Massachusetts Institute of Technology (MIT) to get rid of the 'mental blocks', as they called them, that inhibit creativity. The essential point is to ask them of oneself and of everyone concerned with product development, not just of the few designated creative people.

1. *Do you have difficulty in isolating the problem?*
   The problem well stated is half solved. People in a department cut off from others, unaware of what is going on in the market, not knowing the constraints and possibilities in the plant, are most unlikely to pinpoint the right problem.

2. *Do you narrow the problem too much?*
   You need to get everyone together so they can see the total picture.

3. *Do you study the obvious?*
   Do. Start there. Challenge existing assumptions, as we did with the rivet-setting machines.

155

4. *Do you record all the trivia you can?*
Any detective story will tell you that the small clue sometimes holds the big answer. Again, it is characteristic of Japanese industry to analyse exhaustively a market before deciding to go into it. It is part of the 'slow/fast' way in which they work.

5. *Do you place too much emphasis on past experience?*
This is a tough one. We have to pigeon-hole ideas to live. If every time we picked up a pen we thought all about it, we'd never sign a letter. Such pigeonholing, however, is death to creativity. Indeed, an irritating hallmark of creative people can be their apparent naivety. They seem to see everything for the first time. It is an important asset, not to be mocked.

6. *Do you try to conform too much to the accepted pattern?*
Large companies, in particular, require this. That is one reason for setting up 'skunkworks', where normal rules go into limbo, or design teams where the rules are known to be different, or for bringing in consultants who are outside the corporate framework.

7. *Do you try to judge ideas too soon?*
Designers, I have found, can fall in love with their first ideas. It is important to say, 'Yes, it's great, but try another approach.' Always look for what James Brian Quinn calls 'multiple approaches'. One reason is to speed up the process. Another is to have plenty of options to choose from. There is another angle to this. Ideas are fragile. It is much easier to knock them down than let them grow. It is much better for everyone concerned to let ideas wander freely first. Worry about whether they are any good later.

This, too, is typical of winning companies. They develop lots of choices, then wait a long time before choosing the right one.

8. *Are you afraid of being impolite?*
People may think you rude if you ask too many questions. Encourage your design team to ask all the questions it can think of. It needs facts.

9. *Are you tempted to follow competition?*
MIT says, 'Don't. They may be going in the wrong direction.' This isn't the same as saying ignore them. As we've seen, the more you know about your competitors the better. Instead, MIT may mean that no companies are perfectly perfect. If they are not in the French

market, say, it may be because they have failed to get there, or failed to spot its value. It does not necessarily mean they have decided the French market is not worthwhile for their (and your) business. If they do something else, it may mean they have a special reason, or special connection, or luck, or have simply made a mistake.

10. *Are you afraid of making a fool of yourself?*
Inventiveness demands the risk. You often see imaginative people asking silly questions. How else are they to think new thoughts? The question is whether you create the environment in which they can function. Indeed, do you encourage them to challenge conventional views? You've seen this at board meetings. Some chairmen ask for opinions and spark one person's ideas off against another. Others keep the meeting tight. Intervention slows progress. The chairman frowns, looks at the clock and you soon learn to stop thinking. If that is a microcosm of a company, there is not much hope for innovation in it.

11. *Are you afraid of your client's or boss's reaction to your ideas?*
Don't be, says MIT. Evidently, if you are the boss, the last thing you should do is to provoke this fear. It is much more easily done, particularly in a hierarchical company, then people realise. Irwin M. Stelzer, a consultant economist, once wrote: 'British companies are run by managers who spend less of their time on introducing new ideas, particularly novel ideas from other sources, than managers in any other country.' It is a shortcoming. Unlike most vices, this one is fun to stop.

In circumstances I can't imagine, Lord Chesterfield once remarked that 'from a hayloft a horse looks like a violin'. We may draw two lessons from this. First, we need a different point of view to see things in new ways. Second, it is important to show the design team the way to that hayloft. And know the way yourself.

SUMMARY

In one dimension, at least, people in business are unduly modest. They believe they are not creative. They cannot, as they would tell you, draw a straight line. That link, between imagination and being able to make pictures, is false. That's first. Second, the notion that some people, often called designers, are creative, but the rest of humanity isn't, is equally unfounded. By their deeds successful people in all walks of life, including and particularly in business, prove that they combine both imagination and the courage to change their world.

What is true is that this lack of confidence in their ability causes many business people to downgrade or undervalue the one ingredient that is essential to differentiate their company from its rivals – the imagination to see and do things in a new way. This chapter argues that creative power lies in all of us, albeit to a different degree, and that we do well to draw on it with pride. Corporate systems militate against the creative process. A chaotic, inconsequential, untidy affair, creativity is unlikely to flower in the tightly run, well-organised business.

What is necessary, therefore, is to create the environment that stimulates people to develop and exercise their imagination. This chapter is about how to do this generally, and how a company can draw more from its creative team, in particular noting that a range of disciplines should be included in it, not simply the designated designers. MIT has identified some barriers that we all have to overcome.

9

Give Engineers a New Role

'Anything in process of change is
being changed by something else.'
St Thomas Aquinas

'Success,' says Graham Anthony of the Engineering Council, 'lies in the ability of a company to convert engineering expertise into competitive products through efficient production processes. It requires that engineering be woven in with marketing, research, design and finance.' That's right, except that I'd say that all are parts of the design team. In many companies this does not happen.

You can understand engineering-based companies thinking that their business is about engineering, but that has its own risks. To engineer wonderful products no one buys is best reserved for a weekend hobby. In recent years in Britain there has been a tremendous focus on improving productivity. Overdue and vital as continually improving productivity is, that, too, is a waste of time if we produce goods efficiently that don't sell. No, the whole game is about looking at customers and the competition, then making what people want better than competitors can.

Casio has shifted the engineer into marketing. Their idea is that whoever is closest to the customer will come up with the basic functional design. The other benefit, as we have seen, is speed. Kenichi Ohmae of McKinsey & Co. in Tokyo has claimed that 'for many products turnaround time – from design to market-place – is more critical than labour costs. Close linkages are needed between manufacturing, engineering and marketing.'

That is different from either ignoring the market or misunderstanding it, or treating the various development steps in a line. The linear process is no way to compete. The Minolta Auto-Focus camera was conceived by engineers. Many products are. The difference is that Minolta at once formed a team. Price, design and sales forecast came into their earliest thinking.

In Britain engineers were the great inventors. They threw bridges across broad, roaring rivers, built brave ships to beat their way through towering

159

seas. Factories, from Accra to Adelaide, clattered with the sound of their wondrous machines. Today that genius is rarely seen. Between 1979 and 1989 British engineering exports will have grown 20 per cent. Imports will have risen by 75 per cent. That is according to the Engineering Employment Federation. Naturally, and by ingrained reflex, it blames exchange rates. It also blames skill shortages.

Peter Gorb of the London Business School argues that engineering methodology, and I add 'how to', was 'perverted at the end of the last century by scientific methodology'. Is it a consequence that engineers, once lionised, have given way to financiers as the new heroes?

What a poor swap. Perhaps the time has passed when an Isambard Kingdom Brunel could design a railway, map out the route, raise the money, hire the workers, know where to bridge, where to cut the land and on top of all, by his will, drive the line through. Today, while there are marvellous exceptions, in general engineers fulfil their role best when they fit their skill in with that of others.

Perhaps it is because the practical nature of engineering has been degraded by so-called 'academic drift' in universities and by the search for respectability in the professions that we rely on it less. Yet, as Dr Kenneth Grange of the design group Pentagram has noted, 'Engineering is the single greatest area of opportunity and hazard.' Which is it to be?

Engineers are only a hazard, I submit, when they work in isolation or believe they have all the answers. They provide the most marvellous opportunities when they work with others to tackle new tasks. If industry, confronted by new competition of terrifying intensity, reasserts the primacy of its products, engineers may find themselves thrust once more into the limelight. As rescuers, they can perform a more central role than many have been allowed for years.

Matching their practical skills with those of others, engineers can help to create the new products their companies need. They are better placed than anyone else to lift levels of product quality and reliability. If they care to venture into the plant, they can introduce new ideas, methods and equipment to improve manufacturing. Further, and this may be a new role, they have the sense to identify suppliers worthy of long-term trust.

Not least, engineers can guide their companies into new technologies. Sir Monty Finniston speaks of one West German company whose board consists virtually only of engineers. Who will be more able to spot the new technologies that must be spotted: companies which have engineers in their boardroom or those that don't?

BACK TO BASICS

Today Japan has four times as many engineers per head of population as the United Kingdom does. Sony's chairman, Akio Morita, is a courteous man. Yet he was moved once to say, 'If I criticise the Western world it is that you appreciate the scientist, you do not appreciate the engineer.' It is time for engineers to reassert themselves, though not by polishing the

Isambard Kingdom Brunel, great nineteenth-century engineer. If his great entrepreneurial drive is rare, engineering none the less remains of pivotal importance. Companies that downgrade it run grave risks.

steel wall they have built around their profession. They, like everyone else, need to submit themselves to the demands of the market, turbulent and changing as it is. If they do, their position in any company is most valuable. Why? Because they are concerned with real objects.

Too many companies are bogged down in numbers. Part of 'getting back to basics' is to put numbers in their place, to realise that manufacturing is about making products. Concerned with that, engineers can and should bring a daily reminder to any company of why it is there. Numeracy is a word we know. Literacy is another. Now Edward de Bono has coined a third: 'operacy'. By that he means skill at doing things, making things happen. It is not mathematics and physics that mark out the value of engineers, but their operacy. To be practical, to design objects, to know how they work; that is their role, but not in the echoing silence of a drawing office. Their window on the world must look further than the company car park, be wider than the pages of their engineering journal.

Successful Japanese consumer electronics companies send their product design engineers around the world for up to six months every year. They go to study the latest customer needs and competitive scene. They visit customers and dealers, attend trade shows, hold conferences with dealers and sales people. Not surprisingly, they regard that technique as far superior to sending out questionnaires from corporate headquarters. But would many Western engineers do even that? It is typical, too, for engineers in such companies to switch from job to job. Myopia is taboo. Throughout their careers they mix and mingle and change places with people in other divisions and other parts of the business.

Industry in Britain is desperately short of engineers generally. A recent CBI study of 700 companies revealed that output in one in five of them was restricted by a shortage of qualified staff. One in three of the complaints related to engineering. In part this must be a result of the lack of reward and recognition engineers receive. The United States, too, falls far short of Japan in the number of engineers being trained. When it comes to engineering, the numbers in Japan are stunning. By the early 1980s, 368,000 students were studying engineering in Japanese universities and colleges. In the UK at that time there were 36,000. Fewer engineers have graduated in the USA in the 1980s than in Japan, even though there are five times as many students. During the 1970s, 40 per cent of all master's degrees in Japan were for engineering.

In the UK, Sir Robert Telford, lifetime president of Marconi, believes all engineers should know about electronics. That seems to be a Japanese view. On a per capita basis, since 1977 there have been almost three times as many electrical and electronic engineers graduating annually from Japanese universities as in the USA, four times those in Britain, six times those in France and 70 per cent more than in West Germany.

The gap is widening. The total number of engineering graduates in the USA is growing by 2.4 per cent a year, although the number of electronic engineers is actually decreasing. Between 1967 and 1979 the number of engineering graduates in Japan rose by 7 per cent a year, compound.

I'll stop producing those statistics. But one more shows where we place our emphasis. In Japan, according to Gene Gregory of Sophia University in Tokyo, there are three accountants and one lawyer for every 10,000 people. In the United States there are forty accountants and twenty lawyers for every 10,000 people. Indeed, between 1978 and 1985 the number of accountants in the United States grew by one third, not least because American management focuses on profit and needs more frequent accounts.

MANUFACTURING

Nowhere is the position more acute than in production engineering. While British productivity is catching up, it is still ten years behind French and German performance and twenty years behind Japan. That is according to a survey conducted by PA Consulting Group. This may be partly because Britain simply has too few engineers and even fewer senior executives with primary responsibility for productivity. According to the study, 'they are almost unknown'.

What happens so often is that the production engineers are kept in the dark. A market study done in 1985 among UK manufacturing companies for NEDO showed that six in ten companies have marketing represented at the start of a project, but fewer than four in ten have manufacturing represented either at the beginning or at the end of a development project. It is the linear process in action. Manufacturing is shown the new product after it has been designed, then told to make it. Suppose, as so often happens, that the production people can't make the product as designed; suppose they see a better way? Then the product goes back to design. This process, politely called 'iterate', is bound to be slow. Worse, it can lead to products being more expensive than they need to be. Manufacturing knowledge, at the design stage, can alter the cost of a product.

Mike Burlington, director of design services of the British consultants P-E-Inbucon, believes that 'about 80 per cent of the cost of a product is dictated by its design. It is by design that I see real opportunities for improving profit.' It would be hard for anyone to do this without having manufacturing interests represented on the product development team.

In Japan, claims Masanori Moritani of the Nomura Research Institute, engineers, along with everyone else, are obsessed with improving products and lowering manufacturing costs in order to beat the competition. That is a lesson we can learn. To have everyone in a company aiming at the same goal, not at satisfying his or her own professional ideals, is surely imperative. The idea of diligent and demanding product improvement coming not from dramatic innovation but from narrowing the gap between development and production (and often making outrageous demands of suppliers) may be humbler than seeking the great advances of science, but it is also more rewarding.

Part of the process of getting engineers more involved in the dynamics of their companies is to encourage them to share more fully in the product being developed. One way is to know more about the design. It starts with education. In engineering education in Britain, design is scarcely taught. According to Sir Alex Smith, former Rolls-Royce research director and chief scientist, engineering departments in universities 'don't give a two-penny damn about it'. Mind you, I don't think Brunel, or Stephenson come to that, went to a university.

GIVE TECHNOLOGY A CHANCE

There is another point. A myth has grown up that the only way out of recession for manufacturing industry is through advanced manufacturing technology (AMT) and information technology. As a generalisation that may have merit, although it can frighten us too. Despite exhortation and practical common sense, many companies remain, at best, sceptical – even those that try to be efficient. A Policy Studies Institute report published in November 1986 claimed that the total number of industrial robots in the UK was 3,200. That, it said, is less than the increase in the number of robots in West Germany in 1985 alone.

Colin New, professor of operations management at Cranfield School of Management, conducted a study for the British Institute of Management.

The car industry is using flexible manufacturing systems (FMS) but the true value of robotics takes time to show. Larger scale mass production is less of a benefit than the new ability to change over quickly. Runs can be shorter and variety increased so that companies are more able to meet the individual wishes of their customers.

He looked at 250 manufacturing plants. Two-thirds of the firms experimenting with flexible manufacturing systems (FMS) reported low or negative payoff. Three quarters of the companies experimenting with robotics said the same. Half the companies using computer-aided design (CAD) and computer-aided manufacturing (CAM) said they hadn't made any significant gains from their introduction.

New's findings become more alarming. Less than half the firms interviewed intended to put high or even fairly high emphasis on CAD or CAM. This dropped to one quarter for FMS and to 16 per cent for robotics. The hope is that there are at least equal opportunities to be had in reducing the need for advanced methodology. That can be done by simplifying the design of a product from a manufacturing point of view, and its specification.

Of course, it works two ways. In their study of five winning companies in Japan, Ken-ichi Imai and his colleagues noted that production staff are encouraged to help with market research. Without that sort of perspective and encouragement to put their work in the right context, production managers can be defensive too. They can reject ideas because they don't come from specialists. James Fairhead came across this folly in the international study he carried out for NEDO. 'You don't have to be able to change a die-set in thirty minutes to understand the process,' he suggested mildly. Nor should one be too bound by what the factory says it can make. Conservative and cautious production managers can be quick to say something can't be done. One role of the engineer or consultant designer can be to say to them, 'Oh yes it can.'

If British and even American companies are too short of engineers and if much of our manufacturing is in a parlous state, for all kinds of snobbish and other reasons, this doesn't mean that there is little hope for the companies that do want to innovate.

WORK WITH SUPPLIERS

One characteristic of winning companies is that more and more they buy in all they can. Based on his extensive experience of fast-growing companies, Kenichi Ohmae advises us to 'produce only critical components internally. Buy state-of-the art components from outside vendors.' It makes sense to tap outside sources, noting that the best source can vary by industry. In electronics, it is said, customers provide the innovation. In textiles, materials or equipment the drive can come from suppliers. In biotechnology it could be the universities.

If ever a company was rescued, it was Jaguar. They gave an award to their 'Supplier of the year'. In 1986 Jaguar presented forty-four 'Pursuit of Excellence' awards to suppliers, including four from West Germany. They were judged on the basis of value for money, continuity of supply and quality. At the presentation, Sir John Egan, chairman and chief executive, reminded everyone that 'in this world only excellent products will survive'.

When James Fairhead interviewed a head of engineering at Jaguar, he found they talked repeatedly about Marks & Spencer, the giant retailing group that grew by establishing, long ago, original and strong relations with its suppliers. The honorary president of Marks & Spencer, Lord Sieff, said that, even now, 'I and each of my executives make it a hard and fast point to visit a minimum of forty suppliers a year.'

The PA Consulting Group worked for the rolling stock industry in

Japan. They found companies treated their suppliers as well as their customers. Their 'people relationships' were markedly better than you find in
most firms. These rolling stock companies have 'pushed out the proper
customer-loving attitude to embrace new groups of people, not least their
suppliers,' said PA.

IBM calls its suppliers 'business associates'. They reward them too.
Suppliers whose deliveries are perfect earn a premium price. Prices drop as
defects mount. Ford took full-page advertisements in the *Wall Street Journal* to praise suppliers who had hit high quality standards.

Suppliers can be part of a company's design process. They key is to bring
them in early, let them share in the company's success and be proud of it.
In this direction, everyone has far to go. Sony have people in the design
department with full-time responsibility for links with suppliers.

Rover Cars, in Britain, are co-operating with Honda to produce the
Rover 800 and other cars. Mark Snowdon, Rover's director of product
development, said he was particularly impressed with the way Honda
brought in the parts suppliers at an early design stage. The reasons are not
only to take advantage of their expertise but also to cut the delay that can
occur between design and production. The Open University study, too,
showed that more foreign companies (29 per cent) used suppliers to help
with design and development than did British firms (7 per cent).

When Jaguar tackled the poor quality of its cars, it identified 250 faults;
60 per cent of them were caused by suppliers. Jaguar assigned each problem to teams within the company, and brought in suppliers to work on
them too. The twelve worst problems were left to the board of directors.
All the problems were solved. Today they manage quality, in part, by
taking cars randomly from the line. A system of demerit points provides a
weekly quality index. Jaguar suppliers have to replace all rejected
components. If the failure rate is over 1.5 per cent, the supplier also pays
for labour and handling charges.

Dealers, too, are subject to the same tough attitude. Every three months
overseas representatives meet to pre-empt problems.

Ford Europe are another good example of a growing trend. They used to
design a component, then put it out to tender among as many suppliers as
wanted to bid. Now, according to Uwe Bahnsen, their former design director, Ford choose suppliers early. They base their decision on quality and
reliability, of both products and service. They have whittled the number of
suppliers down from over 30,000 to almost hundreds. Today, they call in
the suppliers, say what they need and, often, design the component with

them. The suppliers do the R & D, testing and validation. In return, Ford offer contracts that may run for several years. This means the supplier can tool up or relocate with confidence. Ford's aim, Bahnsen points out, is to raise the level of consistent quality.

The price difference is always negligible, he says, if you take into account the savings in inspection and warranty payments. He warns that suppliers should not be totally dependent on one company, but should look on it as a long-term partner. The great point is to be clear about the company's needs. You have to give ideas of volume and agree quality standards before you start.

The message is that while being careful about the costs, price isn't everything. Buying the cheapest can lead to lower quality, more expense, lower sales. Without question, winning companies like Ford concentrate on quality, reliability, service. Engineers go for quality and that is a strength. Perhaps a changing role for them is to help their companies identify those suppliers in whom to place long-term faith.

BENEFITS OF QUALITY

Ford say the benefits of better-quality components include less down-time, less inspecting for faults and consequent lower costs because longer runs are guaranteed. Other benefits are lower subsequent costs through claims, and good technological transfer between supplier and customer.

If you are close to your suppliers, they come to understand your company objectives and are better able to work towards them. Importantly, they will know more about your customers. In turn, they know you won't ask the impossible of them, although people in Japan, where this intimacy is usual, do complain of the demands made on suppliers by manufacturing companies.

Nick Garnett, writing in the *Financial Times*, described the unique structure that links the large Japanese corporations with their primary subcontractors and myriad tiny suppliers. The primary subcontractor, he said, 'acts as tutor, policeman, referee, communicator and outright bully-boy among the small subcontractors, on behalf of the main corporation. The subcontractors must shoulder a great deal of the product development whether they like it or not.'

One of Fuji's principal suppliers employs fifty people, but calls in

'How do you feel?' the astronaut was asked. 'How would you feel,' he replied, 'knowing you are sitting on 200,000 parts all bought on the lowest tender?' This is a joke to make a point, no reflection on anyone.

seventy-seven secondary subcontractors, mostly with fewer than 10 employees. These secondary subcontractors develop a high level of competence in problem solving. They are used, both by their customer (the main supplier) and by Fuji, as task forces in product development. Some 90 per cent of the parts of the Fuji-Xerox FX 3500 copier used during test production were made by subcontractors. Fuji-Xerox have another set of six subcontractors that specialise almost entirely in product development. They all work as a team, with a large amount of shared information and a common feeling of shared dependency on the fortunes of Fuji. They do this with few, if any, written contracts.

I have heard business executives scoff at this approach to suppliers. Of course they should fight on price to win business, they say. Many successful companies continue to live like that. There is no doubt, however, that the companies that are clawing our markets away from us point to their relations with suppliers as a key factor. It gives you, and this is the sum, 'a better position in the market'.

Three obstacles can get in the way of developing this relationship with suppliers. First, and much the worst, is NIH (not invented here). More than once I have met companies that think they lose their status somehow if they don't develop everything themselves. The second is secrecy. To be sure, confidentiality can be important, but many companies make this an excuse for not telling anyone anything. Suppliers will be as helpful as they are informed. If they don't know what you want, they can hardly give it to you. Third, of course, is the long-held view that the job of a buyer is to buy for the lowest price possible.

QUALITY

Quality, leading firms are saying, is the way to win markets. Engineers may have a dominant role here too. We all admire the quality and reliability of so many Japanese products. Yet in Japan, only 2 per cent of the workforce are engaged in inspection. In Europe the figure is 10 per cent. How have the Japanese done it? One answer is that everyone is concerned with quality. Another is that they 'design quality in', they don't wait to 'inspect faults out'.

In Europe, the Ford dashboard is an example. The instrument panel is the highest source of defects in a car. All control elements pass through it.

Ford set up a task force of designers, design engineers and manufacturing. In two weeks they visited all their plants in Europe and filmed assembly of the instrument panel. They found that most faults are assembly faults. They were easy to understand. Men lying on their backs, often in mediocre light, could join wrong wires, even though the wires were differently coloured.

Design quality in. Don't wait to inspect faults out. See how Ford did this with a dashboard, and the benefits they found.

The team transferred most of the assembly to a bench. They also reduced the number of connections from sixty to seven, and each became a different shape, so now a worker cannot join wires wrongly. This foolproof system saved Ford money, they found, as well as delivered a more reliable car.

Masanori Moritani of Japan's Nomura Research Institute believes that the Japanese 'total' concentration on manufacturing is the basis of their success. Japanese companies have thousands of graduate engineers on the shopfloor, focusing on improving manufacturing. For example, of 8,000 R & D people in Hitachi, 5,000 are in the factories. Moritani points to

171

the famous 'quality circles' and the leadership of companies by engineers as further evidence of this concentration on manufacturing.

In the United States and other Western countries, with the possible exception of West Germany, there isn't the same 'obsessional' drive to improve quality, Moritani argues. We expect to pay more for high quality. Yet that should not be so. We're the ones who are being fooled. Don Osman from 3M told an audience at the London Business School, 'Our experience shows us that as we drive quality up, so we also drive unit costs down.' A study in 1988 of firms that make air-conditioning units in the USA and Japan showed that designing quality in costs less than inspecting faults out. The US manufacturers' warranty service rate was, on average, *seventeen times* higher than that of the Japanese companies. Yet analysis showed that the cost of quality management in the Japanese firms was half that in the American companies.

Tom Peters claims the work arising from poor quality occupies a quarter of the people in a manufacturing company, one way and another, and 'a staggering' 40 per cent in service companies. The cost of poor quality can be measured in every function, he says, from executive secretaries to engineering and sales to the plant. Peters' advice is just that: to measure it, because 'what gets measured gets done'. A certain rate is acceptable to us. In Japan, he says, they are ashamed if they don't achieve zero faults.

The idea of 'zero defects' is hard to grasp. Dr John Constable, former director of the British Institute of Management, thinks it may be better to think of 'minimum time for reliability'. He points out that there is a difference between the reliability required of a jet engine and the reliability we need in a disposable cigarette lighter.

What is clear is that old standards won't do. We come back to the way competitors set standards. As customers, we now expect products to work and stay working. The quality is not that needed by the engineering department or the machine shop, both with all the tools and knowledge they need to tinker the product back to health, but by the customer who neither knows how machines work, nor cares.

'Quality,' said Sir Terence Beckett, who as head of design at Ford reverse engineered the Mini, 'means selling goods that don't come back to customers who do.' Relentless drive for quality shows up in the market. A major US car supplier surveyed 400,000 replies from readers of *Consumer Reports* magazine. Six per cent of US cars scored well – they had less than the average number of repairs. This compared with 50 per cent of cars made in Sweden and Germany and 89 per cent of cars made in Japan.

When US consultants J. D. Power & Associates surveyed new car buyers to find out which makes gave the least trouble, they found fifteen Japanese cars in the top twenty. Only two US cars were in the list. The research firm asked 30,000 new car buyers how many problems they had encountered in the first three months of ownership. General Motors and Ford owners reported 255 problems per 100 cars. Chrysler owners reported 315. Owners of Japanese cars reported 169 problems per 100 cars.

Ford are doing most to improve this, according to the *Wall Street Journal*. One sideline on this comes from a study they did. John Manoogian, executive director of product assurance at Ford, said studies show satisfied customers tell eight people about their cars. Dissatisfied customers complain to twenty-two people. In the UK Nissan now offer a 100,000-mile guarantee on all parts, making reliability a compelling reason for purchase.

Fashions in these techniques come in waves. A year or two ago, British managers took to quality circles. Half have now abandoned them. They are being premature. It takes up to five years for the benefits to flow. Sony claim their productivity has risen 30 per cent as a result of quality circles. So they sound worth persevering with. Robert Heller, who was US correspondent of the *Financial Times* and business editor of the *Observer* before becoming editor in chief of *Management Today*, believes the benefits of quality circles can be enormous:

> The return on investment is commonly five to eight times. The great discovery was that solutions to problems arise from the interactions of the group. The wonderful consequence is not simply cutting the reject rate but getting the best out of people because they want to give it.

Rank Xerox, hit sideways by Japanese competition in the copier business, has made quality the name of its game. By February 1988 all employees had undergone at least five and a half days' formal training and follow-up activity in total quality management. About fifty people have full-time quality management responsibilities. Standards are reviewed three times a year.

IBM in Havant in the UK won a British quality award in 1984. The citation referred to IBM's success in involving the whole workforce in quality improvements to products and services. According to the former assistant plant manager Peter Doran, what the company learned over four years was that 'the significant gains achieved in quality, cost, productivity, morale and influence were all there for the asking before 1981. The workforce – in common probably with the populations of most other organisations – was just waiting to be asked.' Why did IBM, an exemplary company, bother? A competitor, Brian Androlia, main board director of Apricot, the computer company, says: 'IBM as an organisation was always trying to do the best for its customers and hated losing them.'

One hard reason for battling always for higher quality, as IBM do, is that the expectations of customers are going up. As Dr Steve Smith of PA Consulting Group noted:

> In most cases where an established product has faded from the market it has not done so because it was a poor product, but because customers' expectations had been raised by a product that fulfilled their needs better.

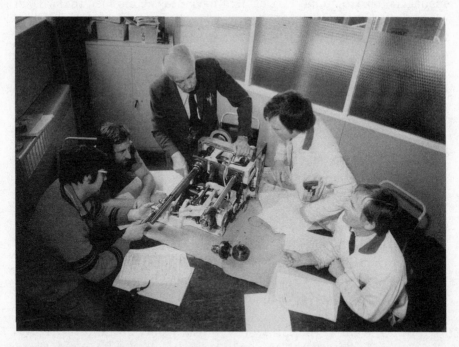

Immense concentration on quality is a major reason for Jaguar's turnaround. Here is one of their sixty quality circles at work. Other companies abandoned this technique too soon.

INVOLVE EVERYONE

Accepting the need for quality, some firms set up quality control departments. There's a danger in that, as Philip Crosby, author of *Quality is Free*,
points out: quality remains 'someone else's job'. It sounds a paradox, but
some companies have raised quality by reducing the number of quality
controllers. The idea is that every employee should care about the quality
of his or her work. This is what Black & Decker did. At first both quality
and productivity got worse. Gradually, however, the reject rate dropped
from 12 per cent to 5 per cent. Today's target is 0.5 per cent. Their quality
attitudes spread to their suppliers too. The essential point, perhaps, is to
stop people thinking defects or mistakes are acceptable.

Steve Smith manages total quality programmes at PA. He says, 'Around
80 per cent of quality programmes are attributable to management . . .
and all responsibility for improvement is theirs.' Exhorting people to 'get it
right first time', for example, won't get far if managers throughout the
business aren't involved to create the means for this to happen.

There are signs of change. In 1986 executives at Austin Rover each
spent a mandatory month on the shopfloor of their Cowley works chasing
faults. Working in teams of four, their task was to sort out faults there and
then, rather than rectify them later. They nicknamed the scheme
'national service'.

You come back to the determined drive we have seen for better productivity. The vice-president of the Electronic Association of Japan, Toshio
Takei, has warned, 'Higher productivity without better quality is no good.'

Given the chance, everyone in the business can contribute to quality or,
as we know, spoil it. The millions of hours invested in an airline can be
thrown away, as far as the passenger is concerned, by a rude hostess. The
same effect can come from a dirty train, or an unfinished car repair. An
unintelligible manual can kill sales of a wondrous computer. I know a
designer whose mother bought a new cooker but couldn't work out from
the manual how to cook a roast. These simple examples show that a company doesn't only have to be good at those aspects of a product the experts
think are important. To compete, a company has to be good all round, as
well as excelling in one thing. Jongi Noguchi, who runs the Quality Centre
of Japan, says that total quality control 'is based on 100 men making one
step, rather than one man making 100 steps'. It is a lot to do with corporate
culture, which we'll come to later.

There is no doubt that quality starts before a new product is even thought of. It is in the company air. People will tell you that in winning companies such as 3M, IBM, Westinghouse and Corning, quality has become part of everyday life. Because quality so often determines sales, it should figure largely all through a product development programme. Equally, much of the product development should be concerned with simplifying and simplifying again the manufacturing or assembly process. John Peake, former chairman of Baker Perkins, put it this way:

> The message is that just continuing to make improvements of 5 per cent or 2 per cent or just 1 per cent through the design process and through people in every facet of the business and its products by sheer hard graft and attention to detail and then going round the circuit again – and again – is a sound formula for success.

It cannot be said that all designers, whether industrial or engineering designers, have this point of view.

The goal for quality improvement Tom Peters recommends is a reduction by 90 per cent of faults in three years, with a 25 per cent reduction in the first twelve to eighteen months.

You have to have a passion for it to get anywhere. You need to persevere. Quality programmes run out of steam after a while. Initial incentives are less attractive, quality leaders get tired. The easy improvements have been made. So it is vital to fight through doldrums of this sort. It can be done. Toyota, even now, is said to be implementing 5,000 improvements a day.

It is important to measure the cost of defects, but improvements should also be measured and shown to everyone. That measurement must be done by the people involved, not by an audit team, or accountant or anyone imposed on the team.

Quality, says Peters, must be rewarded. At Ford between 40 per cent and 65 per cent of the bonus in 1986 was based on contributions to quality, 20 per cent of the bonus related to contribution to profit. For bosses who care only for the bottom line, isn't that something to think about?

Other points Peters makes are: no improvement is too small and everyone should learn about it. Finally, quality improvement is the primary source of cost reduction.

CUSTOMER PERCEPTION

There are two more points to emphasise. First, what matters most to the customer may seem trivial to the engineer or other specialist. Yet the customer is the person to satisfy. It follows, as we have said, that when designers, of any kind, think about a product they should start by knowing what is important to the customer.

Second, being good all around, marvellous as that might sound, may not be enough. Winning demands more. We have seen that a chief executive who invests in improving all functions may make operational

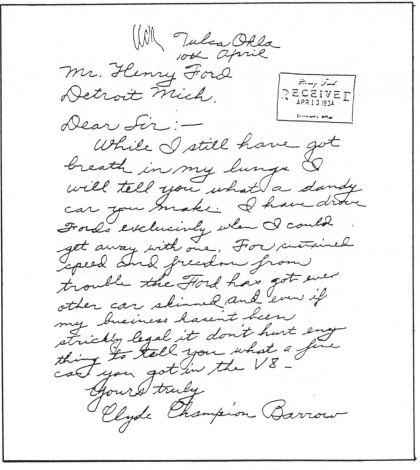

Testimonial from a bank robber

177

improvements, but still lose because the company's performance in a single key function is not as good as that of a competitor. Companies have to choose where to focus.

Certainly, you have to design for ease of manufacture. Certainly you have to look and look again for ways of improving the end quality. As we've seen, a company should buy quality if it wants to sell quality. Of course everyone should know what your policy is towards quality. No doubt many companies, like J. C. Bamford, have signs around the plant to remind everyone, but it goes further.

In the furniture industry, slow delivery times by British manufacturers are one reason for a rapid growth in imports. So quality of performance matters there. Delivery, in that case, becomes part of the essential design process of satisfying the customer. The company that delivers fastest gives itself a competitive edge. And note this: a consultant working for an admired British furniture firm, with a revenue of some £30 million, discovered that about £1 million worth of goods were returned each year because they'd been damaged in transit. The company hadn't realised, nor, it is said, has the industry pinpointed this costly absurdity. The moral is that we have to focus quality standards on customer needs, not on producer convenience. All so plain, yet we don't do it.

BENEFIT OR COST?

Companies that continue to believe that successful business comes from selling at the lowest price will find this talk of quality hard to take. The trouble is that improvement in quality can be a major investment. Edwin Whiting and Malcolm Walsh of the Financial Control Research Institute point out:

> In the short term any quality improvement will probably reduce productivity as more time on fostering quality is at the expense of production . . . In the long term reduction of internal failures should increase the volume of quality assured output.
>
> Standard costs based entirely on production can be the enemy of production volumes.

This implies, once more, that everyone in the business needs to care.

178

The financial people need to evolve systems to cope, and to convince accountants and bankers of the need for quality even at the expense of short-term profit. Quality, as the Ford example showed, saves money. Until that is believed and acted on, the 'cost of not doing it right', as US consultant John MacDonald of Crosby Associates has noted, 'is twenty-five cents on the dollar across the world'.

Anne Humberstone from the CBI went to Japan in the summer of 1984 with a mission to study quality. She found that quality did not increase costs: 'Defects cost money; somebody makes them that gets paid for it.' There must be an end, she said, to the 'spurious conflict' often perceived between costs and quality.

One approach is to work out the costs incurred by poor quality: rejects, reworking, repairs under warranty, and lost orders. According to Humberstone, Japanese industry pursues quality before price because it believes:

- Quality products will always sell because good quality serves the customer best

- Consistent quality actually leads to greater productivity, lower manufacturing costs and therefore competitive prices

- There is, in the end, no conflict between price and quality

This is paradoxical, maybe, but true. More important, it satisfies the customers. In the end that is the only security investors and banks and others who look for quick returns should worry about.

Who, in the company, is more competent or should be more concerned with the quality and reliability of the products it makes than engineers? Their role today is as sure as it should be safe.

SUMMARY

This chapter is written with respect for the great traditions of engineering, yet I am aware that, all too often, engineers have been pushed aside. Their central role has been challenged, if not diminished, not only by financial people but by those irritating *arrivistes* in the marketing department.

Whatever they teach in universities, the unparalleled value of engineers is not their knowledge of mathematics or physics, but their 'operacy', a word coined by Edward de Bono. By that he means 'skill at doing things, making things happen'. Engineers should be proud to be the practical people. With that pride, manufacturing would enjoy a far higher status in the West than it does today.

Four areas of product development, all of the greatest importance to competitiveness, fall within the natural competence and domain of engineers. One, of course, is to 'make things happen' – to stretch the imagination to its limits to create the practical and reliable goods we all want, as *part* of the product development team. Their permanent task is to narrow the gap, every day, between the wishes of customers and the realities of advanced manufacture. Two, engineers are better placed than anyone to 'design quality in, rather than wait to inspect faults out'. But they have to be careful that their idea of quality is the same as that of their customers. Striving for their own idea of excellence if it is not the same is certainly not the point. Three, quality should be everyone's concern, but it is evident that engineers have a more central role than most. Four, it seems to be a hallmark of winning companies that they co-operate with their suppliers in new ways, more on the Marks & Spencer model than on the old one of buying on price. Able to judge which suppliers to rely on, engineers could and should have a key role to play there.

There is a fifth role for engineers, of course. They, too, need to be out and about, finding out what their customers want, which problems are the right ones to address. They won't learn that in a drawing office.

10

What To Do About Technology

'If the truth be told, it is technology
that is creative, because it gives
us new opportunities.'
Ted Happold, consulting engineer

'Whoever is generating new technology will conquer the market-place.'
That is the view of Dr Bruce Merrifield, who is assistant secretary for
productivity, technology and innovation in the US Department of
Commerce. 'Technology,' he adds, 'is now the engine driving the world's
economy.' Where it was once important, it has now become 'essential' for
survival. In 1980 Japan's Ministry of International Trade and Industry
published this: 'The engine that will propel Japan in the 1980s will be
technological innovation.' One study cited shows that 15 per cent of
overall productivity growth in American and Japanese industry came
from changes in the use of labour; 25 per cent came from capital
investment. No less than 60 per cent came from technological change.
And that, as *The Economist* pointed out, was in conventional manufacturing only.

The continuous and driving pursuit of high technology seems vital to
our future. Indeed, Bruce Merrifield once remarked that 'a nation that
does not accord the utmost importance to R & D has made a decision not to
be in business in five to ten years'.

If that is so, put your hands up. The PA Consulting Group interviewed
100 chief executives from the top 1,000 manufacturing companies in
Britain. Their survey showed 'strong recognition' that 'the UK must
generate a continuing stream of new and improved products if it is to
maintain and improve the current competitive position'. But it also
showed that a low priority is being accorded to harnessing new technology and management techniques to product development. Only 4 per
cent of the top executives interviewed thought technology a part of
developing new products and processes. Incredibly, only 1 per cent
thought design had anything to do with it.

In the last five years, as testament to this perhaps, spending on R & D in Britain has gone up less than inflation.

When Gordon Edge was chief executive of PA Technology (now PA's technology laboratory) he put a slightly different slant on the matter: 'In the international markets of the late twentieth century the companies that win in the long term will be those able to use innovation effectively as an integral part of their business strategy.' Things are not as straight-forward as they seem. Richard Reeves at the Cranfield Institute of Technology has regretted that 'in Britain we perpetuate, without examination, the myth that scientific discoveries and inventions are the source of industrial wealth'. He means, does he not, that scientific discovery by itself is no guarantee. The essential task is to couple science, technology and the market-place. Innovation, rather than discovery, is the key to prosperity and that includes, as Dr Roy Rothwell has said, 'all the steps involved in the commercialisation of technological change'.

He hits the nail on the head. Years ago I used the word 'innovation'. A friend who was a scientist said, 'That's just a fancy Yankee word for invention'. It isn't. Invention is part of a process. Innovation is the *whole* process of moving new ideas or products or services successfully into the economy. Understanding the difference is central to knowing how to cope with technology and seeing the links with marketing, design and the rest.

The conventional idea has been to look to science for the breakthrough. As we've noted, R & D invents something, engineers design it, manufacturing makes it, sellers sell it. That view is less strongly held than it once was but, even so, it would be hard to find a self-respecting company without its R & D department. In the UK, tax policy encourages spending on it. But not all R & D departments are focused on the needs of the business. Scientific respectability requires that people in R & D write papers for learned journals, explore uncharted areas and, especially, remove themselves as far as possible from the tawdry world of selling goods. Overstated perhaps, but not without truth.

In Cambridge in 1932 John Cockcroft and E. T. S. Walton split the atom. Lord Rutherford, head of the Cavendish Laboratory, where that experiment and a stream of others of the first importance were conducted, went on record as forecasting that the discovery had little future. One contemporary remembers him saying that splitting the atom was 'a most elegant experiment. The elegance', he explained, 'is that it has no practical application whatever.' Does it linger still, this abstract view of the purity of science?

182

In the 1960s Lord (Wilfred) Brown deplored the private universities to be found in many companies. Of course, it is easy to jest; advanced science and advanced technology do shape our world. 'Industrial design has no meaning, no matter how attractive it is, unless it is backed up by technical excellence.' That is the opinion of Norio Ohga of Sony, a company that devotes 10 per cent of its revenue to R & D.

Each year the R & D department of Honda receives 5 per cent of the company's total earnings. They believe very strongly that R & D should not be organised in the same way or be put under the same pressures as the rest of the company. They have separated R & D from manufacturing and sales. Yet, R & D at Honda is no ivory tower. The department has four centres in Japan and others in America, Europe and Brazil. At each centre there is a group of experts who are split into project teams. They divide the work among themselves and each person has direct responsibility for part of it. They are encouraged to compete for ideas within a team and between teams. Work may be pure research to establish a new technology or prove a theory, or it may be product development based on something the

What was the elegant scientific experiment with, it was said, no practical application whatever?

marketing department wants. The R & D department in Germany, for example, helped find European preferences which, they say, are reflected in the styling of recent Honda cars. Even so, products are evaluated regularly by a discussion team made up of research, development, sales and marketing. Though separate, therefore, the goals of R & D at Honda are quite clear. As the company puts it, 'R & D has a fundamental aim to turn out products that win appreciation and give satisfaction to customers in every corner of the world.'

Riccardo Berla, chairman of Olivetti in the UK, among the most famous of design-led companies, remembers that when their technology fell behind, their sales fell. It was as direct as that.

A COSTLY CONFUSION

Science and technology are two different words. I am told that it is only in Britain that we muddle them. The confusion is costly, as people in research and development (two more words that shouldn't be joined as they are) strive to push boundaries of knowledge as far as scientists should.

I want to expand on this. First, however adventurous they are, most companies in the world cannot afford to keep up with the frontiers of science. A few giants can, and a handful of specialist companies do. But for the majority, most of the time, it is a game that they'd better be cautious about. Realise, as Lord Marshall said, that 'big science, like opera, is a cultural embellishment'. And like opera, I was going to quip, it is certainly better when paid for by someone else.

Already that causes anxiety. Vanity comes into it, too. Once I worked for a pharmaceutical company. Proudly, the president told me that he was investing $2 million a year in research. At the same time I was working for a German chemical group. Their investment in pharmaceutical research was two hundred times as great. Perhaps partly on my advice, the first company all but closed its R & D function. It put the savings into product development rather than invention, and has not looked back. That is not the way for everyone. Fisons has a world lead in the study of respiratory diseases, such as asthma. It depends heavily on R & D to find new compounds. It succeeds by keeping a very narrow and specific focus. You may be sure it is related to the needs of patients. Years ago the present chairman, John Kerridge, worked for Hotpoint, then an innovative marketing company. One day he was in the laboratory. He asked a scientist what he was working on. When he heard he said, 'How does that benefit the customer?', 'Well, er, not at all, but you see. . .' Kerridge stopped the project.

Norman Macrae, when deputy editor of *The Economist*, quoted one prosperous American management consultant who believes that 90 per cent of the work of research laboratories in large corporations is now wasted:

> The researchers are put in blinkers to try to discover something which they cannot discover. They may start to find some interesting things just outside the purview of the blinkers, but then are told that this does not fit into the corporation's strategy for product mix, or their most important work gets lost within the corporate bureaucracy.
>
> For a lot of innovative products the future will lie with enticing researchers from big labs out into setting up their own firms.

It would be foolish to generalise about how to handle research. What is right for one company may be wrong for another. The main point seems to be to stop funding R & D because you feel you have to. Know why you are doing it and what you expect. Get the scientists, not a whit less than anyone else, to realise that they are there to help the company to satisfy its customers.

There is another reason for looking with a jaundiced eye at pure science as the key to prosperity. Mostly, it doesn't work. Like all kinds of exploration of the unknown, there is more failure than success, but that is not the point. We know we must live with failure. No, so much science doesn't achieve practical results because it isn't truly set up to do so. Nor have the people doing it any great desire to meet your commercial goals rather than their own often academic ones. It is misleading, for all but a few companies, to look to scientific R & D to create new products. I have analysed all the nations that have won Nobel prizes for science, then looked at their gross domestic product. There is no correlation. One statistic makes that clear. Up to 1987, the United States had won 124 Nobel prizes for science. The United Kingdom had won 60. Japan, with a balance of payments surplus estimated by the OECD to be $85 billion in 1986, had won three.

Think of that on a per capita basis. If science was the same as innovation, the UK would be the wealthy country. Where this argument puts Trinity

College Cambridge, which has won twenty-six Nobel prizes (that's more than France), it is hard to say.

CAN WE WIN WITH TECHNOLOGY?

I then turned to a book by Masanori Moritani called *Japanese Technology – Getting the Best from the Least*. Many inventions on which Japanese technology is based do indeed, according to Moritani, come from the United States or Europe. 'Epochal' inventions, as he calls them, are not Japan's strong suit. (An OECD study in 1968 showed that Japan had contributed five of 139 significant technological innovations since the Second World War.) In 1976 a US study claimed that only 34 of 500 significant technological innovations introduced between 1953 and 1973 came from Japan.

A recent survey by the Japanese Ministry of International Trade and Industry (MITI) gave different figures but makes the same point. It claimed that of the significant inventions since the end of the Second World War, 6 per cent were Japanese, 14 per cent were French, 22 per cent came from the USA and an extraordinary 55 per cent came from the UK.

Admittedly, Masanori Moritani is worried. Japanese industry is not creative, he fears, in the sense of developing abstract original ideas. He admires Britain for this quality, where the cultural base is individualistic and quite different. For the next decade, he says, 'Japan has to learn how to let the creative spirit flourish within the co-operative team spirit.'

WHERE THE MONEY IS

Has the USA anything to worry about? With its massive spending on R & D, won't it continue to lead the world? Masanori Moritani thinks not. First, he distinguished between the sort of 'epochal' inventions that win Nobel prizes and steady technological improvement.

Second, he believes Japanese business has proved itself infinitely better at developing technology bit by bit but very rapidly (Figure 20). This, he says, is where the money is. Scientists in the United States invented the

Figure 20 How technology has driven diversification at Seiko Epson

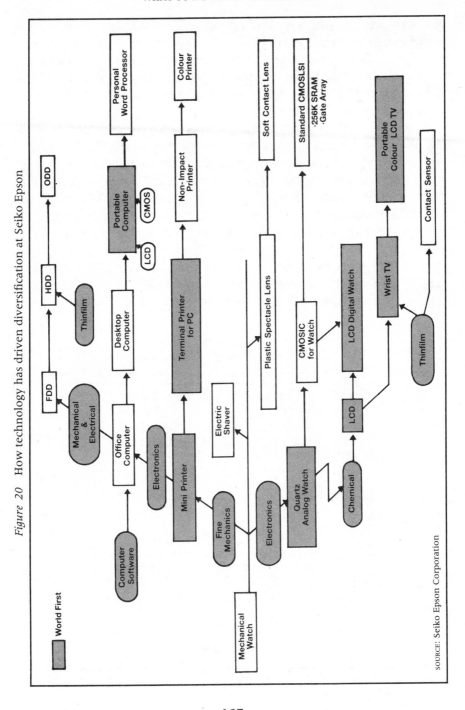

SOURCE: Seiko Epson Corporation

187

silicon chip, but Japanese technology pushed forward the large-scale integrated circuit (LSI) to the very large-scale integrated circuit (VLSI) with up to one million transistors on a 2-mm square wafer. Does this one success matter? Yes, he says, because microelectronics will affect everything and everybody. Not that this is Japan's only advance. Fibre optics, robots, carbon fibres are among others.

When you think that for years Japan was called the great copier, stealing other people's products to market them more cheaply, it is salutary to note that in 1986 alone there were 286 cases before the courts of foreign companies accused of imitating Japanese designs. There were 110 trademark cases of the same kind. Perhaps the ultimate accolade was when Currys, the retailing group, were fined in 1988 for misleading people to think that products made in the UK, Italy, Yugoslavia and Korea came from Japan. They used the brand name Matsui, with a rising sun symbol. Their slogan was 'Japanese technology made perfect'. It is wrong to simplify too much. Japanese industry is engaged in very long-term research. However, according to their own figures, they seem better so far

Figure 21   Where to look for profit-making products

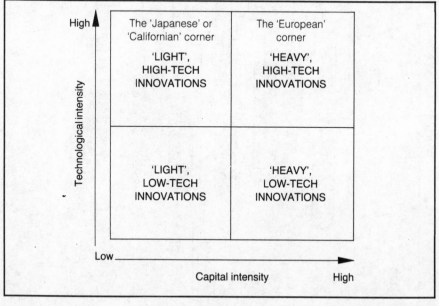

SOURCE: Arthur D. Little

at developing ideas rather than inventing them. A practical point for many companies is that research takes time, and few things take longer than to convert substantially new developments into profit. A study in 1979 by the University of Virginia Business School found that, on average, the cash flow of major corporate ventures did not become positive for twelve years. Average return on investment did not become positive for seven years. Some were quicker, others slower, but the average was more than twice as long as companies expected.

Arthur D. Little are among those who have tried to pin down the main point. They segmented innovations both by their type (process, financial, managerial, structural) and by their technological and capital intensity. According to Arthur D. Little, *innovation management itself may be the main managerial innovation for the late 1980s and beyond.* They drew a matrix (Figure 21). The vertical axis measured the technological intensity of an innovation – low at the bottom, high at the top. The horizontal axis measured money, the level of investment required. Then they divided the square into four boxes. In the top right-hand corner are 'high-tech' innovations that take a long time and cost a lot. Interestingly, they call this the 'European corner' because so many European firms are committed to this kind of innovation. The lower, right-hand quadrant covers capital intensive, but not very technological innovations. Many developments in hotels and retailing, for example, may fall here.

In the lower left-hand corner are the non-technological, not very expensive innovations. Arthur D. Little cite developments of the Club Méditerranée as an example. The top left-hand corner, that is to say, high-tech, low investment, short development cycles, is where many micro-electronic innovations occur. Arthur D. Little put the Sony Walkman here and many of Silicon Valley's electronic devices. They call it the 'Japanese' or 'Californian' corner.

Large corporations, they point out, may have projects in all four corners. Others concentrate on one area. It seems evident that major breakthroughs are more likely to occur on the right, and in the top right-hand quadrant above all. But that is also the most expensive, slowest corner.

It is important to say that not all innovation need aspire to that top-right corner. On the contrary, dynamic growth for most companies will come from 'incremental' improvements. Improving products little by little, all the time. Scientists may think that trivial, the workforce object to altering its settled ways for slight product changes. Production managers may throw up their hands in horror. Everything tells us, though, that this is the realistic route.

'BUBBLE UP'

Japan's Ministry of International Trade and Industry has, according to Arthur D. Little, formalised this. They talk about a 'U-turn' style of decision making; that is, deciding to invest in a long-haul, major development programme comes from the top. Sumitomo Electric invested for fifteen years to develop its optical fibres. Today it is among world leaders. But ideas can also flow the other way, from employees and managers at any level. Some call this the 'bubble-up' approach. It is 'crucial', say Arthur D. Little, 'in the generation of "light" innovations, which often have short cycles and can quickly enhance the competitiveness and success of a company'.

This analysis can be a comfort to the many business executives who would like to be innovative, but who fear they cannot afford it, or who know they cannot compete with the giants. This 'bubble-up' approach is much more appropriate for smaller and medium-sized firms. Still more encouraging, as we see in Chapter 12, small companies are often far better able to generate new ideas and new products than their larger rivals.

THE INNOVATION TRAJECTORY

Michael Posner, who taught economics at both Oxford and Cambridge Universities, a kind of academic gluttony, fears that catching up and overtaking established technological leaders can pose formidable problems for imitators and aspirants for leadership – because they are aiming at a moving target.

Another economist, Joseph Schumpeter, once observed that innovations, like troubles, don't come singly. They are 'more like a series of explosions than a gentle though incessant transformation'. Further, they are not distributed at random but tend to congregate in certain sectors (Figure 22). An innovation doesn't stand alone. It spawns others. Most product innovations lead to further process and product innovations, and

Figure 22   Growth potential for new technologies – a Japanese view

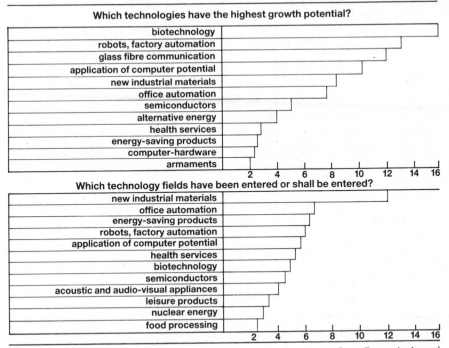

SOURCE: Japan Economics Journal

so it goes on. The expression 'natural trajectory' has been coined to explain the cumulative exploitation of new ideas. The disturbing fact is, if a country or industry misses out on the start of the trajectory, it can stay missed out. By contrast, countries or industries that are quick can benefit in many different sectors at the same time.

Some academics talk about a technology gap. They say, 'As long as the imitation lag is longer than the demand lag a technology trade gap can exist.' In other words, if you invent something you have an advantage. That lasts until someone copies it.

BACK TO CUSTOMERS

There is another comfort, though. Mitch Madique at Stanford University studied 158 high-tech companies in Silicon Valley. Some, of course, performed better than others. What distinguished the winners? According to Madique,

'If you're a technologist, it's easy to delude yourself into thinking that it's the gadgetry that makes the success. But looking back at the research, I now realise that the key was that the product added value to the customer. It is not technology that matters, but how you shape it for the customer.'

But we have to keep the perspective right. As Peter Lawrence, chairman of the Corporate Design Foundation of the US, says, 'While advanced technology makes new products possible, it is ease of understanding and use and attractiveness that makes them sell.' In another context, Sir Monty Finniston, one of Britain's furthest-thinking engineers, made exactly the same point as Madique when Britain's investment in technology was being criticised.

Robert Heller in *The Supermanagers* put it in a sentence: 'The game is played with high technology, but it is won ultimately by marketing.' He added:

The dialogue between the engineers and the marketer has to be continuous in a way that formal rigidities of the classic corporation notoriously discouraged . . . The informal, open structure of the West Coast company, which mimics and maybe derives from West Coast culture, isn't only the natural way to run companies in the information industry – it's the only way.

This puts technology in a context all can understand, and somehow makes it less frightening. If we are closer to our customers than our competitors are, it says, we have a chance. We are back to the multi-disciplinary design and development process. We are back to the need for a team to look at all of it together. If an R & D department works away, however conscientiously, without understanding customer need, and therefore how to adapt technology to it, it will not meet Mitch Madique's criterion.

It may all seem common sense but this co-operation doesn't always happen. In December 1986 *Business Week* reported: 'To bring technology to market faster, IBM scientists and product developers are working together *for the first time* [my emphasis] on projects as diverse as disk drives and silicon structures.'

DIRECTOR OF TECHNOLOGY

Broad as the word 'technology' is, from Star Wars to better toasters, no one should say, 'Well, I can't afford technology. I'll live without it.' Unfortunately some people do. It is hard to see how most will survive. For all of us, resist as we may, continuing investment in new technology is a certainty. As I've tried to say, it doesn't mean we have to invent it ourselves. But what every company (or very nearly every company) must have is someone on the board who understands the subject. What subject? Even that is too broad. The director probably needs to be a generalist. The reason is that if you make water pumps, it is not enough to have a director who knows all about the technology of controlling water. It is likely that advances that will alter the industry will come from outside it, no less than from within. When Charles McCaskie was technical director of Baker Perkins, his brief was summed up by the chairman in one word – innovation. In the same way every company needs a person, a director, with the technical knowledge and enthusiasm to look widely at what is happening and, perhaps with others, to translate their meaning into developments the company can use.

One way, according to Roy Rothwell, is to have what he calls a 'gate-keeper'. You find these often in the US, he says. Gate-keepers attend conferences, read, mix within a network of contacts. They bring technological information into the firm and then spread their news within the company. They can only be effective in a company that values information. But, when allowed to work on a project, the technical results are better.

TECHNOLOGY TRANSFER

Companies, as Sir Robert Telford told me, need more 'technology transfer'. John Bloxcidge described how Wilkinson Sword go about it. 'We have a small team, which we call the four horsemen. Their role is the management of technology transfer.' He gave examples. 'We learned about PTFE [polytetrafluoroethylene] coatings on razor blades from the aerospace industry. We revolutionised our match chemistry [they own Swan Vestas matches] with the help of Swiss textile research.'

Robert Worcester, president of MORI (Market & Opinion Research International) did a study for the PA Consulting Group in 1983. He found that 'three out of four firms have no clear strategy about how they should use R & D'. In 1984 PA Consulting Group published a study on attitudes to technology. It found that 19 per cent of chief executives in the UK thought technology had an impact on their business. In the United States the figure was 42 per cent, in West Germany 44 per cent. Yet over half the British executives thought their products more advanced technologically.

Yet again, sad to say, you see a difference between the average attitudes of British firms and those in Japan. The impact of technology is still not appreciated. In 1985 MORI asked how boards of companies become informed of the potential impact of technology on their company. More than one Japanese company in four gives this responsibility to a main board director. In the UK, no more than three companies in a hundred give this job to a director. You are supposed to 'learn from your own observations', according to a third of the British sample.

The study asked how high-tech research coming from universities has affected corporate strategy. Again, the picture is consistent. Over one-third of Japanese companies said it has led to their investing more in R & D; 28 per cent of top executives in the United States and 25 per cent in Germany said the same. In Britain the figure was 6 per cent.

Of Japanese executives 30 per cent said the effect of technology on their corporate strategy was to focus more on new products. In Britain half as many said that. Here, technology tends to be looked at for short-term, money-saving reasons, much more than anywhere else. British companies look to technology to 'speed production and reduce costs'. *Not one* of the Japanese said that. The vision this conjures up for the future of British competitiveness is not cheerful.

And yet here's a real irony. When the study asked top executives where their competitors in high technology would come from, over half the British sample said Japan. Indeed, the study concluded, 'Japan is taking a far more aggressive stance than its Western rivals in using technology to carry out more research and development and, at the same time, compete more effectively with other countries.'

No more than three British executives in 100 thought you needed new technology to exploit new markets. 'Companies in Britain and the United States have failed to recognise that true innovation lies in pushing back the frontiers to develop new technologies to enter totally new markets,' claims Peter Hyde of PA Consulting Group.

Doesn't it make you wonder? Of thirty-five companies interviewed in Japan, twenty-eight said they have a director responsible for advising the board of key technologies. Of thirty-four companies interviewed in Britain, three said the same.

Compare that general figure with the investment made by small and medium-sized firms in Europe that are acknowledged technological and market leaders in particular niches. The EEC invited Roy Rothwell and Mark Dodgson to study these leaders. They found common characteristics:

- They spent over 12 per cent of their turnover on R & D

- Over a quarter of their staff were technically qualified

- They had very strong links with outside scientific and technological bodies

- They were highly aware of their competitors' technological and market strengths and weaknesses

- They all put emphasis on attracting 'entrepreneurially-oriented' managers

- They were forward looking

- They were strongly market oriented

'One of the most notable features of these firms' said Rothwell, 'is their outward lookingness, their emphasis on forging strong external supplier, customer and infrastructural linkages and their willingness to assimilate external technology that affords them a distinct market advantage.'

MORE R & D

How much we should look to R & D for breakthroughs is hard to say. In the USA, if not in Britain, reliance on or hope in R & D seems to be increasing. *Business Week* magazine monitored a sample of 844 corporations. From 1979 to 1985 their spending on R & D increased by at least 10 per cent a year. Over 3 per cent of their revenue now goes on R & D.

Noting the benefits of 'little-by-little' improvement rather than 'epochal' inventions, the importance of advancing with technology as the handmaiden of industry remains supreme. For many, or even most, companies that cannot afford the fare, there is new hope. New doors are opening. None, however, will avail without a definite strategy for technology.

CLOSER TO UNIVERSITIES

One suggestion for the beginnings of a strategy is for companies to buy in the technology they are going to need, but to have someone on the board, a full- or part-time director, who is able to judge. Sir Robert Telford suggests companies should get closer to polytechnics and universities, using their research assistants.

Gordon Edge, when chief executive of PA Technology, selling £1 million of consultancy a week, met a young man called Clive Sinclair (now Sir Clive, all those calculators, computers and bikes later) who had been to financiers in the City of London with a good idea. Sinclair had been offered a loan of £15,000 for 30 per cent of the equity. Gordon Edge, appalled by this meanness and mistrust of invention in the City of London, tried to create a way to bring the scientists of Cambridge University and the business world closer. He founded a high-tech company called Cambridge Consultants. To his dismay he found the university didn't want to sell science, nor did industry want to buy it.

Although the position is better today, one consequence of this lack of closeness is that companies are missing a source of original ideas. In Britain nine companies in 100, according to an Arthur D. Little study in 1985, consider academic institutions as places from which to get ideas. Forty-five per cent of Japanese firms, by contrast, look to universities for ideas.

Increasingly, this is happening in the USA too (Figure 23). Bristol-Myers made a $3 million arrangement with Yale University. The combination of scientists has led, they say, to three promising drugs in four years. Now the company has built a $150 million laboratory close to Yale. Monsanto make multi-million dollar arrangements with colleges. A senior vice-president at Du Pont, Alexander McLachlan, is quoted as saying the universities are becoming important: 'You have to go there for technology.'

Control Data Corp. has R & D agreements with fifty schools. The reason given by company chairman Robert M. Price is that 'technology is so

Figure 23   US companies are turning to universities to add to their technology

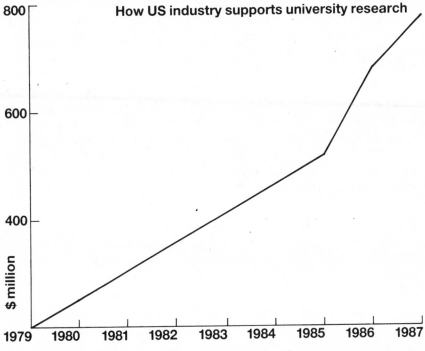

How US industry supports university research

SOURCE: National Science Foundation

complex and changing so rapidly that no one company can maintain all the necessary R & D resources.'

TWO-WAY TECHNOLOGY

There is a refinement in the way this co-operation is performed. When General Electric wanted to develop computer software quickly it set up 'skunkworks' on the campus of nearby Rensselaer Polytechnic. Putting industry close to academics is becoming a feature of British university life too. Between 1980 and 1986 the number of 'science parks' linked to universities grew from two to thirty.

The same is happening the other way. 'Ultra' is the name given by the University of Liverpool to its new technical research advisory service. The idea is to exploit the university's research for the benefit of industry – and

197

no doubt of the university. The government-funded British Technology Group is also giving an extra £15–20 million a year for the next five years to universities. Several universities in the UK have signed contracts that will give them money to conduct market research and identify technology worth developing.

The University of Liverpool's income from research now constitutes about 18 per cent of its total revenue. Salford University employs about fifty people carrying out research projects for industry. Although some bumper contracts pay the rent, the average is about £3,000. In other words, this puts top university research within the reach of small firms.

SHARE YOUR TECHNOLOGY

Another approach is to share technology with other companies. They could be, but need not be, in the same business. A part of technology transfer is to bring in developments from outside one's general circle. Results of sharing technology should be made available on a commercial basis.

In 1988 Roy Rothwell and Mark Beesley looked at 103 very successful technically innovative firms in Britain. Thirty-nine per cent of them contract out some of their R & D. Twenty-six per cent collaborate with other firms to share their technology. Over half (51 per cent) enjoy regular contact with public sector institutions which do R & D. The message is that sharing is better.

Acknowledging the need to fight foreign competition, even the powerful US antitrust law has been altered to allow rival firms to undertake joint R & D projects. There is a new National Cooperative Research Act. A number of US companies have set up 'R & D limited partnerships' with others in the same industry. The big three car makers, General Motors, Ford and Chrysler, want to pool their research into plastic-based composite materials. This could revolutionise car design in the next century.

Well over 200 such partnerships are said to be alive now. These 'strategic alliances', as they have been called, are interesting examples both of recognition of a problem and of a practical response. One Wall Street broking firm is raising $100 million to finance such co-operative ventures. Co-operation is becoming the name of the game in Japan too. In 1986 there were over 3,000 'strategic alliances'.

This interchange can work in other ways. Perkins Engines is offering its R & D arm, Perkins Technology, which claims to be one of the largest operations of its kind in the world, as an independent technology consultancy. Perkins Technology is aiming for a major share of the £400 million world market for diesel engine R & D, but it is also available to other firms. One outside job it has is for seat belts, another for breakfast cereal.

Agreeing to share technology seems an increasingly important step in another way. Sony was first to develop the video cassette recorder. Its system, Betamax, was thought superior to the VHS system used by Matsushita and its half-owned subsidiary, JVC. But Sony didn't share its invention. JVC did. As a result, over nine tenths of the 100 million video recorders sold have been VHS. Learning from this, when Sony developed its 'camcorder' video camera and recorder, it agreed an 8 mm standard with 127 other companies around the world. Although these are early days, Sony's production of camcorders has already climbed to 3.5 million.

Gordon Edge recommends that we take a leaf out of the Japanese book. They built their high technology by learning from other countries. Today the circle is complete. Edge says:

> No major [British] company can be really serious about technological innovation if it does not now have some links with Japan . . . it is an excellent window on the new technologies which will, in time, represent either threats or opportunities for existing industries.

BMW is an example. Since it set up a wholly owned subsidiary in Japan in 1980, it has not only seen its sales grow from 3,700 to 20,000 cars but also watched its competitors – Toyota, Nissan and Honda – move into the luxury market. There's another plus: BMW, being on the spot, has kept an eye on Japanese research in ceramic engines, new uses for electronics in cars and new materials.

In a recent survey carried out in Britain of 120 firms, only four or five were found to be monitoring Japanese technology with any professionalism. Nor is this myopia confined to Britain. In 1984 a sub-committee of the US House of Representatives said, 'US researchers may well be in for some surprises from Japanese researchers by virtue of the fact that they are not aware of the majority of research carried out in Japan.'

Two facts make this hard to understand. First, Japan now files almost as many patents as the US. Second, it publishes a lot in English. The Japan External Trade Organisation (JETRO), publishes mountains of statistics, forecasts and reviews. The *Japan Economic Journal*, published weekly in English, also gives insights into new technology. Companies, too, publish much of their information in English. So there's not much excuse for not knowing what is going on – and is going to happen.

BENEFIT FROM DEFENCE RESEARCH

Almost 30 per cent of Britain's total R & D budget goes on defence, far more than most countries. Although carbon fibre came from Farnborough's Royal Aircraft Establishment, as did aluminium alloys, little of the huge R & D defence spending has had much commercial spin-off. Now here is an encouraging and important development. In 1986 an imaginative scheme started to take effect. It came from an innovation seminar held by Margaret Thatcher at 10 Downing Street in 1982. The government has allowed Defence Technology Enterprises (DTE), a commercial firm, to ferret around the secretive defence research establishments. DTE publishes details of new developments in a bulletin and is already beginning to publish a technology catalogue. With hundreds of innovative ideas on file, it even lists ideas which, once thought bright, are now seen to have no advantage over commercial competitors. But DTE is more than a data bank. It works with scientists to advise them how to exploit technology commercially, as well as looking for commercial applications. The concept is off to a fast start. Already some thirty-five technology transfers have taken place. Forecast sales by firms that have taken them are put at £40 million. And this is just the beginning.

IMPORTANCE OF DESIGN

Because they work in a variety of industries, consultants – designers and others – can be a source of information about new technology. I remember seeing a consultant designer recommend three production processes and two new materials, all in use in other fields, to an international maker of 'white goods' (cookers, fridges, etc.), none of which the manufacturer had heard of.

What is important is not to be too dissuaded by people in the company

Technology from defence. British Aerospace's Experimental Aircraft Programme (EAP), built in cooperation with companies in West Germany and Italy is designed to demonstrate fighter technology. With every imaginable avionic advance, leading 'stealth' technology (a 'low radar signature', they term it), carbon fibre wings and fifteen flight control surfaces to give 'dazzling' manoeuvrability, the EAP is flown by computer, commanded by a pilot. Despite hiccups, it flew three years after the contract was signed.

who say that the plant cannot use the new technology. It may be true, it may not. Riccardo Berla described how Olivetti designers Ettore Sottsass and Mario Bellini 'get into the roots of technology'. They insist technologists should find new solutions, new materials. They are imaginative, so they can give engineers tips when they get stuck. Design is part of Olivetti's culture. If they were to justify the need for it they would point to the designer's ability to enhance the technical solution as well as to the unique identity they have created, and to the higher prices they can command.

Citizen is an example of a company that built a commanding share of world markets by constant technological innovation combined with

201

elegant design. First they offered a highly accurate quartz crystal watch. Count Sigvard Bernadotte, the Swedish designer, styled it. Then they offered the world's first solar-powered analogue watch. Then came the high-frequency quartz watches, with a maximum error of plus or minus three seconds a year.

Roy Rothwell and Paul Gardiner, too, see design as a practical answer. Technically backward firms can catch up, they have found. 'Through a vigorous design effort laggard companies can match their more progressive counterparts and even overtake them.' So there is hope and a route open to all of us.

The vital point, for companies that fear they will drop behind, is to uncouple the link between pure science and product development. For major corporations it may be right. For most companies in the world it is unhelpful. More basic is the pressing need to focus R & D effort on meeting the needs, real or forecast, of customers.

SUMMARY

A conventional and widely held view is that the path to prosperity is led by research and development. Foster R & D, the idea runs, and new products will follow. In the United Kingdom, at least, tax policies encourage that attitude. It is doubtless true for a few giants and highly specialised companies, but for most companies it is a risky route. The scientific tradition, so admired, is not for everyone. Science is not the same as technology, research is not the same as development.

It is necessary to be clear what the aim is before investing in any area of science or technology. There is a difference, too, between what have been called 'epochal' inventions, the ones that win Nobel prizes and alter directions, and more humdrum but also more fruitful bit-by-bit development.

Even so, few companies can escape the impact of technology or should want to. They have to learn how to cope with it within their resources. One practical idea is to buy in all they can. Another is to cuddle up to the universities. A third, and fundamental, idea is to have a director of technology able to understand not only what is going on in one's own industry, but in technology more widely.

11

Create the Climate for Success

'Economy does not need an actuary.
It needs a visionary.'
Anthony Jay, *Management and Machiavelli*

This chapter is the hardest to write and perhaps the most important in the book. It is concerned with corporate culture. And even uttering those words will switch some people off. Executives who think that business is mainly about money, which in turn is about buying cheap and quantity discounts or, even worse, cash flow forecasts and strictly financial control, will ridicule what comes next. I have seen it happen.

What happened was this. The National Economic Development Office commissioned James Fairhead to see if he could find out what it is that the winning companies in the world are doing right. How were they developing all these new products? His study, perhaps the most international to date, sought evidence from France, Italy, West Germany, Japan, The Netherlands, the UK and the USA. He presented his results to a NEDO committee in the spring of 1986. Members waited for a description of methods, organisation, lines of reporting and the like. Instead he talked about one element all the winning companies seemed to have in common: the same 'corporate culture'. Reaction was divided and strong.

When they heard corporate culture described, some people on the committee, chosen for their distinguished performance in managing design in large organisations, said, 'Of course. That's what we do.' Academics and business academics, if there is such a term, agreed too. But others present called it 'pie-in-the-sky', 'cuckooland', 'trivia' and a few ruder epithets that I forget. Perhaps, like Goering before them, it was the word 'culture' that made them reach for their gun, or maybe it was the vagueness that was so irritating.

As the chairman who commissioned the study I confess I, too, felt disappointment. It took me some months to see Fairhead's point. Every firm has a culture, whether helpful or not. I am now convinced that getting the culture right is central to success. Not peripheral, not an add-on extra, but central. Get the culture right and the rest follows. Get it wrong and decline cannot be far away. The subject has become as sharp as that.

'Corporate culture' really is a pompous phrase. In the end, the key to competitive success is the way the company sees its mission, the vision it shows, where it focuses and the way it treats its people. Those I take to be expressions of corporate culture. They can take some strange forms and don't always mix. When General Motors bought Electronic Data Systems (EDS) in 1984 they found a rule that employees mustn't wear tasselled shoes. Their handbook, according to one General Motors manager, reads like 'something out of a nineteenth-century Presbyterian hymn book'. General Motors themselves are trying to change a heavy, bureaucratic, slow empire into smaller, quicker, more responsive units. Managers carry 'culture cards' in their pockets, to remind them of their mission. Perhaps it is paying off. When Chevrolet marketers asked for specially equipped cars to combat imports in California engineers produced them in less than six months. Until recently, that would have taken three times as long. And maybe there's another sign: in the latest J. D. Powers & Associates quality or reliability tests, three General Motors cars are in the top ten. That speaks not of different equipment in the plants but of a different attitude.

When General Motors bought EDS their aim was not only to unify and update its data processing, telecommunications and factory automation, but also to acquire the company's 'legendary' entrepreneurial spirit. Roger Smith, chairman of General Motors, 'expected the company's aggressive, free-wheeling, can-do attitude to spread throughout GM's bureaucracy'.

Perhaps a clash was inevitable. EDS was founded by a remarkable individualist, Ross Perot. Son of a Texan cotton broker and horse trader, he started the company in 1962 with a capital of $1,000. Seven years later, by the time he was thirty-nine, he was a billionaire. Today one of the richest men in America, he has given away at least $100 million to worthwhile causes.

'Ross feels you don't manage people,' his sister Bette remarked, 'you lead them.' In 1969 he hired two Boeing 707s to carry Christmas gifts to American prisoners of war in North Vietnam. In 1978, when two of his managers had been imprisoned in Tehran during the revolution, he organised a commando team from among his own employees and hired a 'green beret' colonel to rescue them. Incredibly, they succeeded. Author Ken Follett turned this exploit into a book, *On Wings of Eagles*.

Of his management, *Time* magazine says, 'Perot fostered a spirit of no-frills egalitarianism that inspired high standards and fierce loyalty from his workers.' Executive parking spaces and other perks were banned. Perot and the managers are in the same cafeteria as everyone else. Chairman Perot himself described EDS as a place where 'people are treated as full partners. Positions and title aren't important to me, results are.'

Today it is easy to see how his derring-do style, effective as it is, could hardly fit into General Motors' orthodoxy. Speaking of the departmentalised, regimented company he had joined, Perot once said there was a need to 'nuke the GM system'. Another time he likened the problem to teaching an elephant to tap dance. According to *Business Week*, 'the can-do culture of EDS clashed sharply with GM's by-the-book philosophy'. After little more than two years, in December 1986, General Motors bought out Ross Perot. According to one analyst, 'They paid $750 million to have quiet board meetings but they haven't solved any of GM's problems.'

The salutary lesson is that it is not easy to blend opposing corporate cultures, necessary as it may be. Still, the question posed by another analyst is worth considering: 'If you remove the grain of sand, do you still get the pearl?'

When, in the late 1960s, Rene McPherson became president of Dana Corporation, the Toledo-based auto parts firm, he took over a top-heavy bureaucracy, suffering, so critics said, under its own weight. He got rid of 350 out of 500 staff jobs at headquarters and, a point I like, scrapped a 17-inch high pile of operating manuals. He replaced them with a single sheet of paper. McPherson made his managers spend their time with people, rather than send 'faceless memos'. He set up 'Dana University', an ambitious in-house training programme. He said, 'I spend a lot of time on the shop-floor because that is where the action is.' In his twelve years as top executive, Dana's revenues quintupled, to $2.8 billion. Earnings per share rose 15 per cent a year, every year.

Quoting yourself, George Bernard Shaw once said, adds spice to conversation. Not in that spirit, and in no state except humility, I am now going to talk about my own experience. The purpose is to show how a change of corporate culture affects the bottom line.

FIRST-HAND EXAMPLE

With a friend I started a design company in London in 1959, over a garage, in aptly named Adam and Eve Mews. I did and still do believe that you should hire talented people, love them and trust them, give them objectives and clear responsibility and let them get on with it. Most of the many mistakes the company made were mine, because we failed to do one of the above. Nevertheless, we had a marvellous team of very able, very committed colleagues.

Jump twenty-five years. After all kinds of false starts and failures by now the company was being called the largest design office in the world. It had gone public (the first of its kind to do so) and had swung, by acquisition and then organically, into market research and microelectronics. Robert Heller says we were the first design company to become multi-disciplinary. We were certainly first to see all Europe as our home market, with people fluent in all the main European tongues. Organic growth was 70 cent cent a year. With acquisitions, the company grew tenfold in four years.

We had some 600 people in London and Coventry, in New York and San Francisco, in Paris, Singapore and Tokyo. Holding sixteen operating companies together we had a small centre of five people, including two secretaries. Everything was devolved, except a handful of tasks. Vision about where we were going, communications and financial controls were the main ones.

I always said, 'Grow big by staying small.' Don't build mega-divisions. Let people run their own show, have their own identity, develop their own *esprit de corps*. Nor did I mind if they competed with each other, although there is a need to adjudicate sometimes.

Of course it is not easy to liberate companies this way. Achieving results by example and persuasion takes far more time and is far subtler than just telling people what to do. Before we knew of the term 'corporate culture' we none the less spent a lot of time trying to bring our ideas into the companies we bought, by example and persuasion, rarely by direction. There are lots of practical difficulties about this approach. If you give people responsibility for performance, how do you introduce things that they think are wrong? Some become despotic when they become bosses, for instance. How do you introduce a gentler style without demotivating them? Or, indeed, a more rigorous one?

One company in the group refused to discuss the performance of each of its departments at board meetings. The reason was that the head of one department, a founder partner, always lost money. The figures were known but not talked about. Public exposure (even only in the board room), it was thought, would humiliate her. I thought this discouraged those who did well. At the risk of hurting the senior person and after six months' persuasion, the figures were shown. Within one quarter the errant department was showing profits, and others, proud of their results, were doing better than ever.

WHEN TO BE 'LOOSE' OR 'TIGHT'?

Other managers may have no visual taste at all. How do you get them to choose top designers for their brochures and letterheads, rather than dreadful ones, especially if the dreadful ones cost less and they can't see the difference anyway? One approach is that of Olivetti. Every picture in its London office is approved in Ivrea Italy, before it goes on the walls. That is one way. I don't think it is mine. Tom Peters and Bob Waterman's 'loose/tight' control exactly describes the way we tried to manage what had become, in our field, quite a large and diversified group.

We also wanted companies to spend much more on training. We commonly found that leaders at any level slice their training budgets at the first sign of shortfall. How does a devolved company cope with that? Hire good people, trust them, love them – that was our attitude. Most of the time let them, indeed, make them, decide. That is hard too. Bosses think they're there to boss. People expect to be told. If you say, 'Well, this is what I would do, but you make up your own mind,' you find it takes time for people to see that that is not abrogating responsibility, but a way to develop confidence and pride. I always drew the organisation 'upside down' as some would say, as an inverse pyramid. The people serving clients every day were at the top. The board was at the bottom. The idea was to let everyone see that serving clients well is the essence of good business. The job of more senior people was to help people under them do that well. One way, perhaps the single most important, is to create a vision for the business everyone shares.

NEED FOR VISION

Vision consists, partly, in sensing the way society is evolving, looking out to see the way the world is going. It includes making connections others don't make and running with ideas because you know they'll be right at the right time, some years away. It means smelling burning before there is a fire, and caring about details that no one else notices. I used to think that was amateur management. I don't any more.

Vision also includes keeping finance in perspective. Accountants are there to serve the business. You are not there to serve them. Customers and quality and employees are more important. Caring, in my book, and as success story after success story shows, counts more than counting. Nor is that the paternalism of a small, private company. Listen to Richard Dupree, head of mighty Procter & Gamble:

> If you leave us our money, our buildings and our brands, but take away our people, the company will fail. But if you take away our money, our buildings and our brands, but leave us all our people we can rebuild the whole thing in a decade.

Or listen to Anita Roddick. Although The Body Shop has some 400 of its own people and some 2,700 in franchisees, she reckons to know most by name. She runs the company as a big family, friends say. She's a very caring person, always asking questions, offering praise. She insists on keeping her telephone line open.

> I have nightmares of memos in triplicate . . . You hear businessmen say, 'Our people are our greatest asset.' What a stupid remark. People are not merely an asset, they *are* the company. People rather than things will be the focus of business in the future; it will be individuals who herald change in the future.
>
> If we don't love our staff, our neighbours, the environment, we'll all be doomed.

And if clever businessmen reading this smile at the innocence of it all, let them go back to numbers, language they do understand. Every year Body Shop profits have more or less doubled.

For many years it was my job to sell. It is healthy for bosses to keep their hand in. For one thing, you bring in business. For another, people in the company see you do so. 'Nothing will endear you more to everyone here,' I once said to a managing director I recruited, 'than bringing in business.' (He didn't. He drew matrices. He left.) For another, selling keeps your mind out, where it should be, serving customers. No, that is not for some-one else to do, that is for everyone to do. Next, there is no better way of knowing what is going on, how the competition performs, the problems your own people have.

At a more august level, Remington's Victor Kiam says the same.

> I still visit stores. I still make calls on customers, still handle some of our accounts, which means literally going out with a sample case and making a sale . . . The closer you get to the ultimate consumer, the more you'll learn about your business.

One of the hard parts of devolving responsibility is to make sure people in different groups mix. In my experience, they get insular and protective quickly. How much of my time as chairman went on this I don't know, but it must have been a quarter or a third.

Knowing the ups and downs, I do not say we did everything well. Certainly not. But the long-term, general line of advance was right. One of the important achievements, if you are lucky, is that very able people work very hard, producing excellent results.

One rainy day I lent an umbrella to Beryl McAlhone, then editor of *Designer* magazine. It was her custom to go into her office on Sundays. Not thinking, she rang my office to say she was returning the umbrella. A designer answered. Later she realised it was Sunday. So she rang a number of other design offices to see who was in and who wasn't – then wrote a piece about it.

High motivation, high commitment, if guided, lead to high results. Steve Jobs, co-founder of Apple Computer, said just that about his staff. They all got stock options, but many halved their pay to join Apple. Why did they come? Jobs told a conference organised by the US Design Management Institute:

> They come for the opportunity to work their butts off and not see things get all screwed up before they get out the door. They come to do it right. They have a personal conviction about the way to do it and they've seen it screwed up and the way they know it should be done.

Four years ago (1985) Jobs was pushed out of Apple by the man he hired, John Sculley. With five 'disciples' he created a new company, NeXT. He put in $7 million of his own money and attracted Ross Perot to invest $20 million and join the board. Then he set about designing a new computer. When he hired people he wouldn't show it to them. Susan

'Whether or not it's a nice day, Mrs Delaney, is for the board to decide.'
Reproduced by permission of *Punch*

Barnes, his chief financial officer, said, 'We want people to join because of the quality of the people they'll work with, not because of the product.'

When it was launched in October 1988 to an audience of 3,000 executives, analysts, educators and journalists, that product, the one they *did* work on, was called 'the most exciting computer in years'. 'It's a neat, neat box,' said one analyst. 'Wow', 'cool', 'insanely great' were words others used. Whatever words Jobs uses, there is no doubt that he understands, encourages and benefits from a charged, creative, demanding climate.

NEED FOR CARE

However, there is a solemn rider to this. It takes a while to alter the long-settled ideas of how a business should be run. To shift it from a hierarchy to a truly devolved company needs patience and persistence. In days, by

210

deeds you don't think of, the open trust you work to create can evaporate.

'If you want to influence a whole organisation,' said Sir Christopher Hogg, chairman of Courtaulds, 'your actions (and those who are seen to be acting on your behalf) are more important than your words.' He added, 'If you want the company to do the right things, you'd better darned well do the right things in the centre.'

It is fantastic how quickly a corporate culture can deteriorate. Because my company was growing, I thought it was time to bring in someone able to manage the group 'properly', in place of my amateur ways. To replace myself I appointed an exemplary, business-school trained, big company chairman. The new man replaced a glass door to our little suite of rooms with a heavy wooden door. Within a week it was called 'the Kremlin'. Control of the group became centralised. Central overheads more than tripled. Some parts of the company, the original ones, kept their open culture intact and continued to grow. Others were 'co-ordinated'. (Having separate companies within one division competing with each other was thought to be untidy. They could save money by rationalising.) Key people, their autonomy lessened, left to start their own companies.

Profits slowed down, the share price more than halved. It wasn't long before the impact was felt on successful parts of the company. Their budgets were cut to meet shortfalls in other parts of the group. Top people from those successful companies left too. Thirty-three months after the new man took over the company was sold to a competitor for half its former value.

Of course there is luck in this, but also ample evidence to show that the 'culture' of a company affects its financial performance. No doubt about it.

Budgets, reports, memos, numbers, are all necessary in a big company. But, as you so often find, they can smother initiative and even divert good people from the right, simpler, goals. John Bittleston found that when he was head of planning at Rank Hovis McDougall, the big food group. They planned in millions, made deals to move thousands of 'cases' through supermarkets, worried about decimal points of market share. 'Somehow,' remembered John, 'the simple truths of running a business never came up.' To keep his feet on the ground – and while still in the company – he started his own little business. It was a DIY shop for wine buffs. In the evenings he'd talk to the manager. At weekends he'd serve behind the counter all day. Business, Bittleston believes, is about satisfying customers and you have to talk to them to know how to do that. In time he had nine shops. Now chairman of Cerebos Pacific in Singapore (a 70 per cent subsidiary of Rank Hovis McDougall), he has kept this touch. Profits have more than doubled since he's been there.

You may see and accept that you need to look after your people and have some sense of corporate culture in a small company, a private company, a service business, a 'consumer goods' business. But what about bigger, heavier industry? Turn to what is claimed to be the world's largest construction company. With a £5 billion a year revenue, Bouygues, in France, leads work on the French end of the channel tunnel and put up the astonishing 110m high Arche de la Defense in Paris, to dwarf the Arc de Triomphe and commemorate the Republic's bicentenary.

Francis Bouygues, the group's founder, puts his success down to the company's 'culture of action'. Management, he maintains, is 'nourished and enriched' by it. Claiming that he has been able to safeguard the spirit that enabled the firm to start, he says that the greatest force is to share the same convictions in all the companies of his, by now, diversified group.

'If we are leaders in a large number of our activities,' Bouygues said

In Versailles, sympathetic in plan to the great palace, is a new office complex for Bouygues, the world's largest construction company. It is called 'Challenger'. Francis Bouygues, the founder, urges everyone to accept this paradox: 'The way to stay leaders is to behave as a challenger.' The building underlines the company's attitude to its people.

recently, 'that is thanks to our imagination, our techniques and our concept of management.' He urges everyone to accept the paradox: the way to stay leader is to behave as a challenger. As in other winning companies, he is using his whole corporate environment to foster his 'culture'.

Challenger, indeed, is the name he has given the group's dazzling new head office in Versailles. There, 3,000 people, each linked by IBM's latest communication technology, work in an open, light, environment, a tangible demonstration of the company's attitude. 'A principal aim,' declared the architect Kevin Roche (an Irishman who studied at Illinois Institute of Technology and won the Pritzker prize), 'was to develop an atmosphere that stimulates employees and helps them interact.'

The same ideas flow from Jan Carlzon, president and CEO of the Scandinavian airline SAS, which recently opened a new head office on the outskirts of Stockholm. Designed by Norwegian architect Niels Torp, it comprises five small buildings about a central, glass-roofed 'main street'. 'A service company cannot be a hierarchy,' says Carlzon.

> Our people must have a great deal of liberty and a great deal of responsibility . . . for this to happen they need the right kind of environment. Good ideas are rarely created when you're sitting at your desk feeling alone and tense, but during creative encounters between human beings. The new office has been planned to foster that kind of communication.

Again, you see the same spirit in Honda. In their Tokyo office tower block the president sits in an open plan office and keeps the door open. Anyone can see the president whenever he wants, without an appointment. Tadashi Kume said he learnt the need for this when he was a young engineer. He had had a good idea and if he hadn't been able to convince the president of the day, it would have cost the company millions.

In short, Bouygues, Carlzon and Kume believe the environment in which people work can influence their behaviour, performance and loyalty. This is not to say, however, that if the building you are in is wrong, an open culture is impossible. When Ian Hay Davison, one-time chief executive of Lloyd's of London, became chairman of Crédit Lyonnais' British financial house (CL-Alexanders Laing and Cruikshank) he visited one dreadful building. People were squeezed in, conditions were poor. He asked to see how secretaries were recruited. There was nothing to see; the staff didn't leave. Somebody had created a spirit they liked.

213

The environment people work in has a profound effect on their performance.
This is the new SAS head office outside Stockholm. Five low office blocks are
clustered around one central covered main street. When you're there, you are in
the world of SAS. It feels good.

214

CREATE THE CLIMATE

A major aim of this book is to help companies create market-winning products, and to do it quickly. If you say all this talk of 'corporate culture' is OK, but it is not about developing products, still less is it to do with design, I reply that coincidence or not, all or most of the winning companies are moving in this direction. The true competitive edge is not design method, nor is it any of the conventional, numerate, controlled ways of managing. It is attitude.

Let me quote Christopher Lorenz, management editor of the *Financial Times*. Speaking at a design management conference in London in 1986, he was asked why more companies don't learn from 3M, whose product development methods are exemplary. Lorenz replied, 'Many try to copy 3M. They fail because they adopt the system, but not the culture.'

· Writing their paper 'Management Perspectives on Innovation' in 1985, Arthur D. Little were emphatic about this:

> It is important to point out that management's most critical role in maximising potential benefits during all . . . phases of the innovation process is to provide a climate that will promote and sustain innovative efforts. Creating a favourable climate is the most important single factor in encouraging innovation.

This sounds, and is, woolly. But that is the essential point. In *A Passion for Excellence* Tom Peters and Nancy Austin wrote: 'We advocate a change from tough-mindedness to "tenderness", from concern with hard data to a concern for the "soft stuff" – values, vision, integrity.'

One of the most important of tomorrow's management functions, according to Francis Kinsman, who advises on 'futures', is 'equated with sympathy and compassion and a deeper than usual knowledge of the self, particularly the emotional and intuitive aspects of the brain'. He believes that management faces the need to come to terms with a new set of human demands. Individualism rules. That applies to the company's staff no less than to its customers. Kinsman believes that 'tomorrow's successful organisation must balance the head, the heart and the will'.

It is common sense, isn't it? 'Techniques don't produce quality products,' say Tom Peters and Nancy Austin to all those managers worrying about advanced manufacturing technology and the latest esoteric management control mechanism. 'People do. People who care.' At Sony they

215

say, 'You have to know people before making any product.' Takio Fujisawa, Honda's partner who took the company from nothing to being the world's largest motorcycle manufacturer in twenty years, emphasises that 'people make the company, not its rules and organisation'. And that's not just words. 'The first object of our organisation,' he said, 'was to create conditions whereby everybody could spend his career in a situation he likes.'

Of all the audiences that a company has to be understood by, employees come first. As David Bernstein of The Creative Business says, 'Clarity begins at home.' Isn't it distressing that in a Korn/Ferry International study conducted in the United States and published in February 1986, only one director in 100 thought 'communications/public relations' one of the three most important issues?

INDIVIDUALS NOT 'WORKFORCE'

It is popular to believe that Japanese companies produce high-quality products because they have a docile, slavish workforce. But that is not fair. A three-year long study by the London School of Economics found that Japanese companies in the United Kingdom obtained output levels that were more than double the average for British manufacturing companies and 50 per cent higher than US-owned manufacturing companies in Britain. Reject rates were one quarter those of British companies. Within 18 months, indeed, they dropped to one eighth. The reason, according to the LSE, was to do not so much with inscrutable oriental ways, but with straightforward, if too little practised, ideas of motivating, supervising and rewarding people. A key feature, indeed, is an emphasis on each individual's achievement in improving his or her performance. Higher pay comes from higher individual quality performance. Because these standards constantly rise, the notion of 'acceptable quality levels' is obsolete.

Only four years after they came to Wales, Yuasa, the Japanese battery makers, had captured 60 per cent of the UK market – and won a Queen's Award for Exports. Kazuo (Ken) Murata is the managing director in the UK. Each week he delivers a talk to his 200 employees. His job, he believes, is to see that all his workers have genuine interest and satisfaction in their work. 'Everyone must enjoy their eight hours of work to enjoy life,' he says.

According to Buck Rodgers, former vice-president of marketing at IBM, IBM have three sacred cows: respect for individuals, the service provided, and the pursuit of excellence. Get those right, the message is, and the profits will follow.

DIRECTOR OF VISION

'Economy,' wrote Anthony Jay in *Management and Machiavelli*, 'does not need an actuary. It needs a visionary.' Vision, according to James Brian Quinn, is not fluff. It attracts top people.

One of the results of a brain-storming weekend led by Ron Baker at Ashridge Management College in 1986 for members of the NEDO design working party was the same. What a company needs, they concluded, was a 'director of vision' whatever he or she is called. One critic retorted, 'that is the same as planning. We've had that. It is discredited.' Weeks later, addressing the same group, Edward de Bono remarked, 'The most destructive words are "That's like . . . we do that already".'

A 'director of vision', the group reckoned, helps to shape the future. He or she prevents corporate myopia and adds a 'conceptual quality' to a board bothered about day-to-day worries. A 'director of vision' can provide an element of magic. Companies shouldn't be afraid of that. He or she helps the company to aim for products of the future, ones that meet future customer aspirations.

Importantly, a 'director of vision' strikes a balance between short-term and long-term profits. Such a person allows risks. He or she looks for new approaches to products and customers, and creates the environment. Further, such a person is necessary because directors have too little time to think. A trained, free mind on the board will help, members of the working party said. 'The director of vision shapes the way you want to be and how to get there.' He or she defines what you need to do, links unrelated things and is less concerned with the past. Such a person, they argued, makes the company look out, more widely, towards the future.

J. Quincy (Quince) Hunsicker runs McKinsey & Co.'s operations in Switzerland. He, too, emphasises the need for vision. He describes it as 'the ability of the top manager to construct and evaluate the implications for the enterprise of scenarios of the future'. Hunsicker lists these qualities for his 'top manager':

217

Sir Terence Conran, a 'director of vision' if ever there was one and innovator in every dimension of business, built a £1 billion business by attacking mediocrity with style.

- To see and understand the pattern of forces underlying superficially unrelated events and phenomena
- To know when to reassess or challenge assumptions that may have been part of the tradition of a company or industry for so long that they have been accepted as 'givens'

218

- To see the value – and limits – of insights derived from analogous situations in other fields

- To recognise and understand 'hybrid' behaviour and avoid falling prey to the tyranny of averages in observing and dealing with it. (To understand that, I looked up 'hybrid'. It means the offspring of two animals or plants of different species or varieties. It also means a thing composed of incongruous elements. And it means cross-bred, mongrel, if that helps.)

- To balance qualitative and quantitative judgements in reaching conclusions (e.g. analysis versus experience or intuition)

Is it expecting too much for one individual to possess all these qualities? With luck, the chairman or chief executive harbours them. If not, then someone should be brought in who does. In 1986 NEDO commissioned a study to see how some companies achieve sharp and sustained improvements in performance. They dubbed them 'sharp-benders'. In the companies they looked at the swift change often came from new people taking over. 'An important feature of the new management in the "sharp-benders" was that they tried to create a new set of values or vision, to drive the company forward.'

Field Marshal Montgomery had the tanks and the plan to win a great victory at Alamein. But he had a vision, too, and he took pains to make sure everyone knew it and shared it. Of the many thousands of men in the desert army in 1942, a commentator wrote, 'He lifted their hearts and hardened their wills,' essential prerequisites for the years of success that followed. But which is the right order? Don't you have to have the vision first and communicate it, then make the plan, then get the armour to carry it through?

Not only do many companies lack vision, demonstrably so, since they are battered by every wind that blows, but, according to research carried out by the Taylor Nelson Group in 1985, an astonishing 45 per cent of British manufacturing companies don't even have a plan when they start a product development project. When there is no common recognition within an organisation of the ideal goal and the obstacles to its attainment, managers' efforts are all aimed in different directions. Once a common recognition is achieved, all concerned can apply their energies to removing the obstacles to a solution.

219

In Search of Excellence makes the same point. 'The role of the chief executive is to manage the values in his organisation.' David Bernstein, of The Creative Business, puts the corporate philosophy first. He talks of the 'three Ps': a company's philosophy, its personality and its positioning. And again: James Brian Quinn, having studied many companies, listed keys to management success. First he put: 'Atmosphere/vision – and a feeling for people.'

Of course, it would be easy to acknowledge that chief executives set the tone. But they could still get it wrong by a mile. Indeed, many do. It is easy to spend entire board meetings talking about budgets, financial performance unit by unit, debts, cash-flow forecasts, rights issues, loans, acquisitions, without a thought for the products you make or customers you serve. Nor is it safe to suppose that people lower down will look after them. First, since the ability to compete determines whether you have any cash to worry about, it should take priority. 'Without customers in sufficient and steady numbers there is no business and no profit. That says where priorities lie,' says Theodore Levitt. Second, people lower down the company take the lead from you. They see where approbation lies. So they can spend their time fussing about budgets, too, when they should be worrying about customers and competitors and products and people and communications.

It really is like the story of the old shopkeeper on his deathbed. His family were gathered around him. In a coma, with only moments to go, he asked them one by one, if they were there. They all were. 'Then who is looking after the shop?' he asked.

You've seen the attitude: never a word of congratulation for something well done – unless it is a bottom-line figure. Well, that is establishing values, but wrong ones. I don't mean a company can be cavalier about money; of course not. I mean it is the wrong focus and the wrong style for a company that wants to do well today.

> I would not say a man in business needs to know nothing about finance, but he is better off knowing too little than too much, for if he becomes too expert . . . instead of being a businessman he will be a note juggler, trying to keep in the air a regular flock of bonds and notes.

That comes from *My Life and Work*, by Henry Ford, published in 1922. Ford's philosophy, which seemed to work, was that the prime aim of any business must always be to provide 'valued service to the community'. If

In Monty's day they didn't talk about MBWA (management by wandering around) but face-to-face contact was then, and remains today, a cornerstone of leadership, something Peters and Waterman found consistently in their study of excellent companies.

priority were given to merely financial objectives, he believed, industrial progress would inevitably be stifled.

Regrettably, that needs qualifying, too. You'll shine in the City of London or on Wall Street while your profits grow every six months. The snag is, by focusing exclusively on profits you are likely to become less competitive. It won't be long before the financiers look for and find another darling.

CARE FOR PEOPLE

So where should you focus? John Adair tells of the British managing director who expressed surprise to the chairman of Toyota at the amount of time he spent out of his office. The chairman replied, 'We do not make cars in my office.' Tom Peters and Bob Waterman call it 'management by wandering around' (MBWA). It is a good idea, but not new. An officer on Rommel's staff in the desert is quoted as saying, 'I wish he'd show a little cowardice and come back to headquarters once in a while.'

This is the way of leaders. Field Marshal Harding, one of the great post-war generals, said repeatedly that leaders must 'see and be seen'. The sentiment applies equally to business. Victor Kiam, too, believes in getting out of his office.

> I can walk into one of my factories today and there's some sort of sixth sense that tells me whether it's really humming; it's something that the most intense briefing from the factory manager over the phone can never tell me. You can sense if your employees are working to the best of their ability and enjoying what they're doing. You can never get that feel unless you visit a place personally.

As chairman and chief executive of Glaxo, the driving British phar-maceutical group, Sir Austin Bide confirms this. 'Successful innovation,' he remarked, 'depends principally on the leadership and inspiration of individuals.' Sitting in a remote top-floor office drawing matrices and tapping a calculator is not leadership.

One idea we had in my company was this: we said, 'We see people in the office every day for years, and love them all, but have no idea what happens to them away from here.' So we held a party called 'The other half'. People brought along things to show what they do in the 'other half' of their lives. One man had just written a book about a Victorian photo-grapher. A woman had sewn a stunning New England patchwork quilt. Another wrote poetry. One designer heaved in a great table he had made. Another took pictures of laid-up steam engines. It was such a success that people who had not taken part felt they had missed a treat.

We also had a 'chat-in', for everyone, every two weeks. Nothing formal happened. We just all drank wine and had a buffet lunch. If there was news to tell we told it. Occasionally one group would present its current work. But mostly we just mixed.

It is not a set piece event that counts, such as the annual staff party. No. It is how you care for people every day that matters. Steve Jobs, co-founder of Apple Computer, said,

> We don't manage the bottom line. We don't manage next quarter's finan-cial results. We don't manage the stock prices. We manage the top line. The

top line is people, environment and leadership. We think if we can get those things right at the top line, the bottom line will take care of itself.

Fanciful? Well, he was talking about a company that created 100 millionaires.

This focus on the environment was well expressed by Brian Key, chairman of the Business Design Group in London. While at the University of Chicago a professor asked the function of a hospital. 'To cure the sick?' proffered Key. 'No', replied the professor. 'Hospitals don't cure people, doctors do. The good hospital creates the environment in which the best doctors want to work.'

HELP THEM TO SHINE

'Managing change,' Sir Ralph Halpern says, 'is by far the most important skill anyone running a company can develop.'

In Washington, Dr Bruce Merrifield, responsible for productivity, technology and innovation in the US Department of Commerce, says that industrial management has become the management of change. Industrial competitiveness, in his opinion, means mastery of three ideas:

- The innovation process itself, both developing new products and realising the need to accelerate the process

- The lifelong, continuous reskilling of the workforce. 'Any set of skills can be obsolete in five to ten years, just as a product can be'

- The move to computer-integrated manufacturing. Manufacturing, he says, is about to undergo a revolution

But change is brought about by people in an environment that allows them to effect change. The single fact that impressed Tom Peters and Nancy Austin most when they were looking at winning companies was that chief executives in those companies believed in their people and backed up their beliefs in every way. They showed they cared. 'The good news,' they wrote, 'comes from treating people decently and asking them to shine and from producing things that work' (Figure 24). You can't have it simpler than that.

Figure 24   Companies that pay attention to their employees grow faster

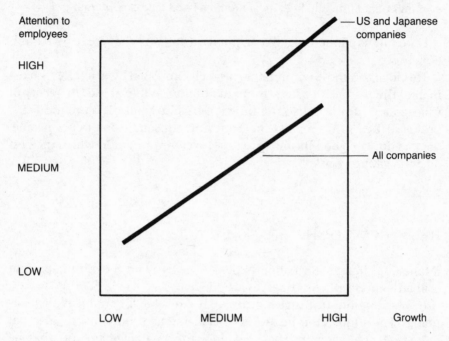

SOURCE: CBI's 'Managing for Success' sample

There are managers who'd agree, and say they care for their people, but don't succeed. Often the hierarchy gets in the way. More than once I have noticed that the most casual, friendly remark can be misunderstood and misinterpreted, only because someone more senior is saying it.

Apparent, if not actual, lack of concern manifests itself another way. Managers can't be everywhere. It is likely that things go on in their company that would make their toes curl. That is why it is essential to spread the values of the management throughout the organisation. Sir Peter Parker is the most caring of men and a fine communicator. When chairman of British Rail – and after he'd been there some years, that is the point – he inspected staff lavatories on a railway station. He was aghast at the primitive facilities. 'Do you expect them to pee in the Boer War?' he asked. His real concern for people hadn't spread through the organisation.

Even in a small firm that gap can exist. Executives in a New York design office were discouraged and unhappy because their salaries were seldom reveiwed. I mentioned this to the boss. He replied 'On the contrary, I take care to review every salary every six months.' He just didn't tell anyone. At the other extreme, Nippon K. K. Shipbuilders say, 'It is our strong belief that an active organisation can be realised only in a system which is based on the philosophy that all employees are equally important partners in successful management.'

Arch-entrepreneur Steve Jobs says it. Mighty shipbuilders who have seen off much of the shipbuilding industry in the world say it. So does Kenichi Ohmae: 'Put good people close to the action and respect their judgement.'

FLATTEN THE PYRAMID

It goes back, does it not, to the hierarchical pyramid. Jan Carlzon, chief executive of SAS, believes it is essential to flatten these organisational pyramids. While societies have changed, he says, companies have not. 'We take people from the new levelled society, and stick them in right at the bottom of the old pyramid company.'

How can people consider themselves 'equal partners' if they never see you or, when they do, you whisk yourself away in a reserved elevator to some carpeted sanctuary close to heaven? Sometimes the attitude can be like that encountered by the new boy in chapel at Eton College. He saw the headmaster walking up the aisle. 'Is that God?' he asked. 'No,' was the reply, 'but while you are here don't let the difference disturb you.' Are any company chairmen like that?

It is not just bosses who foster this hierarchy. Company bosses can get the impression that until it is smashed by showing they themselves don't care for it, the rest of the people in the company expect and respect a pecking order. This has a very practical impact when it comes to evaluating new design ideas. Hierarchical authority can be lethal. That is why Honda's managing director says, 'Ranks and orders of the enterprise should not be allowed to influence the evaluation of the new products.'

Over in California, Steve Jobs explained:

When you're small you're all in one room and I could say, 'God, I think that's a piece of XXXX,' and it's just the same as if somebody else said it. What we found as we started growing was all of a sudden I'd say, 'That's a piece of XXXX,' and they would go, 'Oh well', and throw it away. So we had

225

to instil in people that we operate in a dual mode as management, and they can't talk away the privilege of us being individual contributors or individual jerks either. Then we explicitly say, 'OK, I'm going to tell you what I think about this and I'm going to tell you from the position of being just another person.' In the end, Apple's philosophy is that we pay people a lot of money . . . and it is their job to tell us what to do, not the other way round.

A study comparing attitudes in Swedish, Japanese and British companies found that executives in Sweden and Japan seek respect based on the products they make. In the UK, it said, managers look to their status. This concern for status doesn't figure in many winning companies. Executive dining rooms are not found at Honda. The president, Tadashi Kume, shares his unpartitioned office with his chairman and thirty-one other senior executives. And that office is not at the top of their new tower, but in the middle, on the tenth floor.

In Fremont, California, General Motors formed a joint venture with Toyota called Nummi (New United Motor Manufacturing Inc.). The plant, run by the Japanese, produced 143,652 Chevrolet Novas and 43,726 high performance Tercels in 1987. Already more than 2,000 General Motors managers have studied new methods there. To their surprise, the Japanese have scrapped closed offices, abolished reserved parking spaces, even closed the executive cafeteria. All workers wear the same colour shirts and have four minutes of exercise to Japanese music before they start work.

You might think American workers wouldn't like that. But when General Motors ran the plant there were, according to *The Economist*, 5,000 labour agreements and absenteeism ran at 22 per cent. Today there are twenty labour agreements and absenteeism is 2.5 per cent. General Motors is spreading what it is learning to other plants. Internal audits say a number of General Motors plants have now caught up with Nummi quality levels.

Gordon Edge, when he was at PA Consulting Group, noted:

The primitive urge for a clearly labelled office and title, clearly delineated lines of responsibility, distinctive rules specifying each department's business and proscribing intrusion by others, are all parts of British management culture.

These traits are much less dominant in the more successful economies of the US, West Germany, Japan and Scandinavia.

In those countries it is common, Edge says, to see an interdisciplinary network in which marketing, product planning, finance and R & D 'create and implement strategy together'. He cites Hewlett Packard in the USA, Ericsson and Volvo in Sweden.

My own experience is that it is newly promoted people who cherish status the most. Indeed, one of the forces that drives them is differentiation from their fellows. Recognising this, perhaps a lesson is to provide this distinction in another way. In Minolta the spur is the chance to work on a multi-disciplinary project team. (As a measure of this approach, it is worth noting that the Minolta 7000 was voted outright winner of the Japan Camera Grand Prix and winner of the Innovator of the Year award by the UK magazine *Camera Weekly*).

The real divide seems to be between new industries and old ones. In the new industries, such as electronics, the post Big Bang financial world, design, or advertising, there is little hierarchy. Are they more open because they are growing rapidly and haven't time for anything except high performance? Or do they get high performers because they are open?

GIVE PEOPLE SPACE AND TRUST

John Opel, former chairman of IBM, believes centralisation is a frustrating form of management. 'You have to have people free to act, or they become dependent. They don't have to be told, they have to be allowed.'

Perhaps management style is partly a matter of generation, of age. In Korea, the founder and chairman of giant Hyundai, 70-year-old Chung Ju-Yung, works 100 hours a week and each morning, at 7 am, presides over a meeting of executives. He is said to be autocratic. According to Todd Kilburn, Seoul-based analyst working for stockbrokers James Capel & Co., Chung, wonderful as he is, is 'like a banyan tree under which nothing can grow'.

By contrast Kim Woo-Choong, twenty years his junior and founder of Daewoo, has a more open style. He relies on professional managers and task forces and rarely gets involved. According to *Business Week*, 'this allows the heads of companies within his group to try new products and take risks'. Kim Woo-Choong founded Daewoo in 1967 as a small textile trading house. Today it is one of the largest corporations in the world (revenue $5.6 billion) and Korea's biggest exporter. See where he puts his priorities:

The very future of the company depends on development and implemen-
tation of new products and production processes . . . technological developments and sophisticated quality control systems will enable the company to
increase its competitiveness in international markets . . . management will
reaffirm the value of people in the organisation.

Such a policy towards people is 'both moral and necessary', he says.

As I have said earlier, break the company into small, manageable units.
Give each a high degree of autonomy. Set the managers of each unit clear
goals or, better, let them set the goals within a broad framework you
approve. Get them out of their offices, among customers, into other
departments. Put teams together. Communicate a lot, across functions,
not just up and down. Pay people better. It is mad to lose good people for
marginal sums. Identify their needs. Relate their needs to those of the
company. Bend the organisation, I say, to suit the people, not the other
way round. Tell everyone the company goals, and encourage all to use
their initiative to help the company to achieve its goals. Notice good work.
Praise it. Praise a lot . . . not just the managers, but the switchboard opera-
tors, who can lose customers if they are lazy, and the cleaning people.
Strive to get everyone to put the customer first. Let them see how the
company's product serves the customer. Do that well and they will suggest improvements. Create a good environment for people to work in.
Recognise achievement, knowing that not everyone seeks the same kind
of recognition. Invest in your people and give everyone something to aim
for.

John McDonald at Stanford University has studied Honda. 'More
important than any numbers,' he says, 'is the spirit of Honda. There are a
lot of smart people there, a *joie de vivre*, a sense of humour, and a lot of
young guys with more responsibility than they would have at other
Japanese firms.'

Attractive as it sounds, is this just another way of working or does it produce better results? Honda's sales have tripled in a decade. Already the
world's largest maker of motorcycles and scooters, Honda have leap-
frogged five Japanese car makers and now stand behind Toyota and
Nissan. They are now America's no. 1 foreign car manufacturer.
Observers give these reasons for Honda's success: imaginative management, a highly motivated workforce and 'an almost obsessive attention to
detail'.

That formula has served them well. From fitting surplus army engines

228

on to bicycles after the war, Soichira Honda has built a truly global company, with fifty-eight assembly plants in thirty-two countries. Honda was born the son of a blacksmith. He left school at sixteen, started his own garage when he was twenty-five and started to make piston rings when he was thirty. Now retired, his legend lives on. (Of many stories about him, this is one the company maintains is true: once he had an argument with a tax office that couldn't be resolved. He hired a fire engine. When tax workers left their office to go home he drenched them with a fire hose. The company doesn't say whether this tactic settled his problem.)

Conventional business thinking in both the United States and the United Kingdom is being soundly challenged. Managers educated to act on cool analysis and with numerate rigour are bewildered that these skills no longer seem enough. The hardest message to convey to professional and experienced managers is the rising importance of 'soft' values. Some owners and managers know it instinctively. Others do not. Dynamic product design and development, the effective instruments of competition, are far more likely to come from companies that embrace these new imperatives than from those that go on in the old way.

Let's take a case: Amstrad. Going through hard days now, it nevertheless has lessons for us all. Japanese analysts Nikkei put Amstrad seventeenth in a world-wide review of nearly 3,000 companies. In 1980 its sales were £9 million. By mid 1988 they had risen to £625 million. Profits in that time climbed from £1.2 million to £165 million. Unlike Goldsmith, de Benedetti, Maxwell, Bond and other masters of great companies, Alan Sugar, the founder, who still owns 4 per cent of Amstrad, has not looked to acquisitions for growth.

For years city analysts and technical journalists have been bemused by this seven-day wonder, who doubled his profit every year. Perhaps because they have not understood the unconventional, unhierarchical, even untechnical qualities that make him a winner, they have been unfair. It is true to say that Amstrad's profits fell at the end of 1988 and may stay down for a while. A compendium of reasons are given by analysts. Critics are quick to say that Alan Sugar may no longer appear the wizard he was. We'll see. Incontrovertibly, he took on the Japanese and beat them at their own game. There is much to learn from him. Have faith, I say.

At sixteen, Alan Sugar was selling antennae for car radios from the back of a van in the East End of London. He started Amstrad (the name is culled from Alan Michael Sugar Trading) when he was twenty-one. That was in

1968. Twelve years later he went public. His revenue then was £8.8 million, generated mainly from audio products mostly made in the Far East.

And now this explosive growth – into CDs, hi-fi, word processors, computers, satellite dishes and many more products than people think. How has he done it?

First, Alan Sugar has a clear and sustained *vision*. He popularises high-quality products and sells them in volume. To him, that means a minimum of 200,000 pieces in two years. As *Fortune* magazine said, he is a true pioneer at 'delivering established technology at prices so low that speciality markets are transformed into mass markets'. His hi-fi tower system, launched in 1980, was an example. Buying in the quality of good

Turning high technology into products bought by 'lorry drivers and their wives', Alan Sugar has built one of the fastest-growing firms in the world. He leads the business computer market in the UK and now sells small dishes for satellite TV. Sugar is said to have an uncanny sense of what customers want and the ability to move and switch direction with amazing speed.

Japanese systems, he aimed his product not at 'audiophiles' but at 'lorry drivers and their wives'. His first word processor (1985) was another example of his approach. At that time the British market was taking 60,000 word processors a year. By slicing the price to less than that of a good typewriter (to half or even a third of competitors' prices), he sold 350,000 in eight months. A year later he introduced his first business computer. Three months later he had UK leadership. Now Amstrad expects to sell a million small (24-inch) dishes to receive satellite TV.

Second, Alan Sugar is always *close to the customer*. He is said to have 'an uncanny ability' to know what they want. And he provides it. He is no technical purist who always wants the latest thing. Often experts build in power and features most people don't understand or need or want. Unlike so many in the electronics industry, Sugar is not bewitched by technology. He can use yesterday's technology if, by being more reliable or cheaper, it gives him a competitive edge. 'Eight-bit, sixteen-bit, one-bit,' says Alan Sugar, 'who cares as long as it works?'

Third, he's *fast*. Observers are staggered by how quickly he can switch direction. In 1984 he guessed audio sales would drop. He switched emphasis to personal computers. Audio sales fell 45 per cent. His PCs shot, that year, from £3 million to £90 million. *Financial Weekly* described Amstrad's 'blinding speed in response to signals transmitted from the market . . . an extraordinarily fast reaction time, probably the fastest of any company active today in the consumer electronics and office equipment markets'. This speed is part of the Amstrad culture. They're organised for it. Malcolm Miller, Amstrad's sales and marketing director said, 'We get on with things. If you have a good idea, every day you waste talking about it is a day's lost profit.'

When Ken Ashcroft became finance director he said, 'It was a revelation to me to see the simplicity of decision-making.' That can happen partly because, like so many winning companies, Amstrad has a *lean staff*. Sugar's ship is so tight that the added value he gets from every pound of employee pay is over three times better than the next best in Britain. He pays well, but drives hard. In 1987 with 1,009 employees, Amstrad's market value per employee, according to Extel and Datastream, was over £1 million. Next highest was Saatchi & Saatchi, at £87,000. After Amstrad, the most efficient manufacturing company (and Amstrad is a manufacturer) was Vickers, at less than £36,000.

Until recently, Alan Sugar shared a noisy room, overlooking railway tracks, with his team of four key people: design, marketing, engineering and finance. His 'corporate culture' wouldn't suit everyone. It used to be called 'Oi, you'. But everyone in Amstrad seems inspired by the same urgency, for speed, sales, profits. It is a high-energy culture.

Alan Sugar once said his education began in Japan, where he learned about the need for a Company culture, for everyone in a firm to share the same aims. Two other lessons were a passionate concern for the details of quality, and the need to blast your way into a market with all the guns you've got. Amstrad spend over £20 million a year on advertising in the UK alone, which makes them one of the two or three largest advertisers. While Sugar is not such an inventor with products, preferring to let others point the way, he certainly creates markets, one after another.

Saying that, it is Amstrad's persistent and insistent *drive for new products* that keeps them ahead. I've been looking at the record. Every few months for the last eight or ten years they have come out with an important new product – not a line extension, but something new. Today they probably have twenty products in development. Amstrad use outside firms for product development, but ideas and strategies come from Amstrad. Sugar is central to this. With his remarkable feel for what his customers want (people between seventeen and thirty-five in the BC1C2D socio-economic groups), he thinks of something. He looks at the competition to see whether, by taking out useless features, it can be sold for under £300 and make a profit. If the engineers say yes, Sugar mostly goes ahead.

This is not to say he trims quality. No, he would not build huge markets that way. One reason Amstrad can so under-price competitors is that they have little overheads. They buy or make where it suits the product best, sometimes in Hong Kong or Japan, sometimes in the UK, Spain or else-where. Sugar is unrelenting about staying *flexible*, without great plants that must be kept busy. And he cuts things off at high speed if they don't do well. Amstrad pulled out of clock radios. They withdrew from the CB radio market when laws changed, before most others (and were almost the only firm to leave with a profit). They stopped selling small TV sets.

Still the drive for new products goes on: portable computers, business computers, PCs, camcorders, single unit TV and VCRs, satellite dishes and more to come (Sugar promises white goods one day). In 1988 Amstrad signed an agreement with IBM, giving them world-wide access to all IBM patents.

And look at how Alan Sugar faces adversity. In 1989 Amstrad's profits nose-dived. Characteristically, Sugar described the reasons with candour: 'From an engineering point of view,' he said, 'we had too small a team to take on too big a task, and we are now paying the penalties not only in terms of our ability to design new products but to maintain our existing ranges.' While Sugar admits that he failed to keep a tight grip on the financial reins – and will strengthen it – and sees other faults as a consequence of the company's rapid growth, it is revealing to look at where he places his emphasis: 'We must strengthen ourselves in engineering and design,' he said. 'A top priority must be continuing to design a stream of products and bringing them swiftly to market. . . We can't take two years to design products. It must continue to be other companies copying us two years later.' To satisfy the financial world, many companies would have withdrawn into their financial shell. Not Amstrad.

Amstrad's story, so consistently fooling the experts that Sugar has no time for them, is remarkable. But the principles are easy to state. Jump to chapter 14 and you will see they turn up time after time in the companies that win.

ARE THESE VALUES RIGHT FOR YOU?

There is one attitude even harder to crack. A young British designer designed a new kind of radiator. It was so good it was pictured in many magazines in various countries. As a result, he received many letters from people who wanted to buy it. He took it to a number of suitable British manufacturers. Every one said, 'Very good indeed. But, of course, not quite right for us.'

I tell that story to pick up on that last phrase. Nothing in this book is new. I am describing what winning companies are doing now. But very many companies, the majority, do not have these attitudes. Why not? Some will think the ideas wrong, notwithstanding the evidence. Others will say, as they said to the designer, 'Very good. But, of course, not quite right for us.' That remark could be the biggest single obstacle to progress.

There is a more subtle point. Companies, like individuals, that do well are not necessarily acting differently. It is just that they do each important thing with far more intensity. The worst companies would believe they care about their customers, for instance, or pin faith in their people. But the way they do either would bear little relation to the way successful companies dedicate their minds and resources to the same ideas. Others, I've found, will take an idea, but only do the easy bits of it. Well, maybe that is better than nothing. There is an argument that runs, 'Here are ten things to do. If you do two of them that'll be good. If you do four, that is better still. If you tackle six you are on the path to virtue. If you do all ten you are wonderful.' Starting somewhere is better than nowhere.

In the experience of Uwe Bahnsen, former design director of Ford Europe, it is a mistake to try to change people too quickly. That sounds right, as long as you see the whole vision and resolve to follow it through. The difficulty in large organisations mustn't be underestimated. At Courtaulds, Sir Christopher Hogg has his own coherent vision, but he is allowing four or five years to get it across. At General Motors, they say the new message may have reached two or three levels. But there are still seven or eight to go.

Ford, General Motors (still making 18 per cent of the world's cars) and Courtaulds are all major players, set for the next century. But financially driven executives will still find their concern for a new corporate culture airy-fairy – as though caring for people is a mark of weakness.

For every reason, not least because the climate in which industry operates is changing, the rational, cold, numerate view will be found insufficient. Look at one winner after another and, invariably, you'll find a strong ethos. Something in the air is different at IBM, Honda, The Body Shop, Amstrad, 3M or Sony. They get the money right, but they know the way to do that is to focus on the three fundamentals: their people, their products, their customers. Time and again that triad turns up.

What can happen is that some upheaval forces companies to change their culture. But to achieve a lasting effect takes time. Buying a package of two-day programmes for staff, helpful as that may be, is not enough. In the words of Don Beattie, head of personnel at STC, ICL (Standard Telegraph and Cables, International Computers Ltd), 'It requires consistent signals by top management over an extended timescale.' The reason for embarking on this journey is that, increasingly, the way things are done now will block progress in inevitable new directions. It is hard to see the point of writing plans without encouraging the culture to achieve them.

Changing the direction of a large company is far slower than altering the course of a supertanker, which you almost have to turn to port the day before you need to. Here, then, could be another area in which smaller companies have the advantage.

There is one thing worse than the 'very good, but not quite right for us' attitude – and that is, as Edward de Bono said, the person who hears an idea, then says, 'Ah. Ah. That is like . . . yes, we do that already.' Have you thought that already while reading this book? You may be right. But most companies everywhere are *not* already doing what the winners are, even if they think they are.

Companies that create the endless stream of new products sweeping our shelves, plants and roads have a vision of the future. They focus relentlessly on the customer. They keep the search for new products at the top of their action list all the time. They care for their people and create an open, invigorating atmosphere in which ideas can flourish. They put design, a word combining lots of skills, at the pulsing heart of the business. They aim for market share, not short-term profit. They base their fortunes on speed of innovation, on quality, reliability and service. Not low price. All that adds up to the corporate culture that wins.

SUMMARY

The hardest task for managers who believe they should be 'hard-nosed' is to embrace 'soft' values. James Fairhead was asked if winning companies around the world had anything in common. 'Their corporate culture,' he replied. In his view, nothing so distinguished the excellent from the average or poor performers as this, especially in their attitudes towards people.

At the time, his audience was disappointed. Corporate culture may be interesting, they said, but it is nothing to do with either design or new product development. Not so. First, coincidentally or not, the driving companies share the same values. Second, as Christopher Lorenz has remarked, many corporations have tried to imitate the successful innovators, but few produce the same flow of good products. The reason, Lorenz claims, is that they copy the system but can't acquire the culture. Systems and methodologies don't create new products; people do, people who are given the space to fulfil themselves.

To triumph, people need a vision as well as a plan. The sadly misunderstood and maligned notion of *leadership* comes back to prominence. Companies, all the evidence tells us, need a 'director of vision' whose vision and values must be broadcast and shared. Typical of winning companies are excellent, open communications. When it comes to communications, 'clarity', as David Bernstein pointed out, 'begins at home'.

These notions, of 'soft' values, shared values, genuine faith in the people in the business, may strike the numerate, analytical, planning manager as woolly, if not wet. Their vagueness makes them hard to create and manage. But they do seem to be an integral part of winning in the modern world.

12

Can Smaller Companies Compete?

'When it comes to innovation, small . . . is
more beautiful than even we had ever imagined.'
Tom Peters and Nancy Austin,
in *A Passion for Excellence*

The greatest worry is this: the world seems so dominated by giant corporations that you wonder whether smaller companies have a chance. This matters both because most companies are small or medium-sized and because they are the ones that create jobs. So let's talk about them.

James Brian Quinn, Buchanan professor of management at the Amos Tuck School of Business Administration, Dartmouth College in New Hampshire, is encouraging on this point. Rather than feel disadvantaged, he believes that smaller companies have many of the qualities larger companies should copy. Indeed, some do. He has reviewed many innovations, often from individuals or small companies. Here are some of the reasons why small firms can win.

Quinn thinks large companies have the odds stacked against them. First, the boards of large companies are *removed from market needs*. They can't keep up with all their products and all their markets, he argues, so any change is perceived as a risk. It is safer, the boss thinks, to acquire a company already in the field, or with the product range the company wants.

Second, large companies *can't cope with fanatics*. Suppose, through some mutual mistake, the fanatic joins in the first place. Conflict with the system means that soon he or she will leave or stop being fanatical.

There is a timescale conflict, too. That is Quinn's third point. With their eyes on the next published report, companies find it *hard to invest in long-term projects* that may take seven to ten years to bring in profits.

Fourth, large companies *spend too much too soon*. Quinn has noted how a product development project joins the system like anything else. It gets an account number in the financial department and is expected to carry its share of costs, indirect as well as direct. I have made this mistake: expecting new ventures to carry their share of the overheads. Equally bad and, in my experience, as common, is the opposite. I've often invested too little. You don't get able enough people. They haven't space to turn. They become neutered by the short-term return expected from them.

The next familiar fault, according to Quinn, is that managers in large companies *approve plans, not products*. These companies don't reward risk. 'How many people have been made millionaires by large companies?' he asks. The trouble is, rewarding innovators upsets the pay structure. He asks: 'Do you want innovation or organisational stability?'

DO YOU WANT 'NO SURPRISES'?

Control systems in large companies discriminate against innovation, Quinn believes. In the famous remark of Harold Geneen, former chairman of ITT, large companies want 'no surprises'. Innovation is full of surprise, both ways. Quinn fears that since most new ideas don't work, the bosses are better off saying 'no' to everything. If they say 'no' to everything they will be 95 per cent right, Quinn estimated.

All this is gloomy, but the fact is that large companies have got to innovate to compete. It gets worse. Large companies are large because they have been successful with what they've got, including their existing technology. This puts them, often, in the position of defending their existing investment. Large companies, Quinn says, don't understand risk perception, the 'nose' that people closer to the market can develop. They think new developments are higher risks than they are.

In short, Quinn points out, innovation and change are harder for larger companies. It is harder to change the culture, harder to change the technology and harder to change any plant. Then they may face organised opposition, from unions who fear redundancy, for instance, and even from central government. Large companies have psychological pains of change, which may include the pressure of sacking people, seeing local communities suffer, losing faithful suppliers.

For all these reasons it is no surprise to learn that every highly innovative group in Quinn's sample emulated the small company.

WHAT'S GOOD ABOUT BEING SMALL?

According to James Brian Quinn, smaller companies are 'need-oriented'. They've just got to come up with something that works. They often have 'a fanatic with expertise', a person with knowledge and an idea and the exhausting fanaticism to keep trying until it works. Quinn described Howard Head, developer of the metal ski. Head, who likes skiing, made his metal skis and took them up the mountain. On the way down they snapped. He went back to his workshop and made another pair. They broke too. In the end, and a lot of bruises later, he got it right. That is Quinn's next point. Smaller companies can have a long-term view. Because the innovation stages can be lengthy, it is vital to keep early costs low. Small companies do – they have little choice. Larger companies are tempted to start building departments, assigning overheads and dooming a new venture to the same budget expectations as established product lines.

Smaller companies are also flexible. They can 'turn around fast' Quinn says. And that, he believes, is important. If one idea doesn't work they can switch to another. Better, smaller companies try what he calls 'multiple competing approaches'. Several ideas at once, in other words. How different that is from the conventional, linear, one-stage-at-a-time approach you so often see. IBM adopted this small company approach when they developed their personal computer. Don Estridge, who headed the team, was given a small company brief, and freed from many of the 'Big Blue' constraints. According to a colleague, Estridge introduced some 'very healthy concepts which were consciously used by the corporation – in design, marketing, distribution and manufacturing'.

Hard or impossible for the conventional large company, small companies 'tolerate chaos'. Evidence and practical experience tell us that innovation, change, creating something new, are essentially a disorganised, leaping, jumping, rambling sort of process. Some giant corporations, seeing this, have set up ways to cope with it, as we have seen. But small companies have this free style naturally.

Interestingly, Quinn claims that successful innovators have 'few early formal plans'. That, too, gives the small company an advantage. 'Just do it and see what happens' doesn't sound like the language of the cool-headed financial controller of a major corporation. Quinn talks, too, of incentive rewards, a point that comes later, and the way small companies can work with venture capitalists. If the venture capitalists are good, they know that one success will pay for twenty failures.

So, yes, the smaller company can compete. When the printing machinery company within Baker Perkins launched their advanced 32-page web offset equipment in the USA their revenue from printing was £8 million. Their principal competitor had sales of £200 million. Within three years Baker Perkins had clawed out 60 per cent of the 32-page market. Of the many reasons for their success, one was their determination to aim for higher quality and more advanced technology. They did not focus on low price in order to gain market entry.

'When it comes to innovation,' say Tom Peters and Nancy Austin, authors of *A Passion for Excellence*, which stayed on the *New York Times* bestseller list for more than ten months, 'small . . . is more beautiful than even we had ever imagined.' That is what McDonald's, the fast-food giant, think. They have nearly 10,000 restaurants, a revenue of $14.3 billion, earned in 47 countries, but, according to *Business Week*, not one MBA. Instead, perhaps, they have a 'vice-president for individuality', whose job, they say, is 'to make the company feel small'. That is another feature they seek from franchisees. The entrepreneur partners 'help McDonald's act smaller and younger than it is'.

HOW APPLE STARTED

Check James Brian Quinn's findings with the story of the birth of the Apple computer. It is classic, even the name. At a meeting that got stuck looking for a name, Steve Jobs, the co-founder of Apple, said: 'If we don't think of one in five minutes we'll call the company after the apple I'm eating.'

Steve Jobs was working at Atari. Steve Wozinak, his partner, came from Hewlett Packard. Using 'liberated' parts they made something that seemed to work. Jobs sold his VW bus, Wozinak sold his HP 65 calculator. They raised $1,300 and started their business in a garage. A friend laid out a printed circuit board for them. They sold 200 and made $10,000. While that was going on they designed the Apple II. They spent the money on tooling for a plastic case. The design and tooling drawings took three weeks.

Jobs and Wozinak took the drawings to a shop whose owner said, 'Great, we'll take fifty of them.' But he wanted them fully assembled and ready to sell. So they went to two or three electronic parts distributors. They needed $20,000 worth of parts and got them from one distributor on thirty days' credit. 'On thin air,' said Jobs. 'We had no assets at all.' They delivered the fifty computers that had been ordered, got paid cash and paid the distributor in twenty-nine days.

The first Apple II was shipped in 1977, when Jobs was twenty-two years old. Sales hit $744,000. Four years later their sales had multiplied 432 times, according to Robert Heller in his book *The Supermanagers*. Apple kept early costs low. When they went public in December 1980 their most expensive capital equipment, according to Jobs, was the Herman Miller furniture. They also kept the number of employees down. In 1981 sales per employee in the semiconductor industry were about $25,000–40,000 a year. The figure for IBM was about $150,000–160,000. Apple Computer had sales per employee of $250,000. They did that, Steve Jobs said, by hiring exceptionally able people.

Following these ideas, perhaps, Ross Electronics, a British company based in north London, is taking off. In 1983, after a decade as an importer, it decided to start making its own electronic products: headphones, radios, speakers and now compact disc storage racks. Revenue to end March 1988 was over £4 million. Its headphones are market leaders in the UK and ranked number two throughout Europe. A stylish radio launched in 1985 now sells in Japan, a kind of accolade in the small electronics world, as well as in West Germany, Italy and elsewhere.

Ross Marks, the founder, gives three explanations for this growth. First, the business is design led. 'Of course low cost manufacturing is important,' he says, 'but the real point is to create products customers demand to buy.' He uses the outside design consultants Brand New, a Michael Peters subsidiary.

Second, Marks believes in pumping out one new product after another. 'We don't want to milk a product,' he says. Talking on the eve of launching a new range of 'Stylers', fashion headphones for women, Ross Marks explained, 'We try to leave no room for competitors.'

Third is something Marks has learned from his competitors. 'The Japanese sub-contract as much as possible. At Ross we have learnt to do that. Now we just pull in the subassemblies and finish off the product in-house.' 'No screws, no glues' is how he describes his simple subassembly.

In the 1960s Stuart Turner was running a grocer's shop in the Midlands. On holiday in Spain he came across a wall plug made of plastic. He thought it a good idea badly done. He talked to a friend who was a specialist in

Steve Jobs sold his VW bus to start Apple Computer with partner Steve Wozinak. When they went public their most expensive equipment was their office furniture.

injection moulding. Using a second-hand machine, he made his improved version of the wall plug.

Very soon the £330 he had spent was recouped. In his first year, selling to hardware shops, door-to-door, he made £36,000 profit. That was in 1970. By 1988 his revenue was £15 million.

How has Turner done it? He has two right-hand men. One is Stuart Draper, now manufacturing director. The other is Paul Hepworth, a free-lance designer (also now a director of the company). They all believe that the close relationship between managing director and designer, for over fifteen years, is a key factor in their success. They think it important, too, that the designer is not on their staff. He is free to take other work.

Next might be called an 'input of ignorance'. That is not as unkind as it sounds. Stuart Turner professes that he is not very technical and can't do DIY jobs in the way many can. So any product has to be simple enough for him to understand. This point is important: too often experts who design products assume customers will understand things as they do.

Stuart Turner keeps close to customers and is, without question, the company's product champion. Turner shows prototype ideas to major buyers before going into production. Very often their opinion helps him decide whether to go ahead or not.

Plasplugs has grown by constant product innovation. Today there are over 200 products in their product range. Each year about twenty are launched. Further, they have added value. From simple wall plugs costing a few pence, the company now sells a floor tile cutter costing £29. At first that product sold 50,000 a year. Forecasts put the total volume at over one million. Now the company is thinking about battery-powered tools.

Another lesson is that Stuart Turner ploughs most of his profit back into new product development. Over the years, sadly, he has had little help from banks. (Caution on the part of investment agencies is, in his view, a major contributor to the decline of manufacturing in the UK.)

His simple formula for success is:

- Get an idea that works

- Make sure it looks right so people will buy it

- Make sure you make a good profit on it

THE BODY SHOP

In another field, look at Anita Roddick OBE. In 1985 Veuve Cliquot named her Business Woman of the Year. In 1988 the CBI declared The Body Shop, Company of the Year. *Business* magazine placed it second in a forecast of 200 business leaders in the year 2000. Her company is now large, but it is instructive to see how Ms Roddick started and grew.

Anita Roddick was thirty-three and had two small children and no retail experience when in 1976 she opened 'the smallest shop I could find' in

Brighton. The truth about her is that she has enough energy, imagination, personality and drive for six people. She moves and talks at speed; she wears flat shoes – 'high heels slow me down.' She would make a go of whatever she tackled. Even so, turning a loan of £4,000 into a world-wide company with assets of £200 million is more than making a go of things. With her husband Gordon, she built The Body Shop.

Anita Roddick was born near Brighton in 1942, the third of four children of Italian immigrants who ran a café in Littlehampton. After school she taught for a year, then joined the International Labour Office in Paris, wanting to travel. She did, to far places – Madagascar, Mauritius, La

Anita Roddick OBE, Business Woman of the Year and founder of 1988's Company of the Year, started The Body Shop after seeing how women in undeveloped countries care for their skin. She 'never stops asking questions', friends say.

243

Reunion, New Hebrides. It was that experience that gave her both the idea and leitmotif for her life. She had seen how indigenous people, spared from modern advertising and other cosmetics 'education', cared for their skins and bodies.

> From that year I learnt that certain things cleansed, polished and protected the skin without having to be formulated into a cream or shampoo; what's more, they work brilliantly and have been doing so for more than 2,000 years . . . We can learn an awful lot from women in other societies. They know that these well tried and tested ways work and don't need a scientist or advertising agency to sell them.

She wanted to make these natural products. The big producers had never heard of the ingredients and wouldn't help. Leafing through the Yellow Pages, she found a herbalist who knew the ingredients and who would make up some products. Roddick borrowed £4,000, then opened her first shop. She got the name 'The Body Shop' from the side of a car repair truck she'd seen in the United States. Her neighbour, who ran a funeral parlour, thought she was laughing at him. He objected. But the name stuck. She paid a local art student £25 to design a logo, the one in use now.

Natural products, untested by animal experiment, that was her proposition. Plus honesty. 'The cosmetic industry is bizarre,' she says.

> It is run by men who create needs that don't exist. They have this incredible belief that all women want is hope and promise . . . They've got this obsession with not telling the truth. It's just like the 1950s when the 'magic X' ingredient proclaimed science and development through washing powder . . . Buy this mixture of oil and water and suddenly you will become a movie star. How can they believe women will go on falling for it.'

On the first day's trading, Anita Roddick took £130, selling 'products stripped of hype'. Filling bottles in her kitchen, sticking on labels, putting up shelves, she opened her second shop within six months. Having no money to grow further, she and her husband started to franchise. Today they have more than 300 shops in thirty-three countries and a list of some 5,000 people who want to become franchisees. (It takes three years to get a franchise. 'Unless you're absolutely obsessed you don't get a look in,' said Roddick. Even so, the questionnaire is strange: 'How would you like

244

to die?' candidates are asked. 'What's your favourite flower? Who's your heroine in history or poetry?')

However it is arrived at, there is a remarkable uniformity in all the shops. Hers is a truly international, cross-cultural business.

When the company went public in 1984, 5p shares were offered at 95p. They soared to 480p. If you ask how Anita Roddick has done it, all the rules of success are there, though not those taught by business schools. She has no time for them. She kept early costs low; she had no choice. She puts the customer first. She cares like mad about her products. She tries every one herself and makes them the focus of staff training. 'Others train for a sale. We train for knowledge,' she says. (Because the only training programmes she could find were 'a yawn a minute', she started her own video company.)

Even now, Anita Roddick spends two months a year looking for natural ingredients that are new to her and testing those she already uses. She has watched Polynesian women scoop up untreated cocoa butter and apply it to their skins and seen Sri Lankans using pineapple juice as a skin cleanser. She has lived with Bedouin women in the desert and travelled with reindeer herdsmen in Lapland. She has persuaded Japanese pearl fishermen to test her products under water.

She never stops asking questions, another characteristic of people who build winning companies. 'She'll approach anyone,' said Mark Constantine, her herbalist, 'taxi-drivers, shop assistants, your mother-in-law – and ask how they wash their hair, their skin, their feet.'

Marketing, as it is taught, means little. 'Marketing means an excuse for gathering around the table to talk. To talk on and on around every function other than the most important function which is selling the product, understanding the product and valuing the product.' The Body Shop has never advertised and hasn't much time for the way other retailers work. 'I look at what the cosmetics trade is doing and walk in the opposite direction . . . They've become huge corporations . . . They seem to be led by accountants and become versions of the Post Office or Department of Motor Vehicles.'

The Body Shop sticks to its first principles: no animal testing, close to source ingredients, no hype, no advertising, no pressurised selling, minimal packaging, respect for people and the environment. Anita Roddick adds one more thing. She points to a pink sign pinned beside her desk: It's simple. It reads 'We *will* be the most honest cosmetic company.' Full stop.

According to Anita Roddick, who has created the company with 'shares that defy gravity', as one financial man put it, 'business should be about innovation and ideas and nurturing a spirit in people.' You've got to go into life being a bit more cheeky, being mischievous, not in a childlike way, but just saying 'why not?' all the time. 'Be daring, be different, be first,' she says.

And see where she puts her priorities: she is looking at the future in terms of products, training, communications. Nor is there much chance of The Body Shop slipping into what she calls the 'fat cat mentality'. Anita Roddick uses the company's money to fund a number of important social programmes. She believes business should look after the back street as well as the high street. They are corporate members of Friends of the Earth. Their packaging and publications are printed on recycled paper, their stores broadcast social issues. Every franchisee is required to undertake community work. In India they support a boys' town where destitute youngsters are taught local crafts. Money from the sales is put in a trust fund. When the youngsters leave, at sixteen, they are given enough to buy a herd of sheep or horse and cart. So far 3,000 jobs have been created under this scheme. In a Tibetan refugee camp, they are turning bananas into paper. Elsewhere they are helping old people. Staff working in her shops do this community work in company time. Roddick believes it adds to their sense of purpose and dignity.

VISION AND DETERMINATION

In case there is a risk of making business growth sound too easy, the story of Hille, a British furniture company, shows the need for vision and a great deal of determination.

Destroyed by bombing during the Second World War, they restarted after 1945 with six employees. At first obliged to work on repairing war damage, the principals went to the United States to compete for a contract to make reproduction breakfront bookcases. They won, and supplied ten a week.

At the furniture show in New York in 1949, Leslie and Rosamind Julius (grand-daughter of Hille's founder) were impressed by Robin Day and Clive Latimer, young English designers who had won an international prize for low-cost furniture. Leslie Julius commissioned them to design on

Hille Ergonom 'Supporto' chair, designed by Fred Scott. Some 60,000 have been sold in ten countries.

a royalty basis. 'We will make anything you design,' he promised. Together they were early in exploiting the technology of moulding plywood. When the results were shown the trade press was alarmed. 'Hille's go mad,' ran one headline. 'They're ruining Hille,' said another. None the less, sales of Day's Hillestack chair soon rose to 200 a week and continued to climb.

Faith and salesmanship came into this too. To convince one government department of the robustness of his product, Leslie Julius threw the chair out of a fifth-storey window. Happily, it landed on grass, one leg piercing the ground like a quivering arrow.

Hille decided to focus on selling to architects, designers and other specifiers. This was a further turning point. In 1952 they opened their own showroom, another innovation that made the trade furious. Wanting to 'market the best that could be designed and made' they made a licensing arrangement with Herman Miller, the American leader, to complement their own range and in 1970 they bought the English subsidiary of Knoll International USA to manufacture their range in Britain.

However, their true innovation, the one that places Leslie and Rosamind Julius in the history books, was their development of the first elegant, tough and reliable polypropylene chair. To move from timber to plastics was revolutionary at the time, especially in the furniture trade. It is a dramatic example of innovation achieved by harnessing new technology, however removed it is from the traditional culture of an industry.

With designer Robin Day, Hille sought technical help from Shell and from Britain's Furniture Industry Research Association (FIRA). Even so, the development work became overwhelming and costs soared. One tool, for instance, cost a quarter of their profits. After anxious all-night meetings, they resolved to persevere. 'We could stay longer,' Leslie Julius says in retrospect, 'than people in bigger firms could.' They launched their polypropylene chair in 1962. Twenty-four years later, in 1986, sales have still not tailed off. Some 12–15 million have been sold.

Imagination, courage, determination and insistence on the best are all part of the story. Another important point is that from the beginning, the chair was not conceived in isolation, but as part of a programme. Further, development did not stop there. Always employing and drawing on the best from outstanding designers, Hille continued to generate one outstanding product after another. When Leslie and Rosamind Julius retired in 1983, Hille had more than 300 employees. That is an important point.

Small companies create jobs. The more that succeed the better. In the United Kingdom, according to economist Irwin Stelzer, firms with fewer than 100 employees were responsible for more than half the new jobs created between 1971 and 1981, even though they accounted for only 29 per cent of the jobs at the beginning of the period. It is the same in the United States. Between 1966 and 1976, 80 per cent of new jobs were created by firms with fewer than 100 employees, according to an MIT study.

SUMMARY

Can smaller companies compete? One observer, James Brian Quinn, has analysed innovative companies of all sizes. His firm answer is 'yes'. Smaller companies can compete very well. Indeed, large corporations should emulate them. Some do; IBM is one of them. This chapter reminds people in smaller companies of their many advantages.

13

Double the Time
You Give To Training

'All education is a vision of the future.'
Alvin Toffler

In the nineteenth century a Japanese proverb said it was abominable that innocent children should be taught to use numbers, the tools of merchants. How times change. Gene Gregory, of Sophia University in Tokyo, has noted that 'comparative internal tests conducted by UNESCO show that Japanese scores in mathematics and science are significantly higher than those in any other country'. By the age of fourteen, Japanese schoolchildren have learned more maths than most US high school graduates. Gregory claims that as a result of their education the average IQ among young people in Japan is the highest in the world, eleven points above the US and European average. Richard Lynn, a British psychologist, says much the same. He estimates that 77 per cent of the Japanese younger generation have a higher IQ than the average American or European.

This is not the place to talk about education, except to say that if we want to compete industrially we would do well to know what we are up against.

A real guide to economic performance of a country is how long it keeps children at school. Top of the class, according to the OECD, is Japan. Next comes the United States, then The Netherlands and the German-speaking nations. At the bottom are Portugal, Spain and Britain. Another indicator is the number of people in their twenties and thirties who 'drop-in' to rather than 'drop-out' of higher education. In Australia, Denmark and Sweden more than one fifth of people who enrol in higher education are over twenty-five years old. In the United States, thanks to the burgeoning of non-university community colleges, some 5 million adults seek education after hours. They go back to work better able to cope with the changes going on around them.

249

In the UK, according to Sir Peter Parker, four children in ten leave school with no qualifications whatever. Japanese children, it appears, get off to a better start. Then two or three times more go on to higher education, which is likely to be more focused. The current output of graduate engineers in Japan, for instance, is ten times that of the UK.

A TERRIBLE GULF

It must be said that in Britain today great efforts are being made to provide practical education in polytechnics and other colleges of further and higher education. The Council of National Academic Awards (CNAA), Business and Technician Education Council (BTEC), City and Guilds, Royal Society of Arts and others are striving to bring colleges and companies closer, to equip young people for jobs. Government, too, is encouraging this drive purposefully.

Even so, the myth persists in academic circles that somehow this is lesser education. Britain's most illustrious colleges still foster the view that the classics are superior to science and anything is better than business. 'We look on people who go into business as our failures,' an Oxford professor told the son of a friend of mine. Sir Christopher Hogg, chairman of Courtaulds, said recently, 'It is not an easy thing to run a business. I can't think why it is so degraded by academics.' Whatever the reason, the consequence is awful.

The gulf between so many academics and business executives, wide as a barn door, deep as a well, is mutual. The dean of one business school once observed that most of his students steered clear of manufacturing industry. They went into management consultancies and the financial world. The dean regretted it, but didn't blame the students. In these service companies, he said, graduates were better treated, more highly paid and given greater responsibilities. Of course there are many distinguished exceptions to this sweeping assertion, but the general truth seems to be that manufacturing companies in Britain, perhaps more than anywhere else, neither attract nor look after the competent people they need.

Today many companies seem unwilling to invest in training because their people will be poached. This fear has never concerned Procter & Gamble or Unilever, both exemplary. The time may come when training will be seen as an attraction, a way to recruit people. The logic goes like this. First, Sir Simon Hornby told the Royal Society in 1988, virtually all senior managers for the next twenty years have already finished their formal education. How are they to stay up-to-date, to sustain their earning power?

Second, the young population is dropping sharply. By 1995, the number of sixteen- to nineteen-year-olds will have dropped by 25 per cent. It'll be an employees' market. Professor Charles Handy foresees that they will choose not only who they want to work for, but also what they want to do and how they'll do it. The nine-to-five structure will weaken. People will choose other ways: some mostly working from home, or in small, local clusters, and so forth. But a consequence is that individuals have to be responsible for their own development. If they don't keep up, their earning power will fall.

Thus, the company that can provide updating courses or university sponsorship, or whatever, will be attractive. Good companies have known that for years. Others haven't. Of course, this failure to train will catch up with us; it has already resulted in skill shortages that hold companies back. At best, you end up paying more for skills in short supply. At worst, which is more likely, you simply won't attract the skills you need to run your business. In short, to provide attractive and continuing training is a fundamental of success.

One company quick to recognise the need for this is BP. Well qualified manpower, they say, is one of the company's 'feedstocks'. They give three reasons for turning up the pressure now. One, the swing in demographic patterns which will mean far fewer 18- to 20-year-olds in the early 1990s; two, changing technology demanding new skills, and three, the internal market of Europe after 1992.

COMMITMENT TO TRAINING

Winning companies, wherever they are, demonstrate the most determined commitment to train their people. In Japan, education and training are lifelong. West German industry spends twenty times as much on training as British companies do. In the United States, companies spend about £1,500 per person per year on training. In the UK, the figure is £200. The average spent by industry on training in the USA, West

Germany and France is between 2 per cent and 3 per cent of revenue. In the UK the figure is 0.15 per cent.

As the historian Correlli Barnett has observed, 'Japanese, American and German technological growth has not merely depended on superb national education and training at all levels, it has been driven by it.' Perhaps education begets education. In the face of their highly educated and trained competitors, it is a lamentable fact that plenty of British managers don't think it their job to train their staff. Roger Eglin, editor of the business section of the *Sunday Times*, found this. He talked to many managers whose attitude was 'People are here to work. They are supposed to be trained already.'

Coopers & Lybrand, the international accountants and management consultants, looked at the attitude of British boards to training. Over half the boards they interviewed in an extensive survey do not review training. Giving the Smallpeice lecture at the Royal Society in 1986, Sir Peter Parker put this in shocking context. Of the 3.25 million managers and supervisors in the UK, 40 per cent have no qualifications at all and 80 per cent have no qualifications relating to management. Only 7 per cent have a university degree and a further 7 per cent put membership of a professional body as their highest qualification, according to *The Economist*.

This compares with 85 per cent of Japanese company directors who have degrees or professional qualifications. Of course, if our directors made up for that by continuing their education or training, that would be something. But one recent study showed that over half of Britain's senior executives had never attended any kind of management course. You may wonder how they hope to compete.

In the United States 67,000 MBAs were awarded in 1986, up 50 per cent in ten years. In 1987 the figure in Britain was 2,750. *The Economist* reported that most European executives think an MBA does not prepare the graduate for the real problems of running a company, and there may be truth in that. Anita Roddick, of The Body Shop has often expressed her views about this at the London Business School and Cranfield School of Management:

> Anybody who has an ounce of individuality should never go to a business school . . . because you're structured by academics who measure you in the science of business. They use a business language that is predictable, and going out and doing it is not part of the course.

None the less, three quarters of the executives interviewed by *The Economist* would like their children to get an MBA. If MBAs are thought too theoretical, how does one make them practical? One of France's Grandes Ecoles, the Ecole Centrale de Paris, is now insisting that all students work abroad for three months and won't graduate them until they pass a stiff test in English.

In October 1985, Professor Iain Mangham and Dr Mick Silver from the University of Bath were commissioned by the Economic and Social Research Council to undertake a pilot survey into in-company training in Britain. According to their findings, more than half of British companies make no provision at all for management training. That includes one in five of the companies employing more than 1,000 people. Three quarters of smaller firms (20–49 employees) do no management training.

The chairman of a large holding company gave his opinion: 'In the highly competitive sphere in which we trade, time is not available for formal management training. Managers are paid to successfully manage [sic], and if that cannot be achieved they must be replaced.' One third of managers interviewed were happy with this lack of training. They claimed that none is needed because of previous experience or on-the-job experience.

Iain Mangham and Mick Silver found that more than half the managers in Britain did no training whatever in 1985. In companies with fewer than 1,000 people, fewer than one senior manager in ten did any training. They cite time and expense as the reasons.

So much for managers. What about others in the company? In 1985 *The Chartered Mechanical Engineer* published a comparison forty-five matched companies in Britain and West Germany. It showed that about half the German shopfloor workers had an apprentice-type qualification compared with one quarter of the UK. Fourteen out of sixteen UK companies promoted workers to foremen on the grounds of long service. In all sixteen German companies, the production foreman had passed examinations as craftsmen. Thirteen had acquired the higher certificate of 'Meister'. The remaining three had undergone additional training.

This attitude to training is not universal. Tom Peters quoted one US businessman who expressed a common view: 'You train those people,' he said of his workforce, 'and they'll leave.'

UPGRADING SKILLS

In Japan the emphasis appears to be not only on continual training but on upgrading skills. Gene Gregory noted that during the 1970s blue-collar workers were being trained for white-collar jobs. In the same way, hardware technicians were learning to handle software, and mechanical engineers were being trained to become electronic engineers. Shifting people into higher areas of competence is one goal. Another is to see that people acquire all-round experience.

Geoffrey Peaker and Alan Barnes, two British government officials who inspect colleges, went to Japan in 1986 to look at design education. They were surprised to find it was quite general, not specialised as it is Britain. But then they found that most of the training comes from the company a young person joins, and it lasts for years. In a Japanese company a long-term training plan is written for every person. It includes switching from job to job. People hired as designers spend some time in management, some time in marketing, some time in the plant, as well as practising design.

This postgraduate training is practical and is tailored to specific corporate objectives. The managing director of Honda, Nobuhiko Kawamoto, says designers in his company are educated to absorb 'all the knowledge concerning products, such as production, technology, market, sales, services and', heaven help them, 'additional items'.

At least four benefits flow from this switching within the company. First, people learn the business. Second, they meet colleagues in other departments. Third, the walls that divide disciplines in Western companies are far less likely to arise in Japanese ones. Multi-disciplinary teamwork becomes natural; it doesn't have to be contrived. Fourth, employees acquire a larger perspective than could be gained sitting in one section of the company.

THE COMPANY'S ROLE

In Japan formal education, excellent as it is, is only the start of a continuing process of developing people. Companies, rather than universities, provide postgraduate training. One company alone, Hitachi, spends £30

Hitachi spends millions of pounds on lifelong training for all its staff.

million a year on continuing education for its 165,000 employees and this sum doesn't include the cost of on-the-job training.

'To hire a person and not train him is a failure of management', say Hitachi. This company runs four institutes: an institute of technology, an institute of supervisory and technical training, and two technical colleges. All are under the direct control of the president of Hitachi. There is also the Hitachi Institute of Management Development.

The introductory programme for graduates lasts two years. It includes a lecture by top management, three months on the shopfloor and on-the-job training in a specialised field. At the end of the period each graduate has to submit a thesis. They then go into line jobs and continue to receive junior, middle and perhaps senior management training.

A productivity training centre is not reserved for engineers. Rather, it spreads the ideas of production engineering throughout Hitachi. All technicians who join Hitachi have a two-week intensive training, then three-day 'lodge-in' sessions every other weekend for two years. That's not all. A systematic and consistent on-the-job programme gives all engineers and technicians practical know-how. To quote Gene Gregory: 'An engineer joining the company can look forward to a lifelong programme of education to assure the continual upgrading of his technical knowledge.'

Is all this a waste of money, or a way to build irresistible competitive advantage? There will remain managers who say, 'Well, maybe that is necessary in high-tech areas, but my business is simpler. It doesn't need all that training.' That is no answer. The principles apply to everyone.

MRS FIELDS' COOKIES

You'd think you don't need much training to work in a shop selling freshly baked cookies. But at Mrs Fields Inc., whose headquarters are in Utah, training is 'intensive and continuous'. Debbi Fields was twenty when she borrowed $25,000 from her husband, Randall, to start her own shop in Palo Alto, California. Eleven years later, in 1988, she had 450 shops and a revenue of $90 million.

Training, she says, has been a reason for her success. Indeed, pay increases in her company depend, in part, on how well people do on their training programmes. Although each of her shops is only about 700

Debbi Fields borrowed $25,000 from her husband to start a shop selling freshly baked cookies. Nine years later she had 450 shops, a revenue of $90 million and a quotation on London's Stock Exchange. One secret of her recipe: 'intensive and continuous training' for all her staff.

square feet, each has its own oven. Using dough prepared in one of a number of regional centres, people in the shops bake the cookies themselves. Because they help to make the product they are selling, staff feel more involved, Debbi Fields says. Her staff are in touch every day. She has the best communications money can buy. Each day store managers forecast what sales every hour will be. This information is fed to regional centres to help them plan their production, to head office, who prepare daily balance sheets, and to Debbie Fields, wherever she happens to be.

NEED TO RETRAIN

The point is straightforward. If you expect people to perform well and to respond to changing circumstances, you have to train and retrain them. Sir Bryan Nicholson, who headed the former Manpower Services Commission, makes the case with an example from technology, although he would apply it more widely. He points out that electronic engineers recruited in 1980 will already find much of their knowlege out of date.

One consequence is that almost everyone in work will have to 'go back to school'. *The Economist* reckons that knowledge is changing at the speed it takes to learn. Electronic engineers who qualified in 1987, after four years in college, will find half they have learnt out of date by 1992.

It will be hard to keep up. In 1984 the Butcher Committee forecast that within five years nine out of every ten information technology graduates would be gobbled up by nine firms. Few would be left for anyone else. The shortfall is even worse than it looks. Experience in data processing shows that for every qualified person employed by a computer manufacturer, five are needed by customers.

People who joined Japan's mighty NEC between 1960 and 1965 said it took twelve years for a gap to open between their knowledge and the expertise they needed at work. By contrast, people who joined in 1975 felt it took only two years for their university knowledge to be inadequate to do their job properly. This comparison is not because universities are getting worse, but because technology is moving so fast. What you learn at university, in other words, gets out of date that much more quickly.

Nor is it only at university level. The march of technology affects everyone. So, too, does failure to keep abreast of it. In 1986 the London Chamber of Commerce surveyed 700 companies. One in four, they found, said their introduction of new technology was impeded by lack of skilled people. The proportion has more than doubled in six years. Interestingly, this is far worse in manufacturing companies than in service industries. Twenty-four per cent of manufacturing companies complain of serious skill shortages. Fifteen per cent of service companies say the same.

Such shortages are occurring elsewhere, although the position is most serious in Britain. In a recent poll conducted by MORI for PA, 41 per cent of top executives in Britain gave this as the main constraint on their product and process innovation. Interestingly, Japan came next: 37 per cent of executives interviewed said skill shortage was a constraint on their innovation. In Germany the figure was 8 per cent.

If four top British executives in ten say skill shortage will limit their product development that is worrying. Where does the remedy lie? Nissan believe it rests with the company. Before they opened their first plant in the United States, they spent $20,000 per worker to train each one the new skills required.

Alvin Toffler believes 'continuous re-skilling and re-education is the raw material of the economy of tomorrow'. With the vision that led him to write *Future Shock* and *The Third Wave*, he advised unions to grasp the idea. He thinks they should press for a 25-hour week, plus five hours of training each week. He reckons this could be achieved in five years. Whether unions take the lead in education or management does, there is plainly a desperate need to do more.

RESTATING THE NEED

To underline the urgency another way, a NEDO and MSC report published in 1982 found that across a whole range of industries in Britain, from the workbench to chairman's office, almost seven out of ten people employed lacked any formal qualification of any kind. The figure in West Germany is 36 per cent.

Training is an overhead, a cost of doing business. It is part of being better today and ready for tomorrow. Nor is it yet another of those 'hygienes' good managers are supposed to worry about. Training benefits the business. In Britain, a survey conducted by Coopers & Lybrand (1986) found that companies that train more do better. High-performing companies have 8.9 days' training per employee a year. Low performers show only 2.8 days. High performers have increased their training by 25 per cent in five years. Low performers have cut training by 20 per cent.

'It is no surprise to me,' remarked Sir Peter Parker, 'that a characteristic of the most enterprising companies is that they invest two or three times more than the average in training.' The correlation is obvious. Jaguar is one example. It spends eight times the national average on training, as a percentage of sales.

A PRACTICAL ROUTE

Happily, the investment need not be as great or as complicated as people may fear. One rapid route is to ask local colleges to help. In the United

States Hewlett Packard, Intel, Varian and Bechtel are among companies that look to their local colleges to set up training courses for their people. Lockheed and Tandem Computers do the same. It is cost-effective, they say. In the UK colleges around the country are well equipped to provide the same service to industry. The Cranfield School of Management, with the Open University, has just launched a £2 million distance learning programme for people in small firms. This is designed to let them learn at work, by using workbooks, videos, audio and video programmes. Basic modules call for eight hours of study, half at home or in the office, half in group workshops arranged locally. Among their subjects: product development. This is no place to list the provision available for continuing education and training in Britain, but it is vast.

Chairman and directors need to stay up to date as much as anyone else. Where are they to turn? Seminars provide one answer – and it is noticeable in both the USA and the UK how few manufacturing company directors attend seminars – short courses by professional bodies provide another. The cause for regret, as again Sir Peter Parker has remarked, is that 'without an entrepreneurial culture, management education at university level was not designed into the total education process, into the growing up of British youth'.

BUSINESS SCHOOLS

Until that occurs, we have to send people to business schools and recruit from them. But business schools have a lot to answer for. A lot of their beliefs and jargon should have been swept aside by the realities of the market, and by Japanese competition in particular. To give them their due, there is a limit to what they can do without the right starting point or sympathetic climate around them. 'The best endeavours of business schools,' Sir Peter Parker has said, 'could only be a maraschino cherry popped on top of the educational grapefruit.'

Saying that, you have to be careful what you learn from them or don't learn. Marvellous at theoretical strategy, strong on finance and anything to do with numbers, masters of rational analysis, and often not bad at people, almost all omit the fundamental point: the product, the objects a company actually makes.

I went on an international marketing course at INSEAD in France. The programme was hard and marvellous. It changed my view. But not once did we talk about products, nor was the word 'design' mentioned. Peter Lawrence is running a design course at Boston University and is introducing the same course into ten business schools. But these are exceptions. The pioneer was the London Business School, which has a Design Management Unit. Led by Peter Gorb, himself a Harvard MBA. A world pioneer. It has introduced into a business school the importance of products, of design in all forms of business and, particularly, managing the design process. The University of Manchester also teaches the same principles. So do a few others. But the shortage means that too many people who go to business school learn, if not the wrong attitudes to business, then certainly not some of the right ones.

BACK TO BASICS

If there is a one-line lesson, it is 'get back to basics'. Business has become too theoretical by half. Someone who should know is Sir Edwin Nixon, chairman of IBM in the UK. He said, 'It is too easy for big companies to become distracted from the basic precepts of business.' Business schools, unwittingly no doubt, foster this. Academic drift, an educational blight, takes another form: everything becomes theoretical. Marketing drifts from caring about customers to abstract analysis; management shifts from leading people to discounted cash flows.

The International Management Institute (IMI), associated with the University of Geneva, has made the same criticism. Late in 1984, it commissioned a study to think about the right way to train managers in an unpredictable future. Listing trends, and the fact that several will converge, it came to the conclusion that tomorrow's manager must be *flexible*, be *open to new ideas* and be *willing to question*.

Old training methods won't help, IMI thought. Too much past teaching has been about analysis, packing in knowlege and rooted in a cause-and-effect kind of analysis. It lacked feel for the subjective or emotional elements in decision taking. Case studies are no longer relevant, IMI argues. Current methods underrate creativity and are sometimes too technocratic to stimulate innovative thinking.

Stanford University has something new: a programme called 'Creativity in Business'. One commentator described it as 'an unorthox blip in the MBA curriculum, even for California'. Michael L. Ray, Stanford's

261

professor of marketing and communications, argues that intuition, imagination, flexibility and 'courage to try the unorthodox' are coming to be the characteristics of creativity in business.

Business schools come in for blame, too, from Masanori Moritani, author of *Japanese Technology*. Moritani slams MBAs who, far from spending years on the factory floor learning about and improving their products, come into companies as an élite, expecting to 'manage' whatever it is the company does. In the corporate hierarchy they are above and removed from toilers on the factory floor. They don't expect to get their hands dirty.

That is the number one lesson. The boards of companies must see that the quality of their products is of prime, strategic importance. How to get them and keep them in front of their competitors should be their consuming occupation. We could hope that organisations that affect the company – governments, financial institutions, trade unions – would accept the same perspective. The approach need not be the same as the Japanese, but it must aim at the same goal: to compete in the modern world and to win. To hope to do that without training and retraining seems optimistic indeed.

You come back to the point that it is competitors who set the standards. We should know that the winning companies commit more and more of their resources to training their people. IBM spend $45 million a year on training already, a figure, they say, that can only rise. Of course, training is a cost. Once more, the short-term view of financiers can get in the way. Presumably IBM, whose margins have shrunk in recent times, could have increased their profits if they stopped training people. But then the obvious question is, for how long would 'Big Blue' stay a leader if they did?

TRAINING FOR PRODUCT DEVELOPMENT

Turning to the training most likely to enhance a company's product development, there may be three broad areas. It starts, as it should, with the board. By belief and example the board needs to spread a heightened awareness of the importance of satisfying customers with excellent products and service. Next, it includes everyone in the business being encouraged to hone his or her own skills. Third, people need to see how their skills fit in with those around them. Engineers have to learn more about modern manufacturing, for example, and new techniques and materials, but also must acquire some sensitivity to the needs of the market. Industrial designers must widen their competence in the same way. We saw how the boards of some Japanese companies look to their designers to 'imagine the company's future'. Designers who only know about design will never do that.

ONE AIM: MULTI-DISCIPLINE

The essence, we have seen, is that effective product development is a multi-disciplinary process. One aim of continuing training must be to 'smash' these disciplines together. The list of new skills to learn is long. Perhaps only two more need be mentioned now. If everyone connected with product development could struggle, consciously, to improve his or her imaginative ability, that would be constructive. Nor should this include only the designated 'creative' people.

That label is particularly misleading. Everyone in a company has creative potential that can help it to prosper. You protest. 'Most can't draw a straight line', you say. The link between art and creativity remains firmly in our minds. But art has little to do with it. One definition of creativity is 'the ability to relate previously unrelated experience'. You don't need to be able to draw to do that. You may, however, need to suspend analysis and logic long enough to let fresh ideas flow. Betty Edwards' understanding of the left-hand and right-hand modes of the brain could have widespread application throughout many companies that want to generate new products.

As for developing designers, in the UK there is an extraordinary paradox. American, Japanese, Italian and other business executives visit British colleges to hire designers even before they qualify. The standard of design education in Britain is often said to be exemplary. But British business executives complain that these same students are often unworldly and inadequately trained. Why is this? Are they looking for the wrong qualities? Or is it because they expect young people to be fully competent before they are hired? That would follow if, as we have seen, they don't believe in training people in their companies.

My final comment concerns management. It really will take some remarkable training and a shift of attitude to encourage the tidy manager to condone chaos, to develop the 'do-it-now' drive that seems essential to rapid product development. Not much less is called for. Conventional management systems just do not deliver the goods.

I have compared the different views and practices of winning companies. They train their people, then train them again. The inference is that anyone who seriously intends to compete had better do the same. I find I keep asking the same question: in the contest for the excellence needed to win world markets, including those close to home, who is likely to win? Will it be the companies that see no need to develop their people? Or will it be those that never stop?

The story is told of a man who returned to his university after thirty years. He asked to see a current exam paper. To his surprise, the questions were the same as he had been asked all those years before. 'Oh yes,' explained his host, 'the questions are the same. Only the answers keep changing.' Today you may wonder whether even the questions confronting business haven't changed.

SUMMARY

At the risk of seeming to wander, this chapter describes another gap between winning companies and the rest – training. Many companies do none at all. Few, it seems, recognise the desperate need to train and retrain all the time. This is generally true, but reinforced today by the need to be ever more skilful, by the explosion of knowledge and by the rapid advance of technology.

It is hard to imagine how companies believe they can keep up without continually increasing the competence of their people. Yet it is common to hear even good managers say, 'We're too busy. We haven't time for training, or, 'People are supposed to be competent already.'

If we want to know about the 'winning ways' of winning companies, constant training is one of them. In Japan lifetime training, both in the classroom and on the job, is usual. In the United States, the level is high. In the UK the average spending on education is one twentieth the European average. Who, it is easy to ask, is likely to win? Who is likely to lose?

14

What Makes a
Winning Company?

'You've got to have clear
objectives and fire in your belly.'
John Bertrand, captain of *Australia II*,
the boat that won the Americas Cup in 1983

If evidence taken from many sources becomes repetitive, you may feel it adds up to sound advice. This chapter provides a telegraphic distillation of the findings of experts who have studied companies of all sizes in a number of countries. One hallmark of these companies is that they are introducing new products rapidly and successfully; this is our concern now.

Critics may protest that many of their observations stray from the narrower focus of developing new products. Perhaps that is the main lesson. To be innovative, companies must embrace a whole set of new attitudes. Strengthening the design department, by itself, won't do the trick.

THE ESSENTIALS FOR WINNING

Here are the essentials for a company that wants to win, according to Tom Peters and Bob Waterman in *In Search of Excellence*. They wrote primarily about successful US companies they had studied, but the qualities they found surely have universal relevance. Virtually all are far from the orthodoxy of the modern industrial corporation. That is the bad news. All, encouragingly, are closer to the natural state of smaller companies, especially those in new industries. That is the good news.

1. *'A bias for action'*, for getting on with it. Who would argue with this? But, we have seen, this does not mean at the pace we are used to. Nor

does it mean being satisfied with the best that can be done the way we organise today. Bringing people together in teams – a concept at the heart of this book – is an example of doing things more quickly by doing them differently.

Earlier we saw that Arthur D. Little spoke of innovation in management. It is hard to retain much 'bias for action' in a conventional hierarchical company. Decisions take too long. Forces at work tend to be negative rather than positive. The 'flatter', devolved organisation is faster.

2. *'Close to the customer'*. So many of us say we are but we are not. Not close in the way General Electric was when it wanted to improve its position in the business of making locomotives, or Sony proved it was when it decided to launch an 8-inch TV in the United States, or Honda is when it sends out its designers all the time. Being close to the customer is much safer than being close to the plant or the financier. As the customer shifts, so will you. How many companies have been bemused to discover, too late, that their customer has gone away? That is, at least partly, because they have been looking in the wrong direction.

3. *'Autonomy and entrepreneurship'*. Peters and Waterman found both, even in the largest corporations. Divide the company into bits, small bits. Encourage all the bosses to achieve their own goals. Don't second-guess every move they make. For example, I know the financial director of one public company who may not write to his accountant without the chairman's permission. Heaven knows how they work lower down in the company. Of that chairman, someone said, 'He's typical. He likes to hold all the marbles.' That is yesterday's world.

Of course, you can't just leave people. There is more to creating the environment of autonomy and entrepreneurship. It includes telling everyone your goals, for instance, and permitting risk, and recognising success. It includes sharing the same attitudes, brought about through fostering a questioning, open culture.

4. *'Productivity through people'*. Looking at the winning companies, Peters and Waterman saw a high level of this characteristic. Steve Jobs' experience at Apple is a perfect case. He achieved five or six times the industry average by hiring highly talented, highly charged people and then letting them run.

Almost all of us have far more ability and energy than we are allowed to exercise. So often, the system holds people back. Procedures are necessary in large organisations, but procedures and rules can be based on trust as easily as they can be repressive. Having layer upon layer of managers or officials, who feel it necessary to interfere, doesn't encourage 'productivity through people'. 'It is not too difficult to motivate innovators,' say Arthur D. Little. 'It is very easy to demotivate them. Indifference and bureaucratic hassles are the most commonly cited demotivating factors.'

Criticising people for what they don't do, instead of praising them for what they do do, doesn't help either. 'Productivity through people' must be sensible, but a lot goes with it. When it comes to developing new products, there is everything to be said for it. Everyone in the business can help – and will, if they see the point and know they will be appreciated. Ideas, for instance, can come from anywhere, not just from the 'designated thinkers'.

Maybe 'productivity through people' is another of those areas where managers say, 'We do that already,' because they have personel managers and pension schemes. This is not the same, not the same at all.

5. *'Hands-on, value-driven'*. Peters and Waterman found that these are the companies that win. That means the chairman of Sony carrying his products around with him. It means the head of McDonald's seeing the tables are clean. It means being in touch and on top. There's another, old-fashioned word – 'leadership' – and one way to lead is to show what you think is important by the way you act.

Sir Christopher Hogg, Chairman of Courtaulds, told an audience at the Royal Society of Arts how he sees leadership of a company. 'I have been shifted a considerable distance in the spectrum away from administration orientation, in which it is all too easy to forget that a company exists only by reason of its ability to satisfy customers and markets – away from that and towards market, customer and product orientation.'

6. *'Stick to the knitting'*. If you have found the right way to stay in front, Peters and Waterman say, keep on doing it. There are so many claims on our time it is easy to be distracted. It is also easy, perhaps particularly for imaginative people, to become bored with focused effort. There are so many other possibilities. Sticking to the knitting is not the same as sticking in the mud. Stick-in-the-muds don't alter, don't adapt, don't

267

take risks. People who stick to the knitting do all of these. The key is to drive relentlessly to improve the things that matter.

7. *'Simple form, lean staff'*. Peters and Waterman noted that the companies whose performance they admire avoided excessive central staffs and bureaucratic systems.

8. *'Simultaneous loose/tight properties'*. Be vigilant about a few issues, delegate the others. As for product development, if I may interpret Peters and Waterman's views, perhaps one needs to be 'tight' about the need to stay close to customers and tight about putting constant product improvement in the front of everyone's mind, but loose about how the team works. Experience shows that teams like to be close to, but not sat on by, the board. Be tight about the need for results, loose about the company's usual yardsticks for good behaviour.

If people in the UK think, 'Well all that might be right for the United States, but Britain is different,' they should see the results of the 'sharp-bender' project carried out for NEDO in 1986. This looked at British companies that had turned around sharply, that, in a short term, contrived to do much better. Here is what it found:

1. A bias for action. (There it is again.)

2. Willingness to take risks – we've heard that too. Business executives who turn around companies take decisions rather than avoid them and exert continuing pressure for change and improvement.

3. Short-term cutting waste and overheads.

4. Improvement in organisation, planning and control.

5. Investment in the future (Note, these are companies that turn around quickly.)

6. Concentration on the product, market and requirements of the customer.

7. Motivating the workforce and consulting and involving them in the process of change.

8. Flexibility.

As you will note, the two lists of points are much the same.

All very well, I have been told, but that is about management, not about developing new products. My thesis is that if you get the overall attitude in the company right, the new products will come. Roy Rothwell and Paul Gardiner make the connection better than I may have done. From numerous studies they prepared their own list of 'critical factors for success'. Again there are eight points.

1. Management must establish good communications with customers and other sources of external ideas.

2. Innovation is a corporate-wide task. It is not, they insist, simply a matter of research, design and development. Note that they highlight the importance of good internal communication and co-operation between departments.

3. Watch your product to the market-place. Too many would-be innovators have produced designs that were technically satisfying in themselves but which failed to meet the needs of potential customers. This is 'a sure prescription for disaster'.

4. Companies should eliminate technical bugs before the commercial launch urge Rothwell and Gardiner. This, I suggest, need not be at odds with Peters and Austin, who want us to try new products with real people in real situations as fast as possible. That's the best way to find out what the bugs are.

5. Innovation is difficult. Companies need managers of high quality and ability. Top management must be open minded and progressive. Rothwell and Gardiner add (a recurring theme in this book), 'successful innovation tends to be associated with a participative, horizontal management style, one that emphasises consultation rather than direction from above'.

6. In-house skills are vital believe Rothwell and Gardiner. Companies need internal experts to capitalise on external advice. For example, many attempts at technology transfer have failed because companies did not acquire the necessary in-house skills.

7. After-sales service and user education are important.

269

8. Companies must have a product champion and business innovator, the latter with overall control of a development project.

In case we find these ideas frighteningly new, it is worth noting that some years ago the Confederation of British Industry arrived at similar conclusions. The stern question is: what have we done about them? In its report *Innovation and Competitiveness*, published in 1979, the CBI found there were consistent and significant factors in successful development. It listed seven characteristics:

1. Responsibility for new product and process development is vested in a member of the board.

2. Support and/or participation by the chief executive.

3. Good rapport between marketing, production and development.

4. Effective use of external sources of technological help and advice.

5. Close collaboration with customers in product design.

6. Presence of technologists on the board.

7. Effective screening of ideas and monitoring of progress of approved projects.

Notice how the same themes turn up again and again.

FOCUS ON DEVELOPING WINNING PRODUCTS

You may feel these essentials are too broad for a book about developing competitive products, so then let us focus more narrowly. James Brian Quinn, from his studies of highly innovative companies in several countries, lists the ten characteristics he thinks get results.

1. The need for atmosphere/vision, and a feeling about people.

2. The need for a technology strategy. It doesn't matter whether you look for. major developments, or little-by-little improvement, whether you want to be a leader or fast follower, or whether you

want to buy in or do it yourself. In whichever dimension of a product you seek technological strength. Quinn believes that having a known strategy gives a company a unique cohesion and an ability to perform.

3. The company must be 'market goal-oriented'. The best companies, and not just the consumer goods companies, really are, Quinn says. He cited Bell Labs, where technical engineers deal with customer complaints. The way of working he calls for is 'test/feedback/test/feedback'. There are echoes of Peters and Waterman. Make something. Try it. If it goes wrong, improve it. Try it again.

4. 'Skunkworks' and champions exist. There is always a champion who drives success.

5. Always develop multiple approaches. We've heard that too. 'The nature of innovation is that you don't know.' In any case having several lines to choose from is faster. Sony pursued ten major options when developing the video recorder. Such internal competition is not wasteful. It gets better results quicker.

6. 'Interactive learning', learning from customers, learning from people in other disciplines, back and forth.

7. 'Key targets and chaos', setting up parallel projects, but also placing 'side-bets', lots of small initiatives, beside the main efforts.

8. Don't set up normal structures if you want to develop new products quickly.

9. Rewards and incentives, not only financial ones, are crucial.

10. Innovators are task-oriented and task-driven. Their motivation comes from being able to implement their ideas.

The point is this: all the evidence suggests that if you leave innovation to chance, or leave it to your technical department, or even try to manage it the way you manage any other part of the business, you probably won't get far. Arthur D. Little, who have a three-year programme to look at this subject, are clear about this:

271

Companies with a good record on innovation use specific management techniques to develop new ideas and go out of their way to attract and motivate individuals who are good at innovation. These people are rewarded not necessarily with higher pay but with more interesting jobs and few bureaucratic burdens.

Professor Roy Rothwell leads the Management of Technology group at the Science Policy Research unit, University of Sussex. No one in Britain has studied innovation longer or with more effect than he has. Having looked at hundreds, or thousands, of firms, he is perfectly clear that these are 'essential preconditions' for sustained corporate innovation to take place:

1. *Top management commitment* and visible support for innovation. That's necessary, among other reasons, to overcome barriers that crop up in companies.

2. *Long-term corporate strategy in which innovation plays a key role.* Innovation should be neither a down-the-line nor an ad hoc process. Once in a while you have to respond quickly to competitive behaviour, or to make use of new technology, he says, but it is better to have a sustained policy. That way you can build the technical, marketing and production synergies you need.

3. *Long-term commitment to major projects.* Rothwell sees this as vital, based not on short-term return on investment but on considerations of future market penetration and growth. At least some of any firm's innovation should be funded with 'patient' money.

4. *Corporate flexibility and responsiveness to change.* In some firms, says Rothwell, production sequences get more and more locked in to dominant product designs. This makes them inflexible. And that makes the products obsolete. Bringing in flexible manufacturing systems will help greatly. Flexibility applies as much, of course, to organisation and marketing. You have to be able to adapt both, sometimes, to take advantage of new technology.

5. *Accept risk.*

6. *Innovation-accepting, entrepreneurship-accommodating culture.* Rothwell says you must 'decouple' the creative, innovatory aspects of the firm from its more routine and bureaucratic activities. Create space for 'in-house entrepreneurs'. 3 M has been exemplary at this. You need a free-

272

wheeling atmosphere. You hear that time and again. Innovation, says Rothwell, is essentially a 'people process'.

And here is what Dr Edwards Deming, credited with analysing Japanese economic ills and laying the foundation for their current success, has to say: A positive program of action can be condensed into fourteen points. They apply anywhere, to small organisations as well as to large ones, to the service industries as well as to manufacturing.

1. Create constancy of purpose towards improvement of product and service, with the aim of becoming competitive, staying in business and providing jobs.

2. Adopt the new philosophy of management. We are in a new economic age, created by Japan. Transformation of Western styles of management is necessary to halt the continued decline of industry.

3. Cease dependence on inspection to achieve quality. Eliminate the need for inspection on a mass basis by building quality into the product in the first place.

4. End the practice of awarding business on the basis of price tag. Purchasing must be intregrated with product design, manufacturing and sales, with the close involvement of the chosen supplier. The aim must be to minimise total cost, not merely initial cost.

5. Improve constantly every activity in the company. Improving quality and productivity constantly decreases costs.

6. Institute training and education on the job, for management as well as labour.

7. Institute supervision. The aim of supervision should be to help people, machines and gadgets to do a better job.

8. Drive out fear, so that everyone may work effectively for the company.

9. Break down barriers between departments. People in research, design, sales and production must work as a team, to foresee problems of production in use, which may be encountered with the product or service.

273

10. Eliminate slogans, exhortations and targets asking the workforce for zero defects and new levels of productivity. Such exhortations only create adversarial relationships, because the bulk of the causes of low quality and low productivity belong to the system and thus lie beyond the power of the workforce.

11. Eliminate work standards that prescribe numerical quotas for the day. Substitute aids and helpful supervision.

12a. Remove the barriers that rob hourly workers of their right to pride of workmanship. The responsibility of supervisors must be changed from sheer numbers to quality.

12b. Remove the barriers that rob people in management and in engineering of their right to pride of workmanship. This means, *inter alia*, abolishment of the annual or merit rating and of management by objectives.

13. Institute a vigorous programme of education and re-training. New skills are required for changes in techniques, materials and service.

14. Put everybody in the company to work in teams to accomplish the transformation.

Close to the customer; a reminder before we leave this book.

WHAT TO LEARN FROM THE WINNERS

The ten lessons I gathered from chairing the NEDO study of winning companies are:

1. *Care about products.* Winning companies care about their products far more than most others do. The boards of too many other companies are far more concerned with finance and short-term profit.

2. *Be obsessive about customers.* They have teams committed to studying not only customer needs now, but future lifestyle trends.

3. *Integrate design.* They see design as just one part of developing new products. In the leading companies design is an integral part of a multi-disciplinary approach to product development.

4. *Break down the walls.* Today most companies are organised by function – engineering, manufacturing, design, marketing, finance, etc. Winning companies have largely broken down these walls. They have multi-disciplinary teams, drawn from all these departments, which work together throughout the development of a product. Their communications are more across the company than up and down.

5. *Concentrate on design.* Leading companies give designers and the multi-disciplinary design team a much more central place in the company than in most other companies. Design has been lifted from a functional to a strategic role. Designers are expected to imagine the company's future products.

6. *Havee a product strategy.* This may be dual: both to improve incrementally ('little by little') all the time, and to take larger, more innovative leaps.

7 . *Chase technology.* Many buy in all they can. But note that they say competitive advantage is not achieved by technology but by 'how you relate it to the needs of the customer'.

8. *Co-operate with your suppliers.* More of these companies are developing long-term relationships with their suppliers. Their choice is based on quality and reliability rather than on low cost. They design components together, and see themselves as partners in growth.

275

9. *Demand quality*. The winning companies design quality in, rather than inspect faults out.

10. *Communicate*. A characteristic of all winning companies is excellent communications across the company and all through it.

These ten characteristics add up to a remarkable capacity to create products very quickly, which their customers buy in preference to others.

As almost all the examples in this book show, there are other recurring features in winning companies. Look at people as apparently disparate as Anita Roddick and Alan Sugar, Sir Terence Conran and Akio Morita.

- First, unquestionably, they all have a vision of the future and, indeed, a mission.

- Second, their companies all have a strongly developed 'corporate culture'. Often that is caring, thoughtful, and pins faith in people. Even Alan Sugar, whose corporate culture has been called 'Oi you', and who is brusque and demanding, goes to great lengths when anyone needs help.

- Third, they honour every soul. One way is to create circumstances in which people can shine.

- Fourth, they have clear goals and tell everyone what they are.

- Fifth, they keep it simple. We've made business so elaborate that the simple aims get lost.

- Sixth, they get on with it. 'Try it, fix it, try it' makes sense to me.

- Seventh, I'd repeat the need always, *always*, to run the business to serve and suit the customer. If you mean it, you'll do the right things. Do not run the firm to suit the stock exchange, the factory or, as bad, the administrators. (The only sure way to satisfy these three in the long run is to satisfy the customer).

There are two other words. Love is one. Whatever form it takes, all the people who build winning companies love what they do, love the people around them and the people they're selling to. The final word is persistence. I was recruiting a top manager once and talked with a battle-scarred colonel about qualities to look for. 'Stickability,' he said. By that he meant 'the ability to stay there'. You bet all the men and women who lead winning companies share that quality.

FROM JAPAN TO PRINCE PHILIP

Gene Gregory, professor at Sophia University, Tokyo, gave his own summary of the keys to success he has seen in Japan: education, motivation, innovation. Kenichi Ohmae of McKinsey & Co. in Tokyo tells us that the traditional Japanese success recipe includes mass production, incremental managerial improvement, buy-in technology, fast turnaround time for innovation, small systems and hardware orientation and, of course, strong quality orientation.

Finally, a distinguished American, Robert C. Christopher, who knows Japan well, said in his book *The Japanese Mind* that the key to Japanese efficiency is not low wages or unfair practice but this: 'Japanese managers manage their companies better.' They get more from their workers because they treat them better. The Japanese worker has pay, pride, security. Everybody, in every job, knows that he or she contributes to the success of the company. They know their products better. They have a higher proportion of engineers in top management, a lower proportion of accountants. They believe in quality – not acceptable quality level (AQL) but zero defects. Quality, they believe, should be designed in from the start. Christopher added that the Japanese take a long-term view. They wait for profit. They call it 'patient money'. Top managers, Christopher said, are more people-oriented and more product-oriented. 'Disrespect for our products is a prime source of our difference and difficulty.' Which is where we started.

'It is one thing to have an idea,' Sir Alastair Pilkington once said, 'quite another to turn it into a technical and then a commercial success.' At Pilkington Brothers they realised that survival would depend on being innovative. But their experience was daunting. When they developed float glass it took them twelve years to break even on their cash flow. Still, he believes, 'If the strategy is good, the profits will come.'

Sir Alastair listed three essentials for success. First, the company must believe in the need for innovation. Everyone must see it as vital. 'It simply must not be seen as peripheral.' Second, the resources must be made available. A definite commitment is much more important than is recognised. Third, a major project will not yield quick returns. Everyone has to know that. You need 'courage and determination' to see it through, he declared, having demonstrated it himself.

In his inimitable way, Prince Philip summed up a discussion about 'the management of new ideas' at the Royal Society of Arts in November 1986.

On a scratch pad he listed seven points he thought important. Possibly because he is, *inter alia*, president of the World Wide Fund for Nature, he spoke first of understanding the environment we are in. Creatures can remain unchanged for billions of years but that is because their environment has not changed. Where change does occur, Darwin's principles of selection and evolution work. Relating this to corporate life, he believes the market operates the selection process. 'The company that is best adapted to its environment has the best chances of success. The environment in which a company exists decides how it should be shaped', he said.

Prince Philip then related the management of new ideas to these issues. First, the need to identify the current and future environment in which a company exists. Second, the need to study competition, which imposes restraints and permits opportunities. Third, understanding customer needs and, he added, public attitudes. He gave nuclear power as an example of the gap that can exist between need and acceptability. Next, he urged the audience to be aware of the availability of new materials and new technology. Design talent was vital. Talent was a word he emphasised; 'You need talent. We talk about design education, but perhaps not enough about design talent.' There is an important need for production skills. The next imperative for the introduction of new ideas is, in his view, good management – its attitudes, policy, structure, competence. Finally, he touched on government policy, which can aid or hamper innovation.

The Open University, working with the University of Manchester's Institute of Science and Technology, interviewed people in 100 companies in various industry sectors. They tried to see whether companies that win design awards, or are recognised as having well-designed products, perform better or worse than companies that have no such accolades. The answer, they say, is unequivocal. Companies that had won design awards or had products accepted for the Design Centre's Design Index showed higher return on capital, higher profit margins, higher growth of turnover and higher capital growth. Sectors they looked at included the plastics industry, domestic heating, bicycles, office furniture, electronic business equipment and computing.

No less interesting is the way companies with better performance manage their design process. The Open University listed these six common elements:

1. The companies with high profitability and growth provide designers with a comprehensive design brief. Invariably this includes details of

278

the market, guidance on appearance and image, standards (ergonomic and other) as well as the function of the proposed product and its target price.

2. The companies with high asset and profit growth rates employ several sources of market intelligence.

3. The companies tend to evolve products, improving their own or their competitors'. Companies that created highly innovative products could succeed brilliantly, but more often found the market hard to develop.

4. These more successful companies put prototypes through systematic customer and user trials, as well as testing the product technically. Less successful firms relied more on 'experience' to judge user acceptance.

5. The companies that performed best shared a commitment to design that ran from top management throughout the firms.

6. The companies with a high proportion of research, design and development staff were more likely to have high levels of profitability and growth.

The same principles come up time and again.

SUMMARY

Listen to authorities in the United States, in the UK, in Japan, and you hear the same truths time and again. The driving companies – not necessarily those yielding the highest profit this quarter or next quarter, but those that are carving larger and larger shares of our markets – all share the same attributes. This chapter tells us what they are. Put together, they add up to a consistent and compelling picture of what companies need to do or, more precisely, where they need to place emphasis and focus, if they are to compete.

The second salutary point is to note that the general run of companies do not practise the same ideas. The third and most astonishing feature when you come across it, in 3M or Sharp or elsewhere, is the depth and totality of such companies' commitment to these beliefs. These vital attributes are not fashionable management techniques, but inherent in the way such exemplary companies wake up in the morning and go about their business.

15

Why Change the Way
You Do It Now?

*'How many of us facing this onslaught will, like Garbo
as Camille, give a cough and wander off to die?'*
after Cole Porter

What we have to do to win is obvious. The ideas have been bandied about
for years. The snag is that we don't follow them.

There are reasons for this that go beyond natural conservatism. The
most important may be that the new imperatives don't sound serious
enough. Only yesterday, a major manufacturer told me that it was the
high exchange rate that had held back British industry. That sounds altogether a more high-minded explanation than anything to do with the
goods a company makes, and worthy of comment by intelligent observers.
It is nicely theoretical, well removed from the hurly-burly of business.
Better still, it is something we cannot influence. We are innocent victims.
Economists debate the money supply. Others point to the relative cost of
labour and a hundred other abstractions, all of which may have something in them.

Stephen Bayley, director of the Design Museum in London, historian
and vivid writer about product design, feels deeply about this. Of so many
business executives he said, 'They'll talk about fluctuating exchange rates,
they'll talk about differences in demand. What they'll never actually
admit is that they make products no one wants to buy.'

That really is the bottom line. The evidence, as if we hadn't enough, is
that some companies do succeed. In the same society, with the same bank
rate, under the same laws, these companies go from strength to strength.
It can be done and is being done. While some companies slump into that
vicious vortex mentioned earlier, others in, or coming from, the same
industry, do not.

Sir Geoffrey Chandler both inspired and led Britain's 'Industry Year' in
1986, which ran on. He points out that, in Britain at any rate, 'we live in an
industrial society with an anti-industrial culture'. Education at all levels

fosters that 'anti-industrial' approach. If I may quote Christopher Lorenz quoting Patrick Nuttgens, 'The ideas of Plato and Matthew Arnold conspired to elevate the privileged world of leisure, discussion and speculation far above the imperfect, flawed and confused world of industry and work in the minds of the middle classes.'

This is not the place to go into all that. Yet, since parallels with Japan have appeared throughout this book, it is interesting that Masanori Moritani sees the same roots in the differences between the Mandarins who ruled China and the Samurai of Japan. The Chinese, he says, looked down on the Japanese as vulgarians. They, in turn, thought the Chinese effete. Mandarins were chosen for their intellect, passing extreme exams to qualify for the civil service. To this day, the most senior civil servants in Britain, those who remain in their great departments as government ministers come and go, are known, amiably, as 'mandarins'. Japan's

Selwyn College, Cambridge. Do our most illustrious colleges still encourage the view that the classics are superior to science and anything is better than business? In a world of change, could they be right?

Samurai were warriors. They extolled the virtues of physical strength. They got their hands dirty.

Japanese industry, Moritani claims, is led by descendants of the Samurai. The picture Moritani paints fits his ideas of American and British R & D. 'Brilliant but abstract,' he calls it. Because, by contrast, Japanese scientists and engineers are close to the factory and its products, he likens them to latter-day Samurai.

Gene Gregory points out that over half of Japan's industry leaders and over half of their elite civil servants hold engineering-related degrees. That is far, far from the British experience. So what is the British picture? When the chairman of a major British corporation was photographed for the cover of a business magazine, he chose to wear tweeds and green wellies, with a gun under his arm and a brace of pheasants by his side. There is a cultural history for all of this, too deep to go into now.

What is it that prevents more companies from behaving as the winners do?

MOTIVATION

Lack of motivation is one thing. Although all the business executives I know work very hard indeed, there is a widespread and, I suspect, growing feeling that the price of competing with Japan is too high. 'Look at their way of life,' I have heard, 'Who wants that?' As support for that point of view someone sent me a clipping from a newspaper. It claimed that while people in Britain and in the United States gave millions to Bob Geldof's Live Aid fund for famine relief in Ethiopia, people in Japan donated only about £70,000. The intended implication was that theirs is an uncaring society. That is not so, as their attitude to their employees shows. As for aid, Japan is set to be the world's largest aid donor. It gives more than the United States now and plans to double its 1986 level within seven years. Between 1988 and 1992 the Japanese government aims to provide more than $50,000 million in aid.

If that is surprising, then figures for crime may be more so: in Japan there are half the murders and one fifth the number of crimes of larceny and theft on a per capita basis that we suffer in the UK. Compared with the USA, Japan has one sixth of the murders and one fifth of the crimes of larceny and theft, again per capita. When a study team organised by the Design Council and PA Management Consultants visited Japan in

September 1986, its first call was at a famous department store. 'What do you do about shoplifting?' one of the visitors asked. After a long, puzzled pause, the Japanese host replied, 'We don't have any.'

There is another way we can contrast the West and Japan. According to some sceptics, Japanese industrial might is built on the backs of exploited workers. Wage rates in the summer of 1986 suggest otherwise. In the United States the average wage then was $9.17 per hour. In Japan it was $8.95, in West Germany $6.90 and in the UK $6.72. By the autumn of 1986 the rising yen had put Japanese workers above even those in the United States. Currency changes alter the details, but it is likely that Japanese workers are better off and, as we have seen repeatedly, better regarded and cared for by the companies that employ them.

Levels of tax and quality of life may seem unrelated to many people. For those who make the connection, it can be noted that, up to 1984 at any rate, the tax burden was lower in Japan than in any other advanced country – 27.4 per cent of their gross domestic product in comparison with 29.0 per cent in the USA and 38.5 per cent in the UK. The OECD average was 37.1 per cent. In other words, in Japan there was more pay and less tax. Unemployment in Japan in August 1987 stood at 3.2 per cent, according to the Management and Coordination Agency. Although unemployment is expected to double, in manufacturing the number of jobs is probably rising. In education we have seen that three times as many children go on to higher education as in the UK.

This is not a mindless paean of praise. It simply says we have less to fear than we think. Japanese culture is sharply different from ours and no doubt will remain so. But many of their values are admirable, even enviable. It is possible to believe we can embrace some of them without losing all we hold dear. The conclusion I draw is that some people genuinely do not want to do what is necessary to compete because they misunderstand the prize.

Of course there are qualities to love and cherish about the way we live. Professor Ralf Dahrendorf who came from Germany to head the London School of Economics used the word 'kindness'. 'It cannot be merely the prices of raincoats and sweaters which bring Continentals to Britain by the thousands; they would not go to Turkey or Finland for the same reason.' People in the United States, or West Germany, France, Italy, Scandinavia, Australia and other wonderful countries don't need to be reminded of the merits of their own way of life. My urgent point is that if we want to preserve these value we must stay prosperous.

Dahrendorf remarked that Britain does not easily break down under pressure, 'perhaps not at all. On the contrary adversity seems to bring out the best in the country and its people.' He added, however, 'One may argue that there should be a little more motivation even without adverse circumstances, indeed, at times one may suspect that adversity could be prevented by timely action.'

FALSE CHOICE

The notion of maintaining our present way of life without change or of a return to simpler values is as seductive as it is false. Stephen Bayley, again, pointed out fiercely: 'The alternative to growth isn't pack horses on the Downs and corn dollying. It is urban decay.' And even those who prefer the rural life of apple blossom and sunny memory still want a good modern hospital with the latest brain-scanner within a mile or two.

Opting out is no option. Certainly we can choose, as Kipling advises in his poem about smugglers, to 'watch the wall, my darling, while the Gentlemen go by'. But the cost will be all we cherish. Rob Matthews wrote in his report for the Confederation of British Industry: 'We can adapt to the changes taking place in the world around us or face continuing decline. It cannot be supposed that the decline will be a graceful one.'

That should be motive enough. Sir James Cleminson, past president of the CBI, stated no more than the obvious but curiously ignored truth that 'only by creating wealth do we have the means to improve the quality of life' (of our own people and of those less privileged abroad).

In *Management Today*, Simon Caulkin, the former editor, wrote: 'Britain has no choice but to be competitive in world markets, that is, compete successfully, if it is to keep its people employed.' It's the same in the United States. That is the motive for competing.'

Others who would like to compete feel they can't. We are back to exchange rates, or whatever external force is cited as a reason. To point out that many companies compete very well seems no comfort. This book suggests practical ways for executives to improve their own performance and that of their company, without magic and without government aid.

But it does call for a new way of looking at business. Old ideas linger, long after their day is done. You still see evidence of the nineteenth century or, to be kinder, post-war attitude of 'filling empty spaces'. That is

'The alternative to growth isn't pack horses on the Downs and corn dollying,' according to Stephen Bayley. 'It's urban decay.'

to say, when the world is short of goods, the ability to make and make in volume is the key to prosperity. And when others can do the same, you make in more volume, to lower prices. You see also the legacy of the scientific tradition, right for some but not for all, and certainly you can't go far without seeing the impact of economists.

UNCOUPLING OLD ATTITUDES

It is too bad that the economists' view of industry is out of date, or, to put it better, that the relationships economists thought fundamental have

285

Letter to *The Times*

Sir. On a recent business visit to
Kuala Lumpur I took a rest by the
hotel swimming pool.

A Japanese businessman in the
pool swam over to the side where
I was sitting and started a conversation. As soon as we reached
some points of mutual interest he
reached into a pocket of his swimming trunks and passed me a
waterproof business card.

What chance have we got
against such competition in the
export marketing arena?
Yours faithfully,
C.M. FOGG.
Arrow Projects Consultants Ltd,
7 Dorset Road, SW19.
September 12.

changed. The explanation comes not from an economist, but from Peter
Drucker, recently at Claremont Graduate School in California. In his view
some basic connections have been severed. Trade and capital flows are
one example, production and employment are another. Growth in the
industrial economy no longer necessarily provides jobs. Because these
changes, according to economist Sarah Hogg, have 'crept up on us', they
have not been properly absorbed into policy making.

The uncoupling of people and rational economics is a third. Comparative wealth and security enable many people to try to satisfy their wants as
well as needs, noting that those wants may be emotional as much as they
are rational. As we've seen, some leading companies appreciate this when
they strive to create new working relationships within their company, and
notably when they develop new products. It goes further. This comparative wealth and security emboldens more and more people to 'do their

own thing' – work part-time, work at home, earn less but do what they want. In the UK now, some 16 per cent of working people are self-employed. The job climate is one reason, but not the only, or even the main, one. Manufacturers should think about this.

One reason why it is hard to grasp the accelerating pace of change, and the central, overriding effect it will have on all of us, is the difficulty governments have in keeping up. The ways they have to pick up information aren't always in line with real circumstance. For example, in the USA some 700,000 new companies are born each year. But the Census Bureau doesn't count any with fewer than twenty employees. So many go unnoticed, even though these small companies are likely to be the pattern of the future. According to Dr Bruce Merrifield of the US Commerce Department, Standard Industrial Classification codes are out of date too. 'Silicon chips and computer software are listed in a category of stone, glass and clay.' In Britain until four years ago design was listed by the Department of Education and Science under 'Music and the Performing Arts'.

Years ago, when George Ball was Secretary to the US Treasury, he said that business was twenty-five years ahead of government. How true that is I don't know, but certainly things are changing. Sir Alan Walters, economic adviser to Margaret Thatcher, is conscious of various governments' failures of nerve and resource. He speaks of Europe's chronic arthritis. But he also believes we stand at what he called 'the door of a new age'. Given the right focus and not a hundred well-meaning but ineffective ones, we could stay in the race, or even do better. 'Is civilisation,' Sir Alan asked on the day Japan launched its first rocket and Britain recorded its highest ever social security payments, 'to collapse under the weight of its good intentions?'

The challenge companies face would daunt the stoutest heart. 'International competition,' Sir Christopher Hogg wrote, 'is neither gentle nor fair. On the contrary, it is tough to face, remorseless and intensifying.' Nor is this struggle confined to international companies and exporters. You can buy JVC video machines and Nissan trucks as easily in the dairy land of Somerset as you can, I dare say, in Tokyo. Virtually every company is competing against world-class players in the global market. But, as many companies show, as do actors, athletes, scientists and soldiers and all who excel, there is no reason we shouldn't take on the best. It is a matter of wanting to. It is up to us.

The qualities needed to succeed in international trade, Sir Christopher added, are open-mindedness, energy, the will to progress, commitment and flexibility. And, I add at a more modest level, to create streams of products that people want to buy.

We have the choice. Are we to be like Lord Galway at Almanza in 1707 who, according to Macaulay, 'thought it more honourable to fail according to the rules'? Or are we, with resolve, to echo Philip Faulconbridge's words in *King John*: 'Come the three corners of the world in arms, and we shall shock them'?

Bibliography

Bhaskar, K. (1986) *Japanese Automotive Strategies*, University of East Anglia, Norwich.

Burns, P. and Kippenberger, A., (1988) *Lessons of Success*, Cranfield School of Management.

Christopher, R. C. (1986) *Second to None: American Companies in Japan*, Crown, New York.

Christopher, R. C. (1984) *The Japanese Mind*, Pan Books, London.

Clipson, C. et al. (1985) *Business/Design Issues*, Architecture and Planning Research Laboratory, University of Michigan.

Clutterbuck, D. and Crainer, S. (1988) *Decline and Rise of British Industry*, W. H. Allen, Mercury

Committee of Inquiry Report into the Engineering Profession (1980) *Engineering Our Future* (The Finniston Report), HMSO, London.

Confederation of British Industry (1979) *Innovations and Competitiveness*, London.

Crosby, P. (1978) *Quality is Free: The Art of Making Quality Certain*, McGraw-Hill, Maidenhead.

Department of Trade and Industry (1985) *'. . . you won't do it!'* (Pacific Basin Study Mission Report), HMSO, London.

Doyle, P., Saunders, J. and Wong, V. (1985) *A Comparative Investigation of Japanese Marketing Strategies in the British Market*, Bradford Management Centre, Bradford.

Drucker, P. F. (1955) *The Practice of Management*, Heinemann, London.

Edwards, B. (1981) *Drawing on the Right Side of the Brain*, Fontana, London.

Fairhead, J. (1988) *Design for Corporate Culture*, NEDO.

Fairhead, J. (1985) *A Framework for Communicating the Full Role of Design in Product Development and Innovation*, NEDO, London.

Follett, K. I. (1984) *On Wings of Eagles*, Corgi, London.

Ford, H., and Crowther, S. (1922) *My Life and Work*, Ayer Co. Publishers, USA.

Foster, R. N., (1986) *Innovation: the Attacker's Advantage*, Pan Books.

Freeman, C. (1983) *Design and British Economic Performance*, SPRU.

Halberstam, D. (1987) *The Reckoning*, Bloomsbury, London.

Handy, C. (1984) *The Future of Work*, Blackwell, London.

Heller, R. (1972) *The Naked Manager*, Barrie & Jenkins, London.

Heller, R. (1984) *The Supermanagers*, Sidgwick & Jackson, London.

Hooley, G. J., Lynch, J. E. and West C. J. (1983) *Marketing in the United Kingdom: A Survey of Current Practice and Performance*, Institute of Marketing, London.

Imai, K., Nonaka, I. and Takeuchi, H., (1985) 'Managing the New Product Development Process: How Japanese Companies Learn and Unlearn', in Clark, K. B. et al (eds) *The Uneasy Alliance: Managing the Productivity-Technology Dilemma*, Harvard Business School Press, Boston, Mass.

Jay, A. (1967) *Management and Machiavelli*, Hodder & Stoughton Ltd, London.

Lawrence, P. (ed) (1986) *Views on Design*, Corporate Design Foundation and Design Management Institute, Boston, Mass.

Levitt, T. (1960) 'Marketing Myopia', *Harvard Business Review*, Boston, Mass.

Little, Arthur D., (1985) *Management Perspectives in Innovation*, Arthur D. Little.

Lorenz, C. (1986) *The Design Dimension*, Blackwell, Oxford.

McLuhan, M. (1970) *Culture in Our Business*, McGraw-Hill, New York.

Mangham, I. L. and Silver, M. S. (1986) *Management Training: Context & Practice*, University of Bath, Bath.

Matthews, R. (1985) *Managing for Success*, Confederation of British Industry, London.

MITI (1988) *Design Policy for the 1990s*.

Moritani, M. (1982) *Japanese Technology – Getting the Best from the Least*, The Simul Press, Japan.

National Economic Development Office (1965a) *Survey of Investment in Machine Tools*, NEDO, London.

National Economic Development Office (1965b) *Imported Manufacturers*, NEDO, London.

National Economic Development Office (1977) *International Price Competitiveness, Non Price Factors and Export Performance*, NEDO, London.

National Economic Development Office (1979) *Product Design* (The Corfield Report), NEDO, London.

Nayak, R. and Ketteringham, J. (1986) *Breakthroughs!* W.H. Allen, Mercury.

Northcott, J. (1986) *Robots in British Industry: Expectations and Experience*, British Policy Studies Institute, London.

Oakley, M. (1984) *Managing Product Design*, Weidenfeld & Nicolson, London.

Ohmae, K. (1982) *The Mind of the Strategist: Art of Japanese Business*, McGraw-Hill, New York.

PA Consultancy Group (1985) 'Attitudes to New Technology', study conducted by MORI (Market & Opinion Research International).

Peters, T. J. and Austin, N. K. (1985) *A Passion for Excellence. The Leadership Difference*, Collins, London.

Peters, T. J. and Waterman, R. H. (1982) *In Search of Excellence*, Harper & Row, New York.

Pick, K. and Schott, K. (1983) *The Effect of Price and Non Price Factors on UK Export Performance and Import Penetration*, Discussion Paper No. 35, University College, London.

Pilditch, J. (1961) *The Silent Salesman*, 2nd ed., Business Books, London.

Potter, S., Lewis, J., Roy, Robin (1988) *The Commercial Impact of Design*, Open University.

Quinn, J. B. (1980) *Strategies for Change: Local Incrementalism*, Richard D. Irwin, Illinois.

Rogers, F. G. (1986) *The IBM Way*, Harper & Row, New York.

Rothwell, R. (1986) 'Innovation and Re-innovation: a Role for the User, *Journal of Marketing Management*.

Rothwell, R. (1981) 'Non Price Factor in the Export Competitiveness of Agricultural Engineering Goods', *Research Policy*, 10, Science Policy Research Unit, Brighton, pp. 260–88.

Rothwell, R. (1988) *The Successfully Innovative Firm: Some Research Results*, SPRU.

Rothwell, R. and Gardiner, P. (1984) 'Design and Competition in Engineering', *Long Range Planning*, Vol. 17, No. 3, pp. 78–91.

Rothwell, R. and Zegueld, W. (1982) *Innovation and the Small and Medium Sized Firm*, Frances Pinter, London.

Roy, R. and Walsh, V. (1983) *Plastics Products: Good Design, Innovation and Business Success*, Report DIG-01, Design Innovation Group, Open University Press, Milton Keynes.

Roy, R. and Wield, D. (eds) (1986) *Product Design and Technological Innovation*, Open University Press, Milton Keynes.

Schott, K. (1976) 'Investment in Private Industrial Research and Development in Britain', *Journal of Industrial Economics*.

Toffler, A. (1973) *Future Shock*, Pan Books, London.

Toffler, A. (1981) *The Third Wave*, Pan Books, London.

Acknowledgements

The author wants to thank people who kindly helped:

Graham Anthony, Uwe Bahnsen, Stephen Bayley, Riccardo Berla, Ron Baker, Win Bischoff, Anthony Bamford, Bob Blaich, Sarah Blake, John Butcher MP, David Bernstein, John Bloxcidge, Sir William Barlow, Nick Butler, Vice-Admiral Sir Peter Berger, Lord Caldecote, Colin Clipson, Sir Terence Conran, John Constable, David Carter, Tom Clarke, Edward de Bono, Pamela Denham, Michael Dale, Peter Doyle, Peter Doran, Gordon Edge, Brian Easton, Betty Edwards, James Fairhead, Kit Farrow, Sir Monty Finniston, Rex Fleming, Rodney Fitch, Michael Frye, Peter Gorb, Paul Gardiner, Keith Grant, Perry Goodman, Allan Graham, James Goodson, Frederick Gluck, Sebastian Green, Kenneth Grange, Lewis Goodman, Gordon Howe, John Heskett, Susan Hirst, Sir Christopher Hogg, Frank Heller, Howard Head, Sir Simon Hornby, Sir Ralph Halpern, Françoise Jollant, Steve Jobs, Chris Jackson, Sibylle Kicherer, Victor Kiam, John Kerridge, Peter Lawrence, Christopher Lorenz, Theodore Levitt, Robin Leaf, Alan Livingston, Rob Matthews, David Maroni, Akio Morita, Donald Massaro, Tony McBurnie, Elizabeth Nelson, Kenichi Ohmae, Wally Olins, Sir Peter Parker, John Peake, Jane Priestman, Sir Alastair Pilkington, Tom Peters, Bryan Quilter, James Brian Quinn, Roy Rothwell, Robin Roy, Neale Raine, Michael Sadler-Forster, Michael Smith, Alan Smith, Mike Smith, Kiyoshi Sakashita, Jocelyn Stevens, Ken Sadler, RitaSue Siegel, Alan Topalian, John Tuchfeld, Sir Robert Telford, Merrick Taylor, Sir Frederick Warner, Garth Wiseman, Roger Ward, Rachel Waterhouse, Brian Whalen, Michael Wolff.

Picture Acknowledgements

Index

technology – *contd.*
  shared, 198–200
  and the short-term view, 34–7
  speed of, 258
  transfer, 193–5, 198–200, 269
  two-way, 197–8
  and universities, 196, 258
Telford, Sir Robert, 141, 162–3, 193, 196
Texas Instruments, 109–10
Thatcher, Margaret, 1, 200
3i, *see* Investors in Industry
3M, 126–7, 149, 215
'threshold countries', 11–12

Thurow, Lester C., 37
Toomey, Bill, 135
Toffler, Alvin, 249, 259
Topalian, Alan, 110, 147
Torp, Niels, 213
Toshiba, 35, 120–21
training
  benefits of, 259
  budget, 207
  commitment to, 251–3, 261
  foreign competitors', 252–6
  lack of, 253
  multi-disciplinary, 254, 263–4
  need for, 249–51, 258–9
Turner, Stuart, 240–42

United States of America
  antitrust laws, 198
  car industry, 6–7, 11–12, 173
  education system, 249, 251–2
  engineering, 162

imports, 3–4
R & D, 194
trade deficit, xvii, 3–6, 12
and trade with Japan, 4–6
Utterback, Jim, 74

Valentine, Don, 131
vision
  director of, 217–21, 230–31, 239–46
  long-term, 29–31, 33–6, 272
  need for, 207–10, 217, 246–8, 270
  short-term, 28–37, 46, 77

Walsh, Malcolm, 178
Walsh, Vivien, 68
Walters, Sir Alan, 287
Warren, Tony, 45–6
Wasserman, Arnold, 62
Waterman, Bob, 41, 207, 222, 265–8
West, Christopher, 81–2
Wheldon, Sir Huw, 102
Whiting, Edwin, 178
Wilkinson Sword, 193
Wiseman, Garth, 29, 34
Wolff, Michael, 27
Woo-Chong, Kim, 227–8
Wood, Sir Martin, 130
Worcester, Robert, 142, 193–4
Wozinak, Steve, 239–40

Xerox, 62–3, 89, 104–5, 108, 127–8, 132

Yuasa, 216

zero defects, 172, 277